Dear Michal

Thank you very much
for your gift of TM
course

Best wishes

Karush
Feb 21, 2017

FINANCIAL INCLUSION

AT THE BOTTOM OF THE

PYR▲MID

CAROL REALINI
and KARL MEHTA

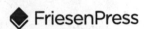

Suite 300 - 990 Fort St
Victoria, BC, Canada, V8V 3K2
www.friesenpress.com

ISBN
978-1-4602-6551-2 (Hardcover)
978-1-4602-6552-9 (Paperback)
978-1-4602-6553-6 (eBook)

1. Business & Economics, Banks & Banking

Distributed to the trade by The Ingram Book Company

Contents

PART TWO

PART THREE

"The book reads like a fast-paced novel. I could not put it down and I can't wait for the sequel to find out what happens next. It should be compulsory reading for every central bank, ministry of finance, and government official who is serious about empowering people. Every senior executive of any bank worth its salt should study this. There is something in it for everybody."

—*Brian Richardson, CEO of Wizzit*

"Navigating the complex layers of the financial inclusion space is not an easy task, but Karl Mehta and Carol Realini manage to paint a clear, detailed landscape of the issues and challenges at hand with an effortless prose that keeps us captivated and informed from start to end. Their grasp of the role of the private sector and the need for a unified systems approach is refreshing and in nice alignment with the work we're undertaking at the Bill & Melinda Gates Foundation. And beyond conveying a keen understanding of the current intricacies at hand, Karl and Carol's concept of financial nomads and banking as a platform are both areas that are new to the community, but absolutely essential for change. I anticipate hearing much more from them as thought leaders and unique voices for progress in this area."

—*Rodger Voorhies, director of Financial Services for the Poor, Bill & Melinda Gates Foundation*

"Increasing financial inclusion is the ongoing revolution that would have received more attention if it were not happening at the same time as the global financial crisis. The book highlights that financial inclusion is a problem in developed and developing countries and spotlights the innovations that have already had an impact on the life of the unbanked and under-banked and others that hold great promise. Serving the bottom of the pyramid requires fundamentally different approaches and collaboration among interested private and not-for-profit actors as well as governments."

—*Gaiv Tata, former director of Financial Inclusion and Infrastructure Global Practice of the World Bank*

"It was a breeze reading this book as the clarity, depth, and breadth of information supported your message. Not only was it an easy and enjoyable read—it was authoritative and credible, written by those who are obvious experts in their field. The personal and real-life experiences supporting the concepts developed around innovation makes the content accessible to anyone—even to those who are new to the concept of financial inclusion. This is a book full of real knowledge and will help readers appreciate what authentic financial inclusion is."

—*Jojo Malolos, former CEO of Smart Hub (Smart MC joint venture)*

Prof. Jeffrey D. Sachs

The end of poverty is coming our way, and this brilliant book explains how and why. The authors, Karl Mehta and Carol Realini, are renowned entrepreneurs at the digital front lines. With remarkable clarity and insight, they bring the readers to the front lines as well, explaining the building blocks of modern financial inclusion through up-to-date and fascinating case studies from around the world. In the race for financial inclusion, they show that the last may indeed come first. Leapfrogging is the order of the day.

Most of us are at least vaguely aware of the financial revolution sweeping the developing world. M-Pesa ("money wallet") is known throughout the world for bringing electronic payments to the unbanked of Kenya and now many other countries as well. Those of us in the richest countries of the world eagerly await such services to arrive in our communities. Ironically, in high-income countries, long-standing regulations often slow the adoption of innovations that are rapidly sweeping low-income economies.

What this book uniquely conveys, however, is a much deeper and systematic understanding of the key concepts and breakthroughs underway across Africa, Asia, and Latin America: mobile banking, mobile payments, micro-credits, micro-insurance, and much more. Each of these involves the creation of ecosystems linking governments, telecoms, banks, merchants, micro-enterprises, and households at the bottom of the pyramid. The structures are rapidly evolving and new business models are being created by the day. This book thoughtfully walks us through a gallery of digital pioneers, showing how dynamic first movers have solved the problems of scale, service delivery, digital security, banking laws, and more to bring financial services of enormous value to the world's poorest people.

The authors profoundly convey the multiple dimensions of empowerment created by new digital financial services. As Mehta and Realini authoritatively summarize, the traditional lack of access to institutional banking has meant that billions of people around the world

> . . . don't have deposit services for security and income
> through interest, no easy way to receive an electronic payment
> from the government, no easy way to get paid other than cash,
> no easy method to receive or send money to family members,
> no access to bank credit, likely no way to buy insurance of any
> kind, and no way to take advantage of electronic bill pay or
> buying online. [p. 45]

These barriers are now falling like dominoes. Through one innovative break-through after another, the poor are rapidly gaining access to deposit services, payments from government, access to cash from merchants, easy ways to send money to family members, bank credit even without credit histories, life and other kinds of insurance, and ways to pay bills online for new services, such as pre-paid solar-powered electricity.

One of the great aspects of this book is that it is written for entrepreneurs by entrepreneurs. That doesn't mean that this isn't a book for large companies and venture capitalists—they will use it, too. The book makes clear that the digital revolution is being created on the ground by visionaries with skill, persistence, insight, and by the readiness to plug away at creating new business models through years of trial and error. Sometimes it's big companies and national governments taking the lead (such as with the Aadhaar Program in India to establish a unique digital identity for all 1.3 billion residents of India), and sometimes it's a lone computer programmer seeking moral and financial rewards in the great fight against poverty.

Every chapter introduces us to the lead personalities, the technical and regulatory challenges they confronted, and the solutions they developed. The chapters usefully conclude with "The Takeaway" lessons from each case study. And the final chapter offers a compelling synthesis in how-to lessons for digital financial inclusion. As the authors make abundantly clear, the greatest successes have been achieved by "addressing a compelling need in a simple way." In each case, the pioneer has solved the chicken-and-egg problem of providing a low-cost service at network scale by finding a way to engage a critical mass of users and usage from the start of the process.

The case studies roughly cover the period of the Millennium Development Goals (MDGs), 2000 – 15. The MDGs have been the world's shared commitment to fighting extreme poverty. MDG 1 called for the rate of poverty to fall by half or more between 1990 and 2015. That has indeed occurred. Poverty in developing countries declined from around forty-three percent in 1990 to around twenty-one percent in 2010, and probably to around sixteen percent in 2015 (once the data are collected and analyzed). Breakthroughs in financial inclusion have surely played their role in these great advances.

Now we are entering a new period of Sustainable Development Goals (SDGs) for the years 2015 – 2030. SDG 1 calls for the end of extreme poverty, and other SDGs call for improved public health, access to education, decent work, sustainable agriculture, renewable energy, smart cities, and more. The SDGs are possible precisely because of the revolution in information and communications technologies. Financial inclusion as described by Mehta and Realini will be an important part of the SDG rollout in the years ahead, but no doubt financial inclusion will also be combined with a growing range of other cutting-edge services, such as access to high-quality health care, education, and renewable energy. Major improvements in governance are also on the way. For example, Nigeria's recent successful democratic election in March 2015 is being credited, at least in part, to the effective use of biometrics for voter registration and honest vote counting.

If the world uses the ICT revolution for human betterment, we can indeed be in the home stretch of the historic effort to end extreme poverty. Visionaries in business, civil society, and government will all play their role. This invaluable volume will give these pioneers and entrepreneurs key insights and inspiration for future success.

Prof. Jeffrey D. Sachs, April 5, 2015

Introduction

Seven hundred years after Giovanni Medici founded the first organized bank in Italy, more than half the world's population is unbanked and consequently cannot get credit to invest in their future earnings.

Compare that with just one hundred years of progress in powered transportation. Today we can reach any part of the world with planes, trains, and ships. We can send space probes to Mars and beyond.

Or consider the amazing progress made in communications. One hundred years ago, the telephone and radio were in their infancy; today, with digital technology, we can communicate anywhere in the world instantly.

Why is the financial system different from transportation, communications, energy, manufacturing, or any of the other industries that have made huge strides—not only during the past century but during our own lives?

Is there something about financial services that is resistant to change?

It's not like the finance industry is neglected or underused by that portion of the earth's population that can access its many services. To transact their daily affairs and protect their wealth, individuals and organizations of means have long relied upon financial services provided by a wide array of government, public, and private entities. Established institutions that fall under the umbrella term "banks"—those formidable buildings with the marble floors and bronzed teller windows—have been, and still are, key players in the financial services sector. But banks have never been the sole providers of financial services to individuals and communities; throughout the years, banks have shared the financial sphere with a dizzying array of providers ranging from the corner loan shark to, most recently, the global retailer Wal-Mart. These providers make loans, offer investment opportunities, keep money safe, and facilitate transactions.

From decade to decade and in region to region across the globe, the stability and quality of both bank and non-bank providers have been, and still are, inconsistent. Some operate with the full faith and trust of their host national governments; some skirt the edges of the law with outlandish products that are more risk than substance; and some have no other purpose than to profit from those who have little.

Yet over the centuries, and in every nation on earth, across the variety of financial services providers who throw open their doors to willing customers, one theme has remained consistent: when measured as a percentage of your assets, if you have lots of money, it's cheaper to do business with an established financial services provider than if you're someone who has to count your cash by the penny.

It's a matter of scale. If you're a big depositor, the less you pay relative to the amount of money you're saving, investing, moving, or borrowing. The more money you deposit or borrow, the lower the percentage in fees and interest rates you're charged. You have access to capital for your business or personal loans. Your prompt repayment of your loans begets you a more favorable credit score, which makes more capital available to you at a lower cost. The more money you borrow and repay, the lower the cost of borrowing each dollar becomes. Fees are waived and perks granted. It becomes easier to make more money because the costs of capital keep going down.

If you're a marginal depositor, or illiterate, or transient, the traditional financial services industry works against you. You pay higher fees, in some cases so high that you actually *lose* your hard-earned money by putting it in a bank or other provider. When you borrow, you pay a higher interest rate. Your bank, if you have one, is as likely to be viewed by you not as a partner but as a predator. If the doors to the bank are closed to you, then you either go without or turn to unregulated providers such as loan sharks and check cashing operations.

In short, for over seven hundred years banks have built a business model that depends on serving the affluent, and that has resulted in the marginalizing of the vast numbers of people at the bottom of the pyramid.

In the world today, over two and a half billion people who earn wages and support families do not use a formally recognized financial services provider.

They are cut off from the institutional services that the wealthy take for granted. For them, the world of old finance is like an Aztec pyramid: broad at the base, with a set of steep stairs ascending to the sacred temple at the top. Not everyone can access the riches and opportunities that lie at the top of the pyramid. The stairs are too steep and the price of admission is too high. These billions of people live at the bottom of the pyramid—abbreviated in this book as BoP. They do the best they can to find shelter, support their families, run their small businesses, and conduct their financial affairs without the benefit of safe and reliable institutional financial services.

They are the financial nomads. They live from day to day, and they climb the steep stairs of the pyramid to use institutional financial services only when they are able or when they have no other choice. This can create a downward spiral due to steep prices, penalty fees, and escalating costs of short-term credit. Because of bad experiences or foreknowledge of the high costs, they avoid the pyramid, and use only cash or patronize the world of alternative financial services—the world of loan sharks and payday loans.

As we shall discuss in this book, being a financial nomad is not a benign lifestyle choice but one that can be very costly.

What's the solution? How can basic financial services be scaled so that the steep stairs to the top of the pyramid are made more level, and that the exalted place at the top of the pyramid is made more spacious?

The solution is twofold. The first part of the solution takes the form of the rejection of one choice: we do not want to simply herd the underserved and low-income wage earners up the steep stairs of the old-school financial pyramid. This system, with its high fees and predatory lending practices, does not work for them. It's why many people who have a choice become financial nomads. They know this system, and they have chosen to avoid it like the plague. Even in the United States, which ought to rank at the very top of the list of countries where everyone has a banking services provider, rational people are abandoning what they believe is an abusive system, and they're going back to cash or embracing alternatives such as bitcoin.

The second part of the solution involves a complete redesign of the pyramid. Around the world, even in what westerners may think of as unlikely places, astonishing innovation is taking place in the finance industry. Far from the sacred temple at the top of the pyramid, new models of grassroots, mobile, and branchless banking are being developed and put into practice. These new models manage to perform the elusive hat trick: they make a profit for the providers, they are affordable for even low-income customers, and they are scalable. This model of new financial services offers a path to institutional banking that has long been denied to over two and a half billion adults around the world—people who are presently left out in the cold.

In every nation, there are dedicated technologists, last-mile distributors, business people, government employees, and operations staff working to transform the way finance is done. The new models require significant changes. Many organizations are stretched and uncomfortable. Too many of these efforts are experiencing the same challenges, confronting the same obstacles, and making the same mistakes. And it's happening so quickly that innovators are not able to take the time to scribe the best practices they're developing or write training material or reach out to others to learn from their efforts. There are too many projects and too few experienced people. And there is still so much that we don't know.

But the prize is too great and the process has already started. It is inevitable that we will live in a world where everyone has affordable access to financial services that empower their life and work. The goal is in sight, but it requires strengthening emerging solutions, then ensuring that the services provided are more widely available.

Change is coming. It has been over a decade since the first evidence surfaced that it might be possible to make basic financial services available and affordable for everyone. And today we can speak of an emerging new finance industry full of accomplishments, setbacks, struggles, emotions, and most of all hard work—harder work than ever expected, but much more rewarding than any of us dreamed possible.

The solution to the inequity of institutional banking is to formulate banking not as a tall pyramid with a temple at the top, but as a broad platform that is accessible to all. It's not about the bank as a sole player delivering products and services. It's about banking not as a pyramid, but as a platform.

The concept of banking as a platform (BaaP) and the ideas and examples put forth in this book are not theoretical. A project first launched in Kenya is but one example of the movement towards banking as a platform. M-Pesa (the name is derived from the words "mobile" and the Swahili word *pesa*, which means "money") allows users to use their cell phones to make a variety of transactions. They can deposit money into an account, use SMS technology to send funds to other users including sellers of goods and services, and redeem deposits for regular money. For sending and withdrawing money using the service, users are charged a small fee. As of August 2014, customers are able to send and receive amounts between KES10 and KES49 to other M-Pesa users at a cost of KES3.[1] As of this writing, one US dollar is worth eighty-eight Kenyan shillings (KES); this means customers can transfer amounts between eleven cents and fifty-six cents at a cost of three cents. For greater amounts, rates are scaled proportionally. Obviously if you're making a transaction of eleven cents, paying a fee of three cents is expensive. But to transfer KES5,000 (US$56) the fee of KES33 (thirty-seven cents) is not a bad deal. Look at it this way—if you pay your fifty-dollar electric bill with a check, you don't think twice about buying a postage stamp to mail your check. Yet that postage stamp will cost nearly one percent of the value of the transaction. To transfer fifty dollars with M-Pesa costs six-tenths of a percent.

The world has taken notice, and the great wave of efforts has been ignited. As of this writing there are 259 different major regional or national implementations around the world—nineteen in Nigeria and fifteen in India alone. And this count refers only to the mobile network operator lead implementations. Within an implementation, there are many projects that are adjacent or connected, and there are the projects that take the traditional banking products and put a mobile front end on them.

This multiplicity of solutions has benefits and downsides. M-Pesa in Kenya proved that decentralized mobile banking could work on a national scale. But similar projects around the world are as yet unconnected efforts to introduce universal banking, and these efforts need coordination and integration.

By fits and starts, a fundamental shift is emerging. These implementations are the tip of the iceberg of a new financial services paradigm where banking shifts from a set of proprietary products and services offered by a bank to a platform for many products and services to be available from many service providers. The bank becomes the enabler. This new framework encourages innovation and enables many "actors" to provide offerings.

---

1   http://www.safaricom.co.ke/personal/m-pesa/my-m-pesa-account/tariffs

In *Financial Inclusion @ BoP*, we'll talk about how to encourage the benefits and remove the downsides through a better architecture for the "ecosystem" of next-generation banking. This emerging approach of banking as a platform will accelerate collaboration and innovation. It's a fundamental change in how we think about delivering radically affordable and universally accessible financial services.

As an outcome, creating a platform of accessible financial services for everyone will have a multiplier effect. First it will contribute an incremental but steady growth in GDP. The banking and financial services industry is fast reaching saturation in over-serving the affluent segment, and the next stage of growth has to come from the 2.5 billion people who are currently underserved or neglected.

Secondly, a platform will create better governments through increased government efficiency, transparency, and decreased corruption. It will fuel better solutions for non-banking industries like health, retail, and consumer packaged goods.

Last, and maybe most importantly, it will create a richer environment for entrepreneurs, wherever they might be.

Part One of *Financial Inclusion @ BoP* will talk about the world today—what is the context of banking, who has good access to banking, who is left out, who is paying too much for basic services, and whose needs are not being met. The underserved financial market is massive, and it isn't just in developing countries. In the United States—the richest nation in the world—financial services are going backwards, with increasing numbers of financial nomads choosing to move away from big banks or even to be "cash preferred."

Our dysfunctional financial services system impacts every country and every demographic. Some ways are obvious while others are invisible. It even impacts those of us who think we're immune by affecting the people and businesses in our lives. It's a universal problem.

We'll take a closer look at the "pain points" of the typical person, family, and business today. The statistics of the financial nomads don't tell the whole story. We need to look at real people and real businesses to get the full picture of the implications of maintaining the status quo.

In Part Two, we'll look closely at key examples around the world where financial inclusion is emerging. These examples will illustrate benefits and challenges.

Although we are unable to write about every example, these will build a mosaic and allow you to understand more deeply what is happening already. Although not all are pure examples of platform finance, these will show the shift from old finance approaches, with banks as the sole provider of institutional products and services with vendors supporting them, to the platform finance approach where banking is a platform and many parties come together to provide innovative low-cost services.

In Part Three, we'll reveal the conditions that are bringing solutions within our reach in the next few years. This is not just about good intentions and hard work. We will demystify banking as a platform. There has never been as fertile an environment for solutions to emerge. We'll take away the mystery and reveal why this is true.

We stand at a time when we have the opportunity to leverage the breathtaking advances that have been made in communications technology during the past twenty years, and use these advances to reconfigure today's obsolete financial services system. What we propose is not a far-off dream but is something that has demonstrated success in real-life conditions. The old way of financial services could fairly be described as *financial services as a privilege*; the new way, *banking as a platform*, is one that is big and broad; and, like any good global platform, it can hold as many people as want to climb aboard.

PART ONE

CHAPTER 1:

Half the World Are Financial Nomads

The world population is roughly seven billion. Of these, 4.6 billion are aged twenty or older.[2] They comprise the pool of adults who could be regular customers of a financial services provider—a bank, savings and loan, credit union, or even Wal-Mart. Estimates suggest that of this eligible pool of 4.6 billion adults, over half—2.5 billion—do not use an established and reputable financial services provider. They are financial nomads who either have no access to financial services or use financial services on a casual basis when they need them.

That's 2.5 billion people who, day in and day out, week after week, month after month, and year after year, use no formal instruments for savings or borrowing. They use no debit or credit cards, have no savings or retirement accounts, and use no checkbooks. They live in a cash- or barter-based economic environment.

It's hard to fathom a number as large as two and a half billion. Some comparisons may help. A typical NFL stadium consists of 70,000 seats, so 2.5 billion people equals 35,714 football stadiums with sellout crowds. It equals 7.9 times the population of the United States, or 19.6 Japans, 38.1 Frances, or 12.9 Brazils.

If you think that 2.5 billion unbanked people is a big number, there's more to the story. Of the 4.6 billion eligible adults who ought to have access to financial services, it's true that 2.1 billion have a relationship with a bank. But many of these have only a simple savings account. In banking parlance, a savings account is *non-transactional*. It's not designed for easy or low-cost transfers of money. A

2   http://www.census.gov/cgi-bin/broker

simple savings account does not come with a debit card or a checkbook. There are likely to be strict limits on the number of withdrawals you can make each month. If you add those who are *non-transactional* banked to the true financial nomads, the numbers swell to 3.5 billion people, or 50,000 football stadiums full, 18 Brazils, 11.1 United States of Americas, 27.5 Japans, or 53.3 Frances.

The numbers of the underserved are not distributed evenly across the globe. In high-income industrialized countries, the percentage of financial nomads is a relatively low eight percent, representing sixty million people. Globally, most of the underserved populations live in Asia, Africa, Latin America, and the Middle East. The highest number of the underserved live in East Asia and South Asia, where 876 million and 612 million people respectively—fifty-nine percent of the population—live apart from any banking system. With 326 million underserved people representing eighty percent of the population, Sub-Saharan Africa is another vast area with large numbers of underserved people. In the Arab states, sixty-seven percent are not customers of an established bank or service provider, representing 136 million people.[3]

There are even a few countries—like Cambodia, the Democratic Republic of Congo, Guinea, the Kyrgyz Republic, Afghanistan, Turkmenistan, and the Republic of Yemen—where less than five percent of adults have bank accounts.[4]

Accepted wisdom might suggest that the income level of the individual would make a difference in his or her access to financial services, and that the people with more income are much more likely to benefit from institutional financial services. Access to formal banking and financial services is presumed to be directly proportional to rise in income levels. In general, this may be true, but from country to country among the global poor there is a surprising difference in use of banking services. Worldwide, for those adults who are living on less than two dollars a day, about twenty-three percent have bank accounts. But the rate varies considerably; in the Middle East and North Africa, only six percent of poor people have bank accounts, whereas in South and East Asia fully twenty-seven percent of poor people hold accounts.

3   http://www. gsma. com/mobilefordevelopment/wp-content/
     uploads/2012/06/110109halfunbanked_0_4. pdf

4   http://www-wds.worldbank.org/external/default/WDSContentServer/IW3P/IB/
     2012/04/19/000158349_20120419083611/Rendered/PDF/WPS6025.pdf

In determining rates of use of institutional banking services, what else matters besides income? Gender, education levels, age? Rural or urban life? The answer is that all of these matter, but especially gender. In developing economies, forty-six percent of adult citizens have bank accounts, but only thirty-seven percent of women do—and this number includes joint accounts held by husband and wife. In developing economies, this disparity exists at all income levels. In high-income economies, the difference is less and only approaches a four percent difference for poor women.

In developing economies, people with more education are twice as likely to have bank accounts as the less educated (in Sub-Saharan Africa, it's four times more likely). Age matters too; people younger than twenty-five or older than sixty-four are less likely to have accounts. In all regions of the world, adults living in cities are more likely to have accounts than rural inhabitants. This last statistic makes sense because many places around the world still use traditional branch banking models, and physical proximity to a branch is key to having access to services.

LIFE AS A FINANCIAL NOMAD

Here's just one example of what life can be like as a financial nomad, without an established financial service provider. I'm not going to provide an obvious story of a low-income person living in a rural area far from a physical bank—there literally billions of those—but will talk instead about someone with a good income living in a fully-banked environment. These are traditional banks to be sure, but for a person with a good income, life at the top of the pyramid is better than being a financial nomad at the bottom.

In 2010, Candice Choi, a reporter for the Associated Press (who at that time lived in New York City) chose to be a financial nomad for a month. She put away her credit and debit cards and suspended her direct deposit paychecks in favor of paper paychecks. She went about her daily business using only cash and alternative financial services such as money orders.[5]

Choi discovered the high costs of money management and of making financial transactions. Her first act was to end the direct deposit of her paychecks.

---

5   http://www. msnbc. msn. com/id/39498483/ns/business-personal_finance/t/
     life-without-bank-fees-confusion-galore/#. UQWhmd3Dwk9

During the course of the month, Choi received two paper paychecks of roughly $1,500 each. But she had no bank account, so to convert her paychecks into specie with value she needed to cash her checks at check-cashing stores. The fee each time was twenty-eight dollars and change, so to cash two paychecks cost her over fifty-six dollars. Choi was lucky to be living in New York where the check-cashing fee is capped by law at 1.83 percent. Florida and Maine both have a cap of five percent, so if Choi lived in one of those two states, it could have cost her up to $150 to cash two paychecks. About half of the states set no limits.

Having cashed her paychecks, she now had a purse full of greenbacks, but Choi had to pay her rent—with a check. So she went to a nearby Western Union to buy money orders using cash from one of her paychecks. Since each money order was limited to $1,000, and her rent was $1,300, she needed two checks, at a total cost of three dollars and fifty cents.

Most of Choi's remaining costs, about thirty-four dollars, went to fees on prepaid cards, which function like bankless debit cards and are available at drug stores and discounters. These cards charge a never-ending stream of fees, ranging from a one-dollar fee for each purchase to five dollars to use the card at an ATM to get cash. One of the cards charged $4.95 each time she wanted to reload it. Prepaid cards are big business; the US government projects that the total dollar amount loaded onto prepaid cards will hit $167 billion in 2014.[6] Imagine the revenues if each card earned just one dollar in profit.

Over the course of the month, Choi spent ninety-three dollars on fees. At that rate, she'd pay over $1,100 a year simply to manage her own money. What's particularly vexing about this case is that most of these fees involved nothing more than converting money from one form into another. Choi received her salary in the form of a paper paycheck, which as a medium of exchange is useless. You cannot go to the grocery store and present your paycheck as payment at the register. You need cash or a card. So Choi's first task was to convert her paycheck into cash. In theory, Choi could have then paid for every purchase with cash, but in reality this is simply not possible. The phone company will not accept cash for payment, and her landlord wouldn't either. So Choi was forced to convert some of her cash into yet another form—checks to pay the rent, prepaid cards

---

6   http://www.consumerfinance.gov/pressreleases/consumer-financial-protection-bureau-considers-rules-on-prepaid-cards/

for other purposes. Every time she performed this monetary alchemy she was charged a fee.

In contrast, consider the ease and economy of electronic direct deposit into your checking account, then using a debit card to make purchases. For one or two big-ticket items, such as your rent payment, you might have to write a check. Chances are good that your bank gave you a box of checks for free.

The burdens of being a financial nomad are not just financial. As Choi discovered, when you're a financial nomad in a big city in America, you experience constant reminders that you're a member of an underclass. So many of Choi's finances had been instantly electronic that it was unnerving to her to waste time going from crummy storefront to crummy storefront, waiting in line simply to cash checks and pay her rent. At the check-cashing place, the clerk counted out her money by visibly snapping each $100 bill in sight of the other customers. Choi's prepaid debit card looked cheap; it didn't have her name on it and the account number was printed, not embossed as on most credit cards.

Choi went to a hotel, which charged her NexisCard $400 in case she incurred any "incidentals." She was told the charge would be refunded at checkout, but to get her money back she had to make several phone calls over a period of three weeks. NexisCard refused to lift the hold until the hotel *faxed* them an official release form! Imagine if instead of being a highly-educated Associated Press reporter, Choi had been a migrant worker. Getting her money back from the hotel would have been much more difficult.

We know Candice Choi's story because she's a professional writer and she intentionally documented every detail of her experience. Imagine her story repeated two and a half billion times—and not just for a month in New York City, but over a lifetime.

CHAPTER 2:

The Barriers to the Traditional Finance System

If the traditional finance system worked for everyone, we would have no reason to write this book, nor would you have reason to read it. But it doesn't work for everyone. If the steep stairs going up the side of the pyramid were made more level, the world wouldn't have 2.5 billion financial nomads living permanently at the bottom, unable to gain access to the benefits that lie at the top.

Why do they live at the bottom of the pyramid? People of a certain mindset might say, "Well, if those people worked harder and got better jobs, they'd have no problem climbing the steep stairs. They could easily reach the top!" People who take this view most often can be found in penthouse offices, smoking big cigars. Anyone who has spent time in the real world knows that the answer is not so simple. There are billions of hardworking people living in every corner of the globe who earn not much more than a subsistence wage. That's just the way the world works. Therefore, our job must be to create a system that leverages technology and human ingenuity to provide basic fairness and access to those who want and need it. In doing so, these financial services will give people more tools to support their families, run their small businesses, save or borrow money to educate themselves or their children, and keep their money safe and working for them. All this will lower barriers to economic and personal betterment.

In order to suggest solutions and create an equitable system, we first need to ask a basic question: Why doesn't every working adult on the planet have a checking account into which they can deposit their paychecks and from which they can make payments? Why can't everyone climb the stairs to the top of the pyramid?

There are many reasons. In the United States, the biggest reason people give for not having a bank account is that they simply don't have enough money to pay for the minimum requirements. Thirty percent of those surveyed say this is the one and only reason.[7] It's not that they are lazy, or that they don't want to climb the steep stairs of the pyramid. It's that the gatekeepers at the top of the temple are also toll takers. It costs *money* to get to the top of the pyramid.

Let's look at this question in greater detail. In order to intelligently and fairly discuss why many people do not attempt to climb the steep stairs of old finance because of the high tolls being charged along the way, we need to analyze the actual costs of opening and maintaining a checking account—the most common form of transactional account—at a traditional bank.

WHAT THE CUSTOMER SEES: OPENING A PERSONAL ACCOUNT

When a new customer approaches a bank or other financial institution and hopes to open a personal checking account or current account (as transactional accounts are called in many places) the experience has many levels. An important consideration is the cost, and we have seen that for many people the cost alone keeps them from climbing the steep stairs to the top of the pyramid. But there are other factors too, including the transparency of the sales materials and, yes, the welcoming feeling the customer gets from the bank. We reviewed the websites of five banks to get an idea of what the typical customer experiences. We encourage you, dear reader, to spend some time online and visit the websites of banks in far-off places.

Before we begin, let's take a look at the global banking landscape. Because the United States is the world's largest economy, Americans may perhaps be forgiven for assuming that the biggest banks in the world are in the United States. Not so; in fact, according to rankings of the world's banks compiled by *SNL Financial,* as of this writing the biggest bank in the US—JPMorgan Chase— appears on the list at number six:[8]

---

7   FDIC Report at http://www.fdic.gov/householdsurvey/2012_unbankedreport.pdf

8   http://www. snl. com/InteractiveX/Article. aspx?cdid=A-26316576-11566

Rank	Bank	Country	Total Assets ($trillions)
1	Industrial and Commercial Bank of China	China	3.06
2	HSBC	United Kingdom	2.72
3	Crédit Agricole Group	France	2.62
4	BNP Paribas	France	2.51
5	Mitsubishi UFJ Financial Group	Japan	2.47
6	JPMorgan Chase	United States	2.46
7	China Construction Bank (CCB)	China	2.45
8	Deutsche Bank	Germany	2.42
9	Agricultural Bank of China	China	2.39
10	Barclays Group	United Kingdom	2.27
11	Bank of China	China	2.23
12	Bank of America	United States	2.13
13	Japan Post Bank	Japan	2.01
14	Citigroup	United States	1.9
15	Mizuho Financial Group	Japan	1.86
16	Royal Bank of Scotland	United Kingdom	1.83
17	Société Générale	France	1.7
18	Banco Santander	Spain	1.61
19	Groupe BPCE	France	1.55
20	Sumitomo Mitsui Financial Group	Japan	1.52

China, Japan, and France each have four banks in the top twenty. The US and UK each have three in the top twenty. Germany and Spain have one each.

If you consider global population distribution, something seems amiss. After China, the second most populous nation on Earth is India; the fourth most populous is Indonesia, followed by Brazil, Pakistan, Nigeria, and Bangladesh. None of these six nations has a bank in the top twenty. Of these six nations, which have a combined population of nearly two billion people, the first bank to appear on the list of the biggest banks in the world is Banco do Brasil S. A. at number fifty-one.

Clearly, in the industrialized nations, traditional banking is well entrenched, and in developing countries is woefully under-represented.

Is this a bad thing? At the moment, yes; but as we will see in the cases of innovative banking in India, Kenya, and other nations, it may very well be the case that the *absence* of institutionalized banking provides a more fertile soil for real innovation.

Let's look at five banks.

Bank of America

In the United States, Bank of America is the second-biggest bank and, at least in its marketing efforts, seeks to attract average-income customers. The following information is paraphrased from the BOA website as of this writing. Of course, these fees may change at any time, and we do not claim that anyone going to the BOA website will see exactly the same fee schedules or services offered.[9]

Let's say you want to open a BOA checking account. The bank gives you four choices or paths of entry. We'll look at two of them—the premium plan and the most economical plan.

Bank of America Premium is the top-of-the-line checking account. The fee is $25 every month—unless you satisfy one of the following two requirements:

1. Maintain a combined balance of $20,000 or more in linked personal deposit accounts with Bank of America and/or eligible linked investment accounts with Merrill Lynch (including Merrill Edge and Merrill Lynch Wealth Management).

2. Have a linked Bank of America first mortgage that BOA services.

To avoid the $25 per month fee just to maintain the account, you need to have either $20,000 with BOA/Merrill Lynch, or a mortgage with BOA. If you have a mortgage, you're probably paying a thousand dollars or more in interest every month, so BOA can easily afford to toss you a free checking account. Plus, BOA knows that if you have both your mortgage and your checking/savings accounts at BOA, the "friction costs" of leaving BOA for another bank are extremely high. You'll stick with BOA.

This plan includes four interest-bearing checking accounts. Up to four regular or money market savings accounts are also included with no extra fee.

---

9   https://www. bankofamerica. com/products/deposits/checking-accounts. go

The Premium plan also provides "select complimentary banking services" that include money orders, cashier's checks, standard checks with no fee, and a standard-size safe deposit box where available.

In addition, BOA offers Premium customers free *inbound* domestic and international wire transfers. If you're enrolled in any of the other three plans, these services will cost you $12 and $16 respectively. For example, let's say you live in New York and don't have a Premium BoA account. Your sister lives in Phoenix and has a Chase account. Your sister wires $100 into your checking account, and BOA will charge you $12 for the privilege. If your sister mailed you a check for $100, and you deposited it into your checking account, it would cost you nothing, even though there are costs associated with processing paper checks.

The fees for *outbound* transfers to another bank are not listed on the basic account information page, but are provided on a page buried deep within the BOA website:

- Three-business-day processing is $3.00.

- Next-business-day processing is $10.00.

- Same-business-day processing (wire transfer) varies by region. (The actual fee disclosure is on the Make Transfer page.)

There are many more fees for things like specialty credit cards and overdrafts, but to keep the discussion simple we'll just talk about the basic services.

All four of the BOA checking accounts offer online banking, mobile and text banking, and online bill pay with customizable alerts and reminders.

Bank of America eBanking is described as an accessible option that is "a basic account for those who want self-service banking (electronic banking)." The fee is $12 each month unless you enroll in and use both paperless statements *and* self-service options (such as BOA ATMs and Online Banking instead of a teller) for all deposits and withdrawals. There appears to be no minimum balance.

In other words, if you never set foot in a branch office and do not ask the bank to mail your statements, this is the one for you. You make all transactions either online or with your debit card. This plan includes one checking account. Additional Bank of America eBanking checking accounts cost a monthly fee of

$5 each. A savings account is not included. To add a companion linked savings account, you'll pay a $5 monthly maintenance fee for each account, or make a automatic monthly transfer of $25 from checking to savings per account, or maintain a minimum daily balance of $300 or more per account.

There is a fee of $8.95 for making a transaction (such as a deposit) through a teller at a branch office. The fee is levied a maximum of one time per month, so if you make three transactions through a teller in one month, it's still $8.95.

BOA's eBank account is the bank's way of competing with the newer online banks such as Ally.

Other banks offer similar no-frills checking accounts designed to woo students who presumably are tech savvy and have lower cash flows than adults.

FirstBank Nigeria Plc.

FirstBank has over 560 branches in Nigeria, eleven subsidiaries, and representative offices all over the world that offer full-suite financial services as well as in involvement in sectors varying from investment banking and funds management to insurance brokerage and microfinance.[10]

As of this writing, the rate of exchange is 1,000 Nigerian Nairas (NGN) = US $6.17.

The FirstInstant Account is described as a "savings product designed for the unbanked and underbanked to enhance financial inclusion." It also offers features associated with a checking or current account, such as a debit card.

Features/Benefits:

- Minimum opening balance of N1,000.

- Minimum operating balance of N500.

- Simplified account opening form.

- Mandatory issuance of debit card. A debit card is mandatory because customers are expected to use strictly alternate channels (ATMs, POS, FirstMobile, FirstOnline).

---

10   http://www.firstbanknigeria.com/products/individual/
     savings-accounts/firstinstant-account/

- Regular savings interest rate applies.

- Can also be opened as a Salary Account.

- Operated primarily via the alternative channels (e.g., POS, ATM, mobile phone etc.).

- All over-the-counter withdrawals attract a flat charge of N150.

- Free e-mail alert; SMS alert at a fee.

Requirements needed to open:

- Minimum opening balance of N1,000.

- Valid identification (including Trade/Market Association ID, valid e-tax clearance card, student ID card (backed with Admission letter), Military/ Paramilitary, NYSC, Government Parastatals ID, etc.

- Two passport photographs.

- Utility bill (e.g., PHCN).

The requirements seem to mean that you need *all* of the above to open a FirstInstant Account, including two passport photos. The required opening balance is a bit more than six dollars, and no other fees are listed.

CIMB Niaga – Jakarta, Indonesia

CIMB Group is a regional universal bank operating in high-growth economies in the Association of Southeast Asian Nations (ASEAN). Headquartered in Kuala Lumpur, CIMB has a presence in eighteen countries, covering ASEAN and major global financial centers, as well as countries in which their customers have significant business and investment dealings. With over 43,000 employees, CIMB Group operates in nine out of the ten ASEAN countries, with exposure to 99% of the region's population and almost 100% of its gross domestic product.[11]

As of this writing, 1,000,000 Indonesian Rupiah (IDR) = US $85.

Current Account Giro Rupiah (Perorangan)

---

11   http://www. cimbniaga. com/index. php?ch=cn_p_db&pg=cn_p_db_cur&tpt=niaga

Features:

- Provides ATM Facility and Internet Banking online in all branches of CIMB NIAGA.

- Receives check or *bilyet giro* that can be used as payment tools.

- Can be used as bank reference.

- Minimum balance: IDR 1,000,000.

- Administration fee: IDR 30,000.

- Costs below minimum balance: IDR 30,000.

- Closing Account Administration: IDR 50,000.

- Check book: IDR 100,000.

Requirements needed to open:

- Copy identity card (KTP / KITAS / KIMS / KITAP) NPWP.

- Complete opening account application.

The account requirements seem to be very simple—the opening balance of at least IDR 1,000,000 and an identity card. Note that while fees are listed, there is no indication of how often fees can be applied. For example, what is the "administration fee"? And is the below-minimum-balance fee applied daily?

Bank of Punjab, Lahore, Pakistan

One of the largest banks in Pakistan, the Bank of Punjab was founded in 1989 by Tajammal Hussain. It functions as a scheduled commercial bank, with a network of 284 branches in major business centers throughout the country. It provides a wide range of banking services, including deposit in local currency; client deposit in foreign currency; remittances; and advances to business, trade, industry and agriculture. Interestingly, the brand tagline for the bank is "Passion Reborn."

We have included this complete text from the bank's website not because it details the costs associated with opening and maintaining a checking or current account—those costs are nowhere to be found—but because it powerfully illustrates the psychological burdens that can come with life as a financial nomad living at the base of the big steep pyramid. This text is the *only* information provided to a customer seeking to open an everyday currency account (not a foreign currency account).[12] Imagine you are a working-class Pakistani and you want to open a currency account. You go to the Bank of Punjab website, click on the choice for "Terms & Conditions," and this is what you see. Here is a small part of the very fine print:

2. Opening an Account

2.1 The Account shall be opened upon submission of duly filled-in Bank's prescribed Account Opening Form properly in the manner provided and on submitting all such documents and information as may be requested by the Bank. Further, the Bank reserves the right to demand such relevant documents and information even after opening of account as deemed necessary. In the event of failure of the Customer to provide such documents and information, the Bank may, at its sole discretion withhold operations of the Account or close such Account.

2.2 The Bank will not refuse opening of account for prospective clients who meet the requirements laid down in the Prudential Regulations, other instructions issued by SBP from time to time and Bank's policies.

2.3 The Account shall be opened with an initial / minimum deposit as stipulated by the Bank from time to time unless specifically relaxed / exempted by SBP.

2.4 A distinctive number will be allotted to every account and this number should be quoted in all correspondence relating to the account and at the time of making a deposit or withdrawal. The Bank reserves the right to change the Account Number or any part of it in order to meet its book-keeping / administration requirement.

---

12 http://www.bop.com.pk/view.aspx?id=38

However, intimation of change in the account number shall be sent to the account holder.

2.5   The Accounts may be opened singly in one name or jointly in two or more names.

That's it! The bank says more than once that it can change the rules whenever it wants, even after you open your account. It does not invite you to ascend the stairs to the top of the pyramid; you must qualify, and the requirements are maddeningly vague. The wall of plain text—there are no graphics—is at best the opposite of "Passion Reborn" and at worst simply intimidating.

If you had a paycheck of one hundred dollars that represented your sole source of funds for living your life, would you hand it over to Bank of Punjab?

The only rational answer would be "no."

YOU CAN'T JUST BLAME THE BANKS

Readers in the United States may be forgiven for assuming that the laws that regulate banks and financial service providers are consistent across the globe. They are not. The degree to which banks operate with transparency—and therefore encourage or discourage low-income customers—varies tremendously. To see this in action, all you have to do is compare the policies of a bank in the United States and the same bank in a very different nation, such as Vietnam. The big US bank Citi happens to operate in Vietnam, and the Vietnamese division of Citi has an attractive English-language website that anyone can access. It's easy to compare the customer experience in both nations.

Here's a sample from the US website.[13] We acknowledge that this information, while accurate at the time of writing, may have changed; we include it here only to demonstrate the tone of the text, not to analyze the content. The page describes four account choices; this is the basic checking account.

---

13   https://online.citibank.com/US/JRS/portal/template.do?ID=PricingPackages

Citibank USA – Basic Banking Package

Package	Basic Banking Package
Minimum Opening Deposit	Checking: None Savings: $100
Combined Average Balance	Checking: $1,500 Savings: $500
Monthly Fee	1.Make 1 Direct Deposit AND 1 Bill Payment each monthly statement period and pay no monthly service fee, OR keep a combined monthly average balance of at least $1,500 in the prior calendar month in either your Basic Checking or with a liked Basic Savings Account and pay no monthly service fee. Otherwise pay a flat $10 monthly service fee.
Per Check Fee	None
Non-Citibank ATMs	$2.00 per withdrawal
Services	The Basics - Option to link Day-to-Day savings account

There's some fine print, but you get the idea. The chart will look familiar to any US banking customer, with the account minimums and fees clearly presented as required by US law.

Citibank Vietnam – Account Opening

The Citi customer in Vietnam has a very different experience. Here's the page describing one of the account options:[14]

Citibank N. A. Vietnam,

Ho Chi Minh City BranchSun Wah Tower,

115 Nguyen Hue Boulevard, District 1,

Ho Chi Minh City, Vietnam.

A simple account that enables you to do your everyday banking.

---

14   http://www. citibank. com. vn/portal/vietnam_home. htm

Application Criteria

- Minimum initial deposit of VND 1,000,000, USD 50, or equivalent.

Documents required for Vietnamese:

- Primary ID: Identification card or Passport

- Secondary ID: Home Registration Book or Driver's License

Documents required for Foreigners: (Resident / Non-Resident)

- Passport

- Valid Visa

- Residence card

Looks simple enough! But how much will it cost? Are there fees or restrictions? Somewhere there must be some fine print that explains the rules. When you search the website for a list of fees, or a description of terms and conditions, you find yourself at a *228-page document*. It's a pdf that you download. Below is reprinted in its entirety the section entitled "Charges/Commissions."[15]

**TERMS AND CONDITIONS
CITIBANK GLOBAL CONSUMER BANKING**

12. Charges/Commissions

12.1 You are authorized to automatically debit my Account(s) with the full amount of any charges, fees (including without limitation legal fees on a full indemnity basis), costs and expenses, interest, taxes (where required by Law or Regulation), commission and penalties (collectively, "Charges") payable to you whether in respect of (i) the Products and/or Services listed hereunder; (ii) any liability of any nature arising (whether in Vietnam or elsewhere) in respect of the Account(s) or otherwise; (iii) any overdraft

---

15 http://www. citibank. com. vn/english/pdf/TERMS-AND-
CONDITIONS. pdf?eOfferCode=VNENBKLNCCA

granted to me and any of its outstanding advances; (iv) any liability of any nature arising (whether in Vietnam or elsewhere) in respect of the Account(s); (v) any overdrawn sums on the Account(s); or (vi) any investment(s) which you quote to or transact for me. You may include such Charges in the price or rate for such investment(s) which you quote to me without having to separately identify them to me. I consent to your retaining for your benefit (or for your compliance with Law or Regulation) any Charges, commissions, rebates and other forms of payment or benefit from any party (including any broker, underwriter or counter-party) in respect of my transactions unless prohibited by the laws of Vietnam.

12.2 A charge will be levied if I fail to maintain the minimum balance required for the Account(s) or if the Account(s) remains inactive for such duration as you may prescribe from time to time. Charges may also be levied if I close any of my Account(s) within such time period as you may prescribe from time to time or if you close my Account(s) in order to comply with Law or Regulation.

12.3 You may, at your discretion and with prior notice to me, modify the prevailing rate and/or amount of any Charges payable by me to you.

12.4 In respect of my use of the Citibank Online Internet Banking Service, I agree to bear all fees and charges incurred in connection with my gaining access to this Service. In the event that you elect to re-extend this Service to me after you (i) have terminated my use of this Service for any reason whatsoever, or (ii) have cancelled my use of this Service at my request, I agree to bear all fees and charges incurred in connection with such re-extension.

Without a clear schedule of fees and conditions—which in the United States the bank is compelled to publish—what rational low-income consumer would willingly open an account with Citibank in Vietnam, knowing that neither the bank nor the government has an interest in defining or enforcing basic consumer rights?

In reprinting this page, we do not intend to single out any particular bank for criticism. The point is that banks, like any other type of enterprise, do business in the culture of their marketplace. In the United States, we have relatively tough consumer protection laws under which all financial service providers must operate. Clearly, in Vietnam the government takes a very different attitude towards regulation, and Citi—or any other provider—adapts its way of doing business to the local legal and ethical standards.

In fact, according to *Bank on it!* forty-two percent—or 8.85 million—of Vietnam's households are unbanked, and eighty-six percent of these unbanked households are in rural areas. People living in Vietnam's remote areas have limited access to formal financial services. Banks are located in cities and towns, and it's no surprise that when rural people visit these urban areas, they don't feel comfortable entering the shiny buildings where banks maintain their offices.[16]

INCOME = OPPORTUNITY

For many reasons—they cannot afford the fees, the banks are too far away, the culture of established financial services providers is intimidating—2.5 billion people are not a part of the traditional finance system. They live at the bottom of the pyramid.

With the exception of some new mobile banking programs, the traditional checking account is designed to accommodate customers who have at least a middle-income base and steady cash flow—that is, they regularly make transactions. Who are these customers? In the United States, according to UNICEF the GNI per capita (gross national income divided by population) is $47,140. At such an income level, the price of admission to traditional banking may be annoying but it's tolerable. In contrast, the GNI in China is $4,260. In India it's $1,340. In Kenya it's $780. In Mali it's $600.[17]

To put that in perspective, the average person in Kenya earns in *one year* what the average person in the United States earns in about *six days*. Imagine earning

16   http://retailbankingblog. wordpress. com/2011/04/11/
      rural-poor-in-vietnam-gain-access-to-formal-savings-services/

17   http://www.unicef.org/infobycountry/index.html

a little over two dollars a day and being asked to pay even one dollar in fees to a bank. The only rational choice is to say "no." Rather than climb the steep stairs of old finance, you'd walk away. But that choice means that you're locked out of the benefits of institutional banking: security for your money, access to loans, easy transactions, and much more.

MORE REASONS TO AVOID TRADITIONAL FINANCE

While thirty percent of financial nomads stay out of the traditional banking system because they cannot afford the price of admission, another thirty-five percent say that while not enough money is a factor, other reasons keep them out of banks, such as the banks' demands for documentation or the high cost of maintaining the bank account. Other common reasons for not having an account include another family member having an account, the bank being too far away, or the person's lack of trust in the bank. Some countries have a chronic problem with the lack of a nationwide banking system footprint, like Tanzania, where forty-seven percent of those surveyed state "too far from a branch" as their reason. Tanzania averages less than one bank branch per two thousand square kilometers. But Tanzania is not alone. In other areas, like rural India, the travel time to a physical bank location can be as long as eight hours.

It may be easy to overlook, but the demand for documentation can be a significant contributing factor. Throughout the world, many people have limited or low-quality documentation such as wet driver's licenses, paper IDs that need to be vetted for forgeries, or they just don't have any identification. Because banking regulators everywhere require the financial institution opening an account to document that they follow strict "know your customer" (KYC) procedures, they must inspect and confirm a customer's identification. If the customer's ID is poor quality or of a type that is easily forged, then the banks must have extensive inspection processes to document the customer. This can be a hassle for all involved and can be costly. It also puts strain on the economic models for the banks that hope to fund new customer campaigns.

Think about it from a business point of view—to sign up a new customer might cost a bank twenty dollars in labor, copying, processing, and approving. This may seem small, but to a bank in a developing economy it might take them two or three years to earn back that amount in income from a new low-income customer. This reality can force them to either limit the number of new customers or focus their marketing campaigns on customers who will generate more short-term revenue or, even worse, charge high fees for basic accounts. This KYC cost can be brought down, but the process will require improved identification systems that take time and, typically, significant government funding.

Another inhibitor to banking is the high cost of basic services. Small depositors are frequently charged annual or monthly fees and fixed transaction costs, making small transactions unaffordable. In the US, the Pew Institute reports that a checking account customer may be charged as many as *forty-nine* different fees. Overdraft fees are some of the most painful since they are more likely to be levied against a tight-budget family or individual. According to BankRate.com, monthly fees on some checking accounts can run about $14 a month or almost $170 a year. And even with monthly fees, people can and do experience other fees. Avoiding monthly fees is also getting harder because banks are raising the monthly minimums for no-fee checking.

And depending on where you are in the world, it can be even worse. Costs can be high due to lack of competition or inadequate in-country infrastructure. In Sierra Leone, forty-four percent of financial nomads report that they avoid banks for reasons of cost. There the fees for a bank account are so high it is equivalent to twenty-seven percent of GDP per capita in annual fees.

Aside from the costs of being banked, many low-income people simply feel as though they are not welcome at a bank. In industrialized cities where banks and bank branches are readily accessible, many low-income people never set foot in a bank because they believe that they would not qualify for and cannot afford the bank's services. A recent study in Mexico City included focus groups consisting of low-income financial nomads who gave the following reasons for not using banks: impossible requirements, high commissions, rigid terms and conditions, low interest rates on deposits, insecurity, and bad treatment.[18] Many focus group members emphasized that their negative attitudes towards banks were rooted in their anticipating bank rejection before the fact.

---

18   Financial exclusion in Latin America — or the social costs of not banking
      the urban poor. Tova María Solo. http://www.sagepublications.com

NON-TRANSACTIONAL ACCOUNTS

As we have seen, nearly half of all adults worldwide have an individual or joint bank account at a formal financial institution—bank, credit union, cooperative, post office, or microfinance provider. And we know that the rate of people who are banked varies considerably by region. In high-income economies, eighty-nine percent of adults are banked, while in developing economies and emerging markets the rate is forty-one percent.[19]

But the functional disparity is actually greater because many bank accounts in developing economies are defined as non-transactional (in India, the estimate is that fifty percent of accounts are non-transactional). They are primarily savings accounts, so the benefit of electronic services for personal and business use is minimal or non-existent. People use such bank accounts for receiving government payments or savings. They travel to branches or post offices when they need to deposit or withdraw, and they do it much less frequently than a typical transactional bank customer. Debit cards, ATMs, and remote deposit are all less common with non-transactional bank account holders.

In developing economies, bank customers deposit or withdraw funds one or two times a month, unlike in high-income economies where bank customers make such transactions six or more times a month. In developing economies, people more frequently go to branches for support, whereas in high income economies they are much more likely to go to ATMs or use electronic payments like debit cards or online bill pay. In South Asia, less than twenty-two percent of account holders have debit cards, compared to eighty-one percent in Europe. During the past year, only five percent of adults in developing economies used any type of electronic payments.

What this all means is that the developing world is dominated by cash transactions. So whereas bank users in high-income countries use banking for a broad range of services, including bill payments and purchases, bank users in developing countries use banks to receive wage payments, remittances, and as a safe place to save. This underutilization of banking impacts as many as one billion more people.

---

19   http://www-wds. worldbank. org/external/default/WDSContentServer/IW3P/
      IB/2012/04/19/000158349_20120419083611/Rendered/PDF/WPS6025. pdf

Many foundations, governments, and development banks are concerned about the global lack of access to institutional financial services. The reason is that financial access impacts opportunity. Lack of access contributes to persistent income inequality and slower economic growth. The poor and women have traditionally suffered from exclusion from formal financial systems. In Chapter 3 we will look more closely at the impact financial exclusion has on individuals, businesses, economies, and governments.

CHAPTER 3:

Measuring the Cost of Being
a Financial Nomad

We know that roughly half of the world's adult population are part of the global institutional finance system and the other half are financial nomads. We call this the finance gap.

Is this a problem we need to solve? And if so, is it a problem for everyone, or just for those who are at the bottom of the pyramid? It's fair to ask why it's a problem for anyone to be outside of institutional banking and to be dependent on alternative financial services. What's wrong with a cash-based economy where you earn your pay and then either save it in a jar under the bed or spend it?

We saw from the story of Candice Choi that managing your money outside of the banking system results in higher costs, both in terms of transaction fees and in terms of time spent going to check-cashing stores, Western Union, and other alternative services. Candice Choi is a reporter who visited the world of financial nomads for a month. She could return to the world of banking whenever she wanted.

We believe that the finance gap impacts human lives, economies, institutions, and opportunity. Lack of access to financial services contributes to persistent income inequality and slower economic growth. The poor and women have traditionally been impacted the most, but the negative effects *trickle up* and touch a wide circle of people who are connected to the nomadic person, including families and the immediate community. If you then consider the wider impact to organizations, governments, economies, and businesses, then clearly the lack of access to financial services impacts everyone.

ALTERNATIVE FINANCIAL SERVICES

The fifty percent of adult humans who are affected by the finance gap are not living in caves; they have jobs, use money, and conduct business, but they do these things without the full range of services provided by institutional banks. They are heavily dependent on cash and services from non-banks. There's a benign-sounding name for the latter: "alternative financial services." These are financial services that exist outside traditional banking institutions, and on which many low-income individuals depend. In high-income countries like the United States, the services may resemble those provided by banks and include pawnshops, payday loans, rent-to-own agreements, refund anticipation loans, car title loans, and varieties of non-bank check cashing, money orders, and money transfers. In developing countries, they have many forms and names, and the services are often predatory and exorbitantly expensive.

The lack of access to institutional banking means you don't have deposit services for security and income through interest, no easy way to receive an electronic payment from the government, no easy way to get paid other than cash, no easy method to receive or send money to family members, no access to bank credit, likely no way to buy insurance of any kind, and no way to take advantage of electronic bill pay or buying online.

Think of something as ubiquitous as student loans. In the United States, college students owe a trillion dollars in student loan debt. In this book we won't debate the wisdom of this massive amount of debt or discuss the rising cost of higher education, but it's a fact that student loans are a significant force for social change and a powerful tool for helping low-income people get education and move up the economic ladder. Access to student loans is through the institutional banking system. If you do not have a bank account, you cannot get a student loan. Period.

Beyond the impact to the individual and the family, if a person is a small- or micro-business owner, then the list gets longer. You have no easy way for your customers to pay you other than with cash. When you need to order and receive from your vendors, the only option is to pay them in cash. You can't accept credit cards at your place of business. If your customers want to buy things on credit, chances are they can't since they probably don't have credit cards, which means you're likely to have to also be in the credit business. And you need to handle cash, which has overhead costs and loss and security issues.

We live in an increasingly digital world where cash just doesn't work very well. If you're not plugged into today's digital communication networks, you have no access to services that your neighbors and competitors have. You run the risk of being left behind. Maybe even more importantly, you risk being left out of all the great future opportunities connected to emerging online and mobile commerce.

For billions of people living at the bottom of the pyramid, cash is king—and it is a tyrant. If you have no other means of managing wealth, not a day goes by that cash impacts your life negatively. Your businesses run slower, your overhead is higher, your personal and family safety is threatened, and the buying and selling of goods and services is more difficult. If your customers need credit, you run a tab, and at the end of every business day you count your cash. Then you lug the bags of cash to a safe place or store it in a safe. Now to some this may sound like a romantic vision of a simpler time, but the problem is that in today's economy, competing stores have retail websites, accept credit cards, and can get bank loans. While you're doing business in the Middle Ages, your competitors have a huge operational advantage. It isn't romantic—it's hard.

If cash is king, then its partner, the queen, is alternative financial services. The queen can be either benign or evil. When assessing the benign aspects of the alternative financial service sector, one should acknowledge that it is addressing an important need, and many providers such as the *hawala* network fit the needs of the unserved. The most successful alternative providers excel at service and reliability, which is essential when dealing with money.

The evil queen—whose minions are the loan sharks—is always high priced and often just plain evil. If you don't pay on time she can be a threat to your life. Physical money can be the worst enemy of the poor, since it is the best friend of violence and corruption.

If you think bank accounts are expensive, try living with no bank account. The total cost of living without a bank account has been measured. Studies by the World Bank indicate the cost to the individual for alternative financial services is six percent to twenty percent of income. The latter estimation comes out of Latin America and looks at the impact to the sole proprietors of businesses. Candice Choi, as we saw, paid roughly three percent during her one-month experience as a financial nomad, and she made only routine transactions; she did not need a payday loan and she did not try to buy a car or a house.

Although countries like the United States offer many more options for consumers and an extensive banking infrastructure, the problems faced by financial nomads can be similar to those faced by financial nomads in developing countries. In the US, the FDIC studies the unserved, and reports an unbanked household with a net income of $20,000 may pay as much as $1,200 annually for alternative service fees, or six percent.[20] One might write this off to a very small segment of high-income economies, but look again. This impacts many American families—according to the FDIC, over 43 million adults and 21 million households. If you count the *underbanked* (who have bank accounts but limit bank use and leverage alternative financial services), the number increases to 100 million adults.

And of course, the problem impacts an even larger percentage of the population of developing countries. In Latin America, for example, where the financially nomadic population varies between fifty percent and eighty five percent, the cost of being outside the system is very high. For those involved in small businesses—who are saving on the side and are using credit—informal financial systems can cost up to fifteen percent of income in Mexico and up to twenty percent in Colombia. For the ninety-five percent of the financial nomads in Mexico who must pay a monthly bill, not having a bank account can translate into a one percent reduction in income. Given these are mostly low-income or poor people, the one percent can represent medicine for a family or a day's supply of food.

Let's look a little closer at the challenges. This is especially useful for those of us who have been removed from the challenges or are not directly touched by them. We find this closer look extremely useful, especially because many people have never experienced being underserved or thought about the implications of it. So bear with us and remember that this book is not really about challenges and problems—it's about innovation. To fully appreciate the opportunity

---

20   http://www.stlouisfed.org/publications/cb/articles/?id=2039, paragraph 6.

to innovate, it's best discussed once we understand the impact of the current banking gap that daily touches half the world.

PAYDAY LOANS

In this book we don't have the stamina, nor you the inclination, to examine each and every way that a low-income person living outside the traditional financial system is forced to pay more for transactional services. There are so many ways! But we'll discuss some of the more flagrant and costly traps that low-income people are compelled to step into.

A payday loan is defined as a short-term loan with an interest rate above thirty-six percent. According to a study by the Pew Charitable Trust, each year twelve million American adults use payday loans. On average, a borrower takes out eight loans of $375 each per year and spends $520 on interest.[21]

Pew's survey found 5.5% of adults in the United States have used a payday loan within the previous five years, with three-quarters of borrowers using storefront lenders and almost one-quarter borrowing online. Overall, in 2010, twelve million Americans used a storefront or online payday loan. Most payday loan borrowers are white, female, and are twenty-five to forty-four years old. However, five groups have higher odds of having used a payday loan: African Americans; those earning below $40,000 annually; those without a four-year college degree; home renters; and those who are separated or divorced. And while lower income is associated with a higher rate of payday-loan usage, other factors can be more predictive of payday borrowing than income, such as home ownership; studies have found that low-income homeowners use payday loans less often than higher-income renters.

Payday loans are often characterized—and advertised—as short-term solutions for unexpected expenses, like a car repair or emergency medical need. Pew's study found that this was often not the case; most payday loan borrowers use the loans to cover ordinary living expenses over the course of months, not unexpected emergencies over the course of weeks. The average borrower is indebted about five months of the year.

---

21   http://www. pewstates. org/uploadedFiles/PCS_Assets/2012/
       Pew_Payday_Lending_Report. pdf

To qualify for a payday loan, you do not need established credit or even collateral. What you need is proof that you have a paying job. The loan is secured by your next paycheck—hence the term "payday loan." Of course, to make the interest rate sound less expensive, payday loan providers don't advertise their annual percentage rate (APR) the same way credit card and personal loan providers do. Payday loan providers state the interest in terms of a fee per $100 loaned. Here's a typical example:

You need a quick loan, perhaps because your car broke down and you need to get to work, or because need to make the rent. You have no access to a bank loan. So you walk into the payday loan office or apply online. Let's say you need to borrow $600 until your next payday, which is in seven days. The payday lender tells you that the fee for your loan is $15 per $100 borrowed. You think, "That's not so bad—it's only fifteen percent." You agree to the loan terms and give the lender a check in the amount of $690, dated in seven days.

When your loan comes due in seven days, the payday lender will cash the check or debit your checking account. If you have $690 in your account, then you are finished and the transaction is completed.

For your seven-day loan you will have paid a fee of ninety dollars. That translates into a whopping annual percentage rate (APR) of 782%. Calculating the APR is complex and involves not only the loan amount and the fee, but the *period* of the loan—how long until you pay it back. If you Google "payday loan APR calculator" you'll find websites that allow you to plug in the loan amount, the fee, and the loan term, and the website will show you the annual percentage rate.

In contrast, as of this writing, credit card APR fixed rates average 13.02%. The highest rates—for folks with bad credit—range up to 22.9%.[22] So-called subprime cards, for borrowers with the lowest credit ratings, such as bankruptcies, have been advertised at 79.9% APR.[23] That's still cheaper than a payday loan.

Aside from the high cost, the big risk to payday loans is that many customers can't pay back the loan on time. Consider the fact that a customer who does not have $600 in his or her bank account this week is unlikely to have $690 in their account next week. Consequently, many customers "roll over" their loans. They

---

22   http://www.bankrate.com/credit-cards/bad-credit-cards.aspx

23   http://www.creditcards.com/credit-card-news/first-premier-79-rate-fees-credit-card-1265.php

cannot pay on the due date, so the creditor charges the $90 fee and agrees to collect on the next payday.

According to the Consumer Federation of America, from a single lender each year the average payday loan customer takes eight to thirteen payday loans or loan renewals.[24] This is called "loan churn." So if you're the average customer, let's say you roll over or renew your $600 loan ten times until you can finally pay it off. To borrow $600 for ten weeks, you will pay a total of $900 in finance charges plus repay the amount borrowed. Your $600 payday loan will end up costing you $1,500.

The structure of payday loans—high fees, short-term due date, lack of underwriting, a single balloon payment, and requiring the borrower's checking account as collateral—fosters not financial independence but long-term indebtedness.

Another example of loan churn would be if you took out the $600 payday loan and managed to pay it back on your next payday. Problem solved? Hardly. Because you're now short $690 during the workweek, you're probably broke. It's very likely that you'll need to take out *another* payday loan to pay for basic living expenses.

There are additional risks and fees. To get a payday loan, you are required to give the creditor a personal check as repayment. If your check bounces, your bank will charge you a fee—often as high as forty dollars. And you still have to make good on both the loan and the check.

The payday loan industry points to repayment plans as a tool that borrowers can use to ease the burdens of loan repayment. But lenders structure these repayment plans to minimize the number of borrowers that receive them. Why? Payday lenders have every incentive to keep borrowers out of these plans because loan churning is much more profitable. Lenders load the repayment plans with fine print to disqualify many borrowers, and make little effort to advertise or promote repayment plans to delinquent or pressured borrowers.

If this sounds terrible—which it is—consider the fact that if you do not have a checking account into which you deposit your paychecks, then even this usurious form of lending is closed to you, and you are left to gaze up at the top of the pyramid and wonder how you'll ever be able to climb those steep stairs.

---

24   http://www.consumerfed.org/news/512

MIGRANT WORKER REMITTANCES

Millions of families depend upon money sent home by family members who are working in some other country. These international remittances constitute a huge flow of funds around the globe. For many developing countries, money sent home by migrant or guest workers constitutes the second largest financial inflow, exceeding international aid. For some individual recipient countries, international remittances from workers living abroad can be as high as a third of GDP.

According to the World Bank, the total value of international remittances has been increasing steadily over the past decade. In 2012, the World Bank estimated that remittances totaled US$440 billion, of which $357 billion was sent by approximately 192 million migrants (or three percent of the world's population) to their homes in developing countries.[25]

The value and characteristics of foreign remittances varies greatly from nation to nation. For example, in 2012, remittances from the United States to other countries totaled more than $123 billion, nearly thirty percent more in inflation-adjusted terms than they were in 2000. Mexico is the destination of the largest amount of remittances from the United States. According to estimates of the Bureau of Economic analysis, in 2009 about $20 billion in remittances was identified in the international economic accounts as going to Mexico; by BEA's estimates, such flows from the United States to Mexico (adjusted for inflation) rose by an average of two percent per year between 2000 and 2009.[26]

In 2012, migrants working in the United States sent a total of $123 billion[27] back to their families, making the US the largest sender of remittances in the world. More than $23 billion went to Mexico, $13.45 billion to China, $10.84 billion to India, and $10 billion to the Philippines, among other recipients. In that same year, data from the World Bank shows the amount of money being sent by migrants across the entire world reached $530 billion, making it a larger economy than Iran or Argentina. This worldwide figure has tripled in the last

---

25   http://econ. worldbank. org/WBSITE/EXTERNAL/EXTDEC/EXT
      DECPROSPECTS/0,,contentMDK:22759429~pagePK:64165401
      ~piPK:64165026~theSitePK:476883,00. html#Remittances

26   http://www.cbo.gov/publication/22012

27   http://www.pewsocialtrends.org/2014/02/20/remittance-map/

ten years and is now three times bigger than the total aid budgets given by countries around the world.[28]

In 2012, remittances sent home to India from Indian workers in foreign countries reached $70 billion, the highest in the world, followed by $66 billion sent home to China by Chinese workers abroad. The sharp increase in remittances to India has come primarily from the oil-exporting countries of the Persian Gulf, where large numbers of migrants from many nations—South Asia, MENA (Middle East and North Africa) and East Asia and Pacific regions—continue to produce robust growth in remittance flows.[29]

In Indonesia, total remittance sent home to Indonesia by that country's more than four million citizens working abroad exceeds $5 billion. There are now 4.32 million Indonesian workers overseas sending money back home, according to studies by Bank Indonesia.[30]

Remittances fluctuate according to regional economies. For example, nearly eleven percent of all Mexicans live outside of Mexico, most of them in the United States, and the money they send home to family members is one of the country's most important sources of foreign income, representing about two percent of the country's gross domestic product. During the Great Recession, yearly Mexican remittance figures experienced a steep decline and then rebounded; the total amount of remittances in 2011 was $22.7 billion, a seven percent rise over 2010.[31]

Most of the remittances are sent through the conventional channel of agents, including MoneyGram, Western Union, UAE Exchange, or Xpress Money Services. However, in recent years, online and mobile phone money transfers from companies such as Remit2India and Xoom.com have seen significant growth.

---

28   http://www.dailymail.co.uk/news/article-2271455/Revealed-How-immigrants-America-sending-120-BILLION-struggling-families-home.html

29   http://www. dnaindia. com/money/report_india-to-overtake-china-receive-70-billion-remittance-in-2012-world-bank_1767576

30   http://www.thejakartapost.com/news/2010/12/09/migrant-worker-remittances-reached-us5-billion.html

31   http://latimesblogs. latimes. com/world_now/2012/11/mexico-immigrants-remittances. html

The Cost of Remittance

The goal of this book is not to analyze the necessity or dynamics of international workers' remittances—that would be a book all by itself—but to highlight the cost of such remittances, particularly for the unbanked and those who are dependent upon alternative financial services.

The cost of remittance transactions is often expensive relative to the amounts sent (which are typically no more than a few hundred dollars per transaction), the generally low incomes of migrant workers, and the income of remittance recipients. Therefore, a reduction in the price of remittance transfers would represent a significant savings for migrants and their families. According to the World Bank, if the cost of sending remittances were reduced by five percentage points relative to the value sent, remittance recipients in developing countries would receive over $16 billion dollars more each year than they do now.

Just how much does it cost to send money home? The cost varies tremendously according to where you are, to where you're sending money, and the channel or service that you use. The World Bank estimates that, on a global basis, sending remittances costs an average of 8.96% of the amount sent. This means that on average, if you send US$200 from one place in the world to another, the fee will be $17.92. This is an *average*; the World Bank has calculated the cost of hundreds of routes or corridors for remitting money. Here is a sample:

Corridors for remitting money	Average cost to send US$200
South Africa to Zambia	$45.87
Qatar to India	$36.56
Global Average	**$17.92**
Germany to Turkey	$12.85
United States to Mexico	$11.13
Singapore to Indonesia	$10.49
United Arab Emirates to Pakistan	$4.92

The most expensive of any corridor in the world is South Africa to Zambia. This means that if you're a migrant worker in South Africa and you want to send US$200 to your family in Zambia, it will cost you $45.87, or nearly twenty-three percent of the amount you want to send.

According to the World Bank, the cheapest corridor is from the United Arab Emirates to Pakistan, where to remit $200 will cost you $4.92, or a bit more than two percent.

The cost will also vary by the service you choose (or are forced to use by circumstance). If you use a bank to remit funds from South Africa to Zambia, the transaction will cost you an average of 26.34 percent. If you use a money transfer organizations (MTO) such as Western Union or Moneygram, the fee will be an average of 11.01%, which is a significant savings.

Conversely, sending money via a bank from Singapore to Indonesia will cost you an average of 3.34%, while choosing an MTO will be more expensive at 4.08 percent.

Remittance prices are high for many reasons, including limited competition, regulatory obstacles, underdeveloped financial infrastructure in some countries, lack of access to the banking sector by remittance senders and/or receivers, and difficulties for migrants to obtain the necessary identification documentation to enter the financial mainstream.

It may be argued that the single most important factor driving high remittance prices is a lack of transparency in the market. Because there can be several variables of which remittance prices are comprised, consumers may have difficulty comparing total fees, or they simply might not bother, and instead choose the agency that is physically the most convenient. The price for a remittance may include a fee charged to the sender, a margin taken on the exchange rate when remittances are paid and received in different currencies, and another fee charged to the recipient of the funds. Fee components may also vary according to the speed of the transfer, how the recipient is given the funds (in cash or by crediting an account), and the information provided by the sender about the recipient (such as a bank account number).

This industry-wide complexity of fee calculation also tends to reduce competition, as consumers gravitate to familiar providers because they are not aware of other providers, or cannot conveniently compare the services they usually buy against another product.[32]

---

32   http://web. worldbank. org/WBSITE/EXTERNAL/TOPICS/
EXTFINANCIALSECTOR/EXTPAYMENTREMMITTANC
E/0,,contentMDK:22121552~menuPK:5978015~pagePK:2
10058~piPK:210062~theSitePK:1943138,00. html

The bottom line is that if you're a worker living far from home, and you're sending funds home to your family through established channels, it's going to cost you, on average, nearly nine percent.

The Hawala System

The exception, of course, is the ancient *hawala* system. Since it exists entirely "off the grid," estimates of its size are difficult to make. In brief, hawalas are unregulated international financing networks. (The word *hawala* means "in trust" in Hindi.) Hawalas are found throughout the world, but most commonly in the Middle East, North Africa, and the Indian subcontinent. Individuals and organizations use the system to transfer cash, locally or overseas, to recipients who do not have access to a bank or who do not want to deal with a bank. Transfers leave no paper trail and offer anonymity to both the originator and the recipient.

Here's how it works. The operator of a hawala is a *thakedar*. A fee, traditionally five percent of the amount to be transferred, is charged for the service.[33] When a person wishes to transfer money, the *thakedar* of one hawala contacts his counterpart in the other location, usually now by e-mail. Within minutes, the originating thakedar receives a confirmation from the recipient thakedar stating that there is sufficient cash on hand to complete the transfer. A password is then shared among the sender, the recipient, and the two thakedars. To receive the money, the recipient then provides his thakedar with the password. In relationships that develop over a period of years, the system is based on trust between the two thakedars. The cash debt is settled later between the two thakedars.

The hawala system as it currently exists is cash-based; if the recipient and the receiver had a direct electronic money-transfer capability, there would be no need to use cash. Of course, for some users of the system, the lack of any electronic or physical record of a transaction is an attractive feature, and it is this feature that makes hawalas of equal interest to law enforcement agencies.

---

33   http://www.cbc.ca/news/background/banking/hawala.html

CHECK-CASHING SERVICES

If you are unbanked, or if your personal finances are day-to-day and you cannot wait for a paycheck or government check to clear to access the funds, you will likely patronize a check-cashing service.

In the United States, there are an estimated 13,000 check-cashing organizations (CCOs) that cash more than $80 billion worth of checks annually. Roughly eighty-five percent of these are individual payroll checks with an average size of five hundred dollars. The remainder of the checks cashed consist of government benefits, income-tax refund checks, and personal checks. CCOs do not require a customer to have an account to cash a check.

While fees vary by state and by store, Financial Service Centers of America (FISCA), an industry trade group representing CCOs and payday lenders, estimates national annual check-cashing revenues at over $1.6 billion.[34]

Check-cashing providers may be small, independent businesses, or large national chains. The largest check-casher in the United States, ACE Cash Express, Inc. , reports over $250 million in annual revenues and has 1,230 stores in thirty-seven states and the District of Columbia.

The check-cashing industry provides a wide range of services, many of which are not offered by banks or other financial institutions. These services include cashing checks, selling money orders, completing wire transfers, and other services related to utility bill payment, public assistance benefits and food stamp distribution, payday loans, and lottery ticket sales. In many lower-income neighborhoods, the corner check-cashing store is the primary provider of financial services.

Check-Cashing Customers

Every year in the United States, over thirty million people submit 180 million checks for processing at check-cashing providers. The primary customers are lower- and middle-income working individuals who tend to be younger than the general population and are living from paycheck to paycheck.

Many CCO customers who are living day-to-day with regard to finances need their checks converted to cash immediately. Many customers live in a cash economy, where businesses that provide staple goods and services will

---

34   http://www. msgcpa. com/files/Check%20Cashing. pdf

not accept personal checks. Many do not trust banks and, with chronically low account balances, are hesitant to write checks for fear of incurring high bounced-check fees.

Direct Deposit

The increase in direct deposit by government and private employers poses a challenge to the check-cashing industry. As states have switched over to Electronic Benefit Transfer (EBT) accounts and direct deposits, the mail delivery of public welfare, disability, tax refund, and other government checks has sharply declined. Direct deposit provides customers with immediate access to funds, eliminating the waiting period for checks to clear, thereby bypassing the primary service of CCOs.

However, to receive direct deposit funds, you need to have a bank account. To step into this new opportunity to serve the unbanked, some CCOs and banks have contracted with counties to receive the direct deposit of government assistance checks. They charge recipients a monthly fee to access their funds.

ACE Cash Express advertises this direct deposit service:

"Get paid up to two days faster when you have your payroll or government benefits check direct deposited to your ACE Elite Visa Prepaid Debit Card. Plus, enjoy the time and savings of not having to pay a check-cashing fee or wait in line to cash your check. Get the ACE Elite Visa Prepaid Debit Card and experience the freedom to withdraw your money when you need it."[35]

Aside from various fees for various services, it appears the ACE Elite Visa Prepaid Debit Card carries a monthly fee of five dollars on the condition that you deposit at least $500 each month. There is no fee for direct deposit.

The Cost of Check-Cashing Services

As reported in 2011 by Claes Bell for Bankrate.com, the real cost of check-cashing services as compared to fees charged by banks can be very high. Financial nomads who patronize check-cashing stores are not getting a good deal. Here is a sample of checking-cashing fees among financial service providers and some large national check-cashing chains.

---

35   https://www. acecashexpress. com/store-services/direct-deposit

Regions: 1.5 percent and three percent of the check amount, with a minimum fee of three dollars.

KeyCorp: One percent of the check amount.

U. S. Bank: Ten dollars.

Wal-Mart: Three dollars for checks of $1,000 or less, six dollars for check amounts of $1,001 to $5,000.

Ace Cash Express: Three percent of the check amount.

Check 'N Go: Up to three percent of the check amount.

If you go online to **Moneytree,** and look for the check-cashing fees, you find this message:

"View the fees for your neighborhood by finding your local Moneytree branch."[36]

Not very encouraging. So then you find a branch office. We found one of several Moneytree offices in Reno, Nevada. For check-cashing fees, the website provides this chart:[37]

TYPE OF CHECK	FEE
Payroll	1.90%
Government	1.90%
Personal (1st and 2nd Party)	4.90%
Money Orders	4.90%
Insurance Drafts	3.90%
Cashier's Checks	3.90%
Tax Checks	1.90%
Moneytree Money Orders	1.00%
Other Checks	4.90%
Business Owners: Ask About Special Rates	
In addition, a $.99 fee is charged on transactions over $20.00	

On a typical biweekly pay schedule, you're looking at a minimum of $494 a year for cashing your twenty-six payroll checks of $1,000 each. That's a significant amount of money, especially when you consider that either depositing a paper check or electronic direct deposit costs you not a penny.

---

36   http://www. moneytreeinc. com/services/check-cashing

37   http://www. moneytreeinc. com/branch/meadowood. aspx

Alternative financial services are not as well regulated or transparent as the checking account operations at major banks. Contrary to banks, which provide detailed fee schedules, check-cashing services often do not post their fees or make their fee schedules easily accessible.

Financial nomads cope daily with the challenges of living without affordable financial services. High fee services, excess time waiting in line, extra effort and travel time to pay bills, expensive remittances to support family members, lack of access to electronic payments—all of this makes their lives a little harder. After all, it is expensive to be poor.

PART TWO

The lack of affordable and adaptable banking services is an issue that should concern everyone, not just the people who are living at the bottom of the pyramid. At its worst, a lack of banking creates a downward spiral of disenfranchisement, widens the gap between rich and poor, encourages outlaw or extralegal behavior, and inhibits the social mobility that keeps any society vibrant and open. An accessible and reliable banking system helps to create stability and overall prosperity. Low-income workers waste less time in check-cashing lines, spend less money on usurious back-alley services, have legitimate identification, feel connected to the economic fabric of their society, are encouraged to save, have access to credit, and participate in retail commerce.

We have seen the costs to living at the bottom of the steep pyramid, and the obstacles that keep many hardworking individuals and families from making the long climb to the top. However, the goal of this book is not only to point out the challenges but to draw attention to the real-world solutions that exist today.

We'll see that in many cases, the future is already here; it's just not equally distributed yet. Innovation is emerging as a patchwork. We're entering a new era where the world will see a shift from incremental advances in financial inclusion to exponential growth. Part of the revolution in personal finance is driven by global social change: the growing empowerment of women, the rise of stable democratic governments, and the increased recognition of basic human rights. Technology is also a major force; the rise of smartphones, improvements in banking infrastructure, cloud computing, social networking, the management of vast amounts of real-time and archival data, mobile technology and networks, and the successful scaling of regional models to national and international scale are all drivers of change.

In Part Two, we'll look at a selection of key initiatives from around the globe. These are systems that really work, and they are all very different from each other. By seeing multiple aspects of the future, we can start to build a model of what's to come. Each of these examples are pieces of the larger puzzle of technology-enabled financial services that are not only affordable but can be used by the entire pyramid. These approaches will light pathways to a future where 2.5 billion additional people have services that can empower their life and work. This will not only impact their lives—it will empower them to be full citizens of the emerging digital world. It will also expand the digital world to include them, allowing other citizens and businesses to serve 2.5 billion additional people. This expanded digital world is the largest emerging market ever.

CHAPTER 4:
The Philippines and Smart Money

With a population of ninety-two million people, the Philippines is an archipelago nation comprised of 7,107 islands. The Philippine economy is slowly transitioning from one based on agriculture—which employs nearly a third of its people—to one based more on services and manufacturing. Despite the changes, the income level of forty-five percent of the population of the Philippines remains less than two dollars a day.

With so many islands, so many small depositors, and widespread dependence on cash, the environment for traditional banking with branch offices is extremely challenging.

Smart Communications is a wholly-owned mobile phone and internet service subsidiary of the Philippine Long Distance Telephone Company (PLDT). Commonly known as PLDT, it's the largest telecommunications company in the Philippines.

In 1991, anticipating the liberalization of the telecommunications industry in the Philippines, Smart Communications was organized by a group of Filipino investors under the name Smart Information Technology, Inc. As of this writing, with 50.9 million cellular subscribers, Smart has become the largest mobile network operator in the Philippines.

In December 2000, when they first launched Smart Money, Smart wasn't the biggest mobile network operator. But by June 2004, they had overtaken their competitors. Their leadership in the Philippines was rooted in their products and services designed specifically for the disenfranchised consumers.[38]

They steadily grew their prepaid subscriber base and focused on products and services needed by the average consumer. Since many people in their subscriber base lacked formal credit, Smart had to excel at prepaid phones and value-added services for the low-income market. Although operating in a relatively small country and modest economy, Smart's success got noticed globally. As mobile operators gathered at their annual GSMA conference, Smart was recognized numerous times for innovative products and services designed for low-income consumers. Their role in prepaid and mobile money was as a pioneer in the Philippines and as a thought leader in BoP mobile for the rest of the world—including Vodafone, who later went on to launch M-Pesa in Kenya.

When this all started in 2000, most of the mobile market worldwide was focused on the traditional "elite customer," where mobile was a nice second line to complement landline services. Penetration was about fifty percent in developed countries but only five percent in developing and emerging economies.

Smart was effective at focusing on the BoP, designing products and services, creating distribution systems, and scaling their execution. Their first affordable product was Smart Buddy, a prepaid cellular phone, text only, where talk time or minutes could be bought at retail in small increments. In August 2002, they continued this focus by offering PurTxt, a service for those who could not afford "call and text." Small denominations of top-up were a key to reaching and serving the low-income consumers.

Between 2000 and 2004, Smart focused on scaling for lower value "ARPU" subscribers. It did a few things that were later duplicated by all mobile operators in emerging markets. First they eliminated the card-based mobile minute sales method (remember those scratch cards?). Instead, they replaced it with Smart Load, an over-the-air method to top-up value on your prepaid phone. Smart Load drastically brought down the cost of top-ups from P300 (roughly the minimum daily wage, which as of this writing is about US$7.00) to as low as P30 (about US$.70). The sale of micro-top-ups electronically by an army of retailers nationwide enabled Smart to reach even remote communities. This helped boost the penetration rate to more than thirty percent, lowered the

---

38   What works: Smart Communications – Expanding Networks, Expanding Profits. WRI, Vodafone, September 2004

distribution cost, and also extended the reach because now all you needed was a feature phone (with voice and text) to be able to sell minutes in rural areas. The number of agents scaled quickly. Smart had 50,000 outlets when Smart Load was launched in May 2003, but scaled to 500,000 retail agents due to success and the new low cost distribution model.

This vast distribution model created incremental income for the Smart retailers, called *sari-sari* or Tagalog storeowners. These sari-sari merchants often provide credit and have close connections with their patrons. Some retailers earned up to $18.00 a day in re-load sales. This not only made mobile communication more accessible, but it also created higher income for hundreds of thousands of small merchants across the country.

Once distribution costs were down, the second step was to lower the minimum top-up value. In May 2003, they introduced lower denomination top-ups that could be done in small increments—P30 (at that time US$.53), P60 (US$1.07), P115 (US$2.06), and P200 (US$3.58). This "nano top-up" made it affordable for almost everyone. Smart realized that most Filipino incomes fall in the lower-income brackets, with as much as fifty-one percent of the population living on US$2.00 per day or less. By December 2003, Smart introduced the Pasa Load initiative, which allowed for loads as in even smaller increments, starting with a P2 load (US$0.03). In 2003, this was a revolutionary idea when only fourteen percent of potential subscribers in developing markets had mobile phones.

Besides innovative products, Smart showed how through great execution and focus on very low cost they could not only grow their numbers but they could grow their top and bottom lines. In this period (2000 – 2004) the jury was still out about profitable, scalable business models for BoP mobile businesses, and Smart showed the world how it could be done. This had a profound impact on the next decade of mobile growth globally.

The mobile wallet idea was percolating globally but mostly in research circles. Smart was the first to ask the question, "How could a wallet be provided to someone who doesn't even use a bank today?" They not only asked the question, but in December 2000 they answered it when they launched Smart Money. They decided to offer the first mobile wallet for the unbanked and distribute it through their airtime top-up agents. After all, they had far more agents and reach in the Philippines than all the banks put together. And they had more customers already than all the banks.

Smart Money was their invention. It was an easy and safe way to make financial transactions. They retooled part of their agent network to act as banking agents, signing up customers for the service, and loading and unloading cash. Once they had Smart Money on their phones, the phone became a combination of a banking website and a debit card in digital form. The services were basic, simple to use, and focused on supporting what their customers needed for their day-to-day lives. Users could transfer money, pay bills, and top-up airtime with their Smart mobile account. To bridge to the traditional banking and payments world, they offered an optional separate Smart Money Card, which also doubles as a MasterCard, letting customers make ATM and debit card transactions, both in-store. Smart Money can be used either through the Smart mobile phone or a Smart Money MasterCard.

Features of Smart Money include:

- Instant money management. Users can check their cash balance through their Smart cellphone. The customer receives a notification message when a successful transaction is made. In 2000, this was done all from a very simple feature phone and on phone text-based applications.

- Transfer funds to and from a bank account to a Smart Money account. Since some people did have regular bank accounts, this created a bridge between the mobile account and the traditional bank accounts.

- Like M-Pesa, Smart Money from Smart is not a bank. Customer funds are held in an account with Banco de Oro, and the bank does not have any individual customer information. This is similar to the model in the US where Wal-Mart, Rush Card, and Green Dot offer prepaid accounts. They don't need to be a bank to do this, but there must be a bank behind the scenes holding the funds. This allows these companies with great reach and trust to be the retail face of banking.

- The customer need not have a traditional bank account to use Smart Money, because of easy over-the-counter reloading at participating establishments. Also, Smart Money agents can do registration for the account even if the customer has never had a bank account. They follow banking regulations and "know your customer" rules which are universal to banking around the world.

To load cash to the Smart Money account, the customer must physically visit an agent at a Smart Wireless Center, a Banco de Oro branch location, or a Smart Padala participating outlet. The customer gives the money to be loaded to their Smart Money account to the cashier. The customer receives a confirmation message on their phone when money has been loaded to their account.[39] They can also transfer funds from their bank account into their Smart Money account using their mobile phone, or accept a transfer of funds from another Smart Money account holder.[40] A similar process is used if they want to withdraw money.

Smart's implementation was innovative and groundbreaking. The idea was simple, but the implementation was complex. It required many years of hard work on the product, the agent relationships and technology, the treasury management, and the marketing to drive adoption of a new category of banking service to a customer base that was mostly unfamiliar with banks.

At a microfinance conference in Washington, DC in 2004, we met Jojo Malolos, who was the key manager on the project for Smart. At the time, the work he was doing was quite experimental and most of the listeners struggled to understand what he was doing—how it worked, the business models, even why he would attempt it. He led the team at Smart from 2002 until 2012 and is now advising other innovative companies on financial inclusion across the world.

We had the opportunity to visit with Jojo and ask him about what he had learned over his decade of work on financial inclusion in the Philippines, and how the mobile banking revolution had impacted businesses and citizens.

"Smart started with an approach that built on their experience with telecom," he said. "In the beginning, Smart could see telecom realizing extensive communications reach, where everyone would have access to communication through mobile phones. Key innovations—prepaid accounts vs. post-paid billing, electronic distribution of prepaid minutes (elimination of scratch cards), vast retail networks for distribution—were dramatically changing the communications landscape.

---

39   http://www1.smart.com.ph/money/what/

40   http://www1.smart.com.ph/money/use/add-funds

"And as we saw the 'communications gap' close, we saw the other impact it had in the Philippines. It did more than connect people; it meant social and economic good. So while we had built a highly-profitable telecom business reaching everyone, at the same time we created new jobs, added new tax revenue for the government, and grew the economy of the Philippines.

"When mobile telecom entered the Philippines, the typical person did not have a landline. There were fewer than two million landlines in a country of approximately 75 million people. Mobile operators understood that the success of telecom required a well-designed 'ecosystem' that included a vast retail network. This retail network created efficient reach to all people, which enabled Smart Telecom to profitably serve even the small customers. (In 2012, the average revenue per user was US$3.25 per month in the Philippines. In Indonesia it was $3.07, India $1.62, Malaysia $13.20, Singapore $34.00, and in China $10.52.) This retail channel has to be mutually beneficial to scale, meaning the business model works for all involved, with each business in the value chain—no matter what size—financially benefitting from participating.

"What was amazing about this telecom success was that it created new businesses and jobs. Some of the retailers already existed and they benefitted with new revenue opportunities. But there were many retailers that were new businesses. This created hundreds of thousands of jobs; Smart, just one of the mobile operators, had 1.2 million retailers enabled to provide telecom services.

"In addition to job creation, mobile telecommunication empowered people's lives and their work. Consumers and small businesses were given great service at a low price. This addressed a massive communicate gap, and the benefits included greater business efficiency, greater security, enhanced family and friend communication, and on and on.

"As the communications gap was being addressed, Smart decided to leverage their assets to tackle another hard challenge, and set out to address the banking gap. When they started, only twenty-five percent of the adult population in the Philippines had bank accounts. The other leading operator followed suit, and in 2004, Globe Telecom launched a competitive offering. So in 2004, before the rest of the world even noticed, both mobile operators were actively marketing mobile financial services targeted at the traditionally unbanked.

"When we set out to add mobile financial services to our product set, we felt if we used the same principles that enabled scaling in our telecom business, we could achieve the same results—scalable, profitable services that reached everyone and benefitted all in the value chain. We aspired to solve a hard problem, which was to give underserved people affordable access to banking and electronic payments. At the same time, we knew this too would bring social, economic, and government improvements to the Philippines."

Smart Communications accomplished all they set out to do, and more. They proved that the mobile phone could be used to deliver low cost, high value financial services at the BoP. They also proved they could do it profitably where banks couldn't, and that in doing so they could enhance customer loyalty dramatically. Not only did their innovative, inclusive products like Smart Money and Pasa Load help telecommunications reach the majority of Filipinos, but their market approach drove revenue and opportunity for micro-entrepreneurs across the country. Their focus on the average—that is, low-income—consumer and their sensitivity to micro-enterprise allowed them to create unprecedented scale and reach for both telecom and banking.

This success was a key industry inflection point, and all that follows—M-Pesa, and 150 mobile network operator mobile wallets for the BoP projects globally—can all be tied back to this first success. And when they took the stage at industry events, the executives of Smart also sent a message to the industry that this is good business, but it is also the right thing to do. People need telecom, entrepreneurial opportunity, and banking, plus everything that comes along with them.

But before we move on, it's important to note one key success factor that influenced the success of Smart Money. This was highlighted by a recent conversation with Don Rae, who led the project in the early years. He says, "One of the real insights that gets frequently overlooked is what it takes to make a payment system prosper—by definition it is a coupon-clipping business model, with low margins and totally driven by volume. It's a classic chicken-and-egg situation—no volumes and no business. Those who have been successful—like transit cards like Octopus—prosper and build because they originate from transit systems which by definition are high-volume and repeat transactions.

"The thing that drove Smart Money adoption was that there was a high volume day-one merchant, which was Smart itself and the top-up business. By marrying these two products, we were able to get over the volume hump by being our own biggest merchant with high volumes. In fact, in the early days when Globe had gone to E-top-ups but did not yet have GCash, their dealers were Smart's second-biggest merchant pool.

"I'm not sure people really understand this concept even to the present day, and it's why so many trials fail to take root. You need volume and repeatability on day one; after you have that base you can add other streams on top incrementally. Companies like Square who are going after Starbucks are hitting the right target, as their customers buy a coffee every day."

THE TAKEAWAY

The pieces of the financial inclusion puzzle we can see from Smart Money and their innovation include:

- A non-bank like Smart Telecom, with great trust and reach to the customer, can be a key actor in delivering financial services. They leverage their distribution and relationships, which helps bring people into the banking system. We think of this as non-banks providing the "last mile to the customer."

- Technology, specifically mobile, can digitally connect people to the banking system. Even without the high bandwidth and fancy applications on a smart phone, this can be efficient and effective.

- Driving initial use through simple daily transactions like topping-up mobile or buying coffee is key to creating the critical mass of usage. Once this is done, then the sky's the limit on what other uses are adopted.

CHAPTER 5:

Kenya and M-Pesa

More than one billion customers in developing markets have access to a mobile phone but do not have a formal bank account.[41] It's inevitable that these two facts should collide, and from that collision new solutions emerge.

M-Pesa is an early success story that demonstrates that basic banking services—keeping cash safe and facilitating cash transactions—can be provided to vast numbers of customers who once lived at the bottom of the pyramid and who now can be said to inhabit an open and accessible financial platform.

In April 2007, Safaricom, Kenya's largest mobile provider, partnered with Vodaphone to launch M-Pesa, a mobile-phone-based payment and money transfer service. ("M" is for "mobile" and *pesa* is the Swahili word for "money.") M-Pesa allows individual users to deposit and carry funds in an account whose balance appears on their cell phones; to send funds using SMS technology to other users; and to redeem their deposits for regular money. Users are charged a small fee for sending and withdrawing money using the service. Since its introduction, M-Pesa has spread quickly and has become the most successful mobile phone-based financial service in the developing world. By 2012, about seventeen million M-Pesa accounts had been registered in Kenya. The number of mobile subscribers in Kenya reached 28.08 million, and mobile penetration

41   http://www.gsma.com/mobilefordevelopment/programmes/mobile-money-for-the-unbanked/programme-overview

increased to 71.3% of the population of forty million people. The number of M-Pesa users represent an astonishing forty percent of the population.[42]

In recent years, M-Pesa has expanded to Tanzania, Afghanistan (as M-Paisa), South Africa, and a limited area in India (M-Paisa). Plans are in the works for a service in Egypt.

M-Pesa is aimed at mobile customers who do not have a bank account by choice, because they do not have access to a bank, or because they do not have sufficient income to justify a bank account. Customer money is held safely in a bank account run by M-Pesa on the customer's behalf. M-Pesa customers do not have any contact with the bank, and the bank does not have their personal details (another example of a non-bank providing the last mile to the customer).

A key part of the concept is that M-Pesa is not a mobile banking service but a mobile prepaid money account and money transfer solution. Mobile banking provides access to perform transactions on an existing standard bank account through mobile phone technology. M-Pesa was designed specifically for people who do not have access to conventional banking. It is different in that the customer does not need a bank account, only a mobile phone to perform transactions. This makes it a sort of hybrid service, which for Westerners might be understood as if Western Union—a funds transfer service—also allowed customers to keep reserves of cash on deposit. Instead of always having to give Western Union the cash you needed to transfer, you could make the transfer yourself on your phone from the balance in your account.

This is similar to Smart Money, but there are differences. M-Pesa does not encourage card usage. Instead, the customer interface is primarily the phone. If I want to take money out, I can go to an agent or an ATM—but I use a PIN and one-time token to access the ATM, not a card. Also, merchants accept M-Pesa directly, bypassing the need for cards for merchant acceptance (more about this later when we look at what Kopao Kopo is doing in Kenya). Another difference is that the initial use case that drove adoption was domestic money transfer, not top-up. Safaricom was able to "paint the countryside red"—their logo colors—and provide a vast agent network. Then they advertised widely to encourage people to use it as a better way to send money home to their relatives in rural areas.

---

42   http://www.cck.go.ke/news/2012/sector_statistics.html

There is no charge to open an M-Pesa account and no charge to make a deposit. There is no minimum balance; an M-Pesa account can have between zero and KES100,000 at any time. The maximum daily transaction value is KES140,000, and the maximum per transaction is KES70,000.[43] (As of this writing, one US dollar equals KES88, so KES100,000 is about US$1,135.) Fees are charged for transactions, and there is a fee to withdraw cash from the M-Pesa account.

M-Pesa has been designed to be easy to use. The service is driven by a secure application on Safaricom SIM cards. Registered customers have a menu on their phone, giving them the ability to move money to other phone based accounts.

To register, a customer goes to an authorized M-Pesa agent and:

Step 1: Replaces the existing Safaricom SIM card in the mobile phone.

Step 2: Registers as a new M-Pesa customer. In conformance with global "know your customer" (KYC) standards, registration requires a Kenya national ID card or other acceptable identification.

Step 3: Activates the M-Pesa account. M-Pesa customers can deposit and withdraw cash from a network of agents that includes airtime resellers and retail outlets acting as banking agents. As of this writing, there are over 40,000 agents in Kenya and many more new outlets are being added daily.

Customers need an M-Pesa PIN to send or withdraw money from their account and while using the M-Pesa menu on the Safaricom SIM.

M-Pesa has been transformative. The Economist explained M-Pesa concisely in an article published in June 2010:

> It is like magic. By clicking a few keys on a mobile phone, money can be zapped from one part of Kenya to another in seconds. For urban migrants sending money home to their villages, and for people used to queuing at banks for hours to pay bills or school fees, the M-Pesa money-transfer service, operated by Safaricom, Kenya's largest mobile operator, is a godsend. No wonder . . . It is used by 9.5 million people, or twenty-three percent of the population, and transfers the equivalent of eleven percent of Kenya's GDP each year; or

---

43   http://www.safaricom.co.ke/personal/m-pesa/m-pesa-services-tariffs/tariffs

that it has inspired more than sixty similar schemes across the world.[44]

By mid-2012, in Kenya there were 19.5 million m-money users (eighty-three percent of the adult population), transferring nearly US$8 billion per year (equivalent to twenty-four percent of GDP). M-Pesa is responsible for more than ninety percent of these transfers, which are growing at nearly forty percent per year.[45]

M-Pesa offers many benefits to unbanked and low-income customers. The unbanked now have a way to save money, to send money, and to receive money. The fees are reasonable. For the unbanked, sending money or paying bills meant using Western Union, which is expensive and inconvenient. It works with just about any phone, so customers can get on the system very easily. The system is simple enough so people can learn how to use it, and it's proven itself to be safe. Safaricom dominates the Kenyan market, so there is a wide reach, which makes life easier for consumers. Businesses can do multiple payments, so business owners can easily pay workers.[46]

Aside from the technological foundation that makes M-Pesa both functional and scalable, a key reason for its success in Kenya is the fact that Kenyan citizens are required to carry a national identification card. While civil libertarians (especially in the United States) may have reservations about the implementation of such a federal ID system, the fact remains that in low-income countries many people do not have the ubiquitous personal IDs such as a driver's license that many people in more developed countries take for granted.

It is mandatory that all Kenyans aged eighteen and above carry the national identity card. The Kenya national identity card is the main and legal identification document recognized in Kenya. Citizens must provide it to open a bank account, register a business, for employment, acquire a driver's license, transact mobile phone banking, and many other uses that require proof of identity.[47]

---

44   http://www.economist.com/node/16319635
45   http://ict4dblog. wordpress. com/2012/11/24/why-m-pesa-outperforms-other-developing-country-mobile-money-schemes/
46   http://ourmobileworld.org/post/35349373601/what-is-mpesa-how-does-it-work-how-did-it-start
47   http://kenya. thebeehive. org/en/content/640/1757

An additional condition that made the development of M-Pesa possible was that Kenyan regulators approved the development of a financial services provider that was not a bank. And while the established banks in Kenya initially resisted this new competitive upstart, they eventually jumped on the bandwagon and have begun to offer their own versions of mobile banking, further blurring the lines between traditional banks and alternative financial services providers.

In 2010 Equity Bank, the largest bank in Kenya by customer base, partnered with Safaricom to launch M-Kesho, a service that allows deposits to, and withdrawals from, one's Equity bank account through selected M-Pesa agents and through the M-Pesa menu. (In Kiswahili, *kesho* means "future.") Like M-Pesa accounts, M-Kesho accounts have no account opening fees, minimum balances, or monthly charges. But unlike M-Pesa accounts, M-Kesho accounts pay interest, do not have a limit on account balances, and are linked to limited emergency credit and insurance facilities. And unlike its regular Equity account holders who can only transact at the bank's 140 branches, Equity's M-Kesho customers are able to transact at any of the 40,000 retail outlets that accept M-Pesa.[48]

In May 2012, KCB, the biggest bank in Kenya by asset base, introduced their mobile banking product, Mobi Bank. Open to all mobile networks, Mobi Bank is accessible via the mobile web and offers a wide range of services:

- Send money directly from a KCB account directly to any mobile number, irrespective of whether the recipient is registered onto M-Pesa or other mobile cash transaction providers such as Airtel Money or yuCash.

- The recipient can collect the money from any KCB branch or KCB Mtaani agent by presenting their ID card and the SMS message.

- Accessible anywhere in the world via the Internet. All the customer needs is an internet-enabled phone, and they can send money directly from their KCB account to a mobile number or any other bank account from wherever they are in the world.

- Direct transfer from KCB account to M-Pesa, Airtel Money, or yuCash. The customer doesn't have to send money to their own M-Pesa, Airtel

---

48 http://www. financialaccess. org/blog/2010/05/m-kesho-kenya-new-step-m-pesa-and-mobile-banking

Money or yuCash account; they can send directly from their KCB account to the recipient.

- Direct airtime top-up from KCB account to any mobile phone on the network. The user can add beneficiaries on their KCB Mobi Bank account. These are all the people to whom the user frequently sends airtime. Any time the user needs to send airtime, they simply select the beneficiary, and the amount is debited directly from the user's KCB account and into the beneficiary's account.

- Credit card balance and mini-statement. The user can check their KCB credit card statements and get a mini-statement.

- Pay bills from a credit card via KCB Mobi Bank.

- Loan payments directly from the user's KCB account into their loan account via KCB Mobi Bank.[49]

In November 2012, Safaricom launched M-Shwari, a revolutionary banking service for its M-Pesa customers. (*Shwari* means "all is well" in Swahili.) The service is offered in partnership with Commercial Bank of Africa, which has held the M-Pesa money transfer trust account since its inception and is the major channel through which agents replenish their e-money reserves. M-Shwari allows customers to save and borrow money through the mobile phone. Unlike M-Pesa, which does not pay interest, M-Shwari accounts earn interest on the money saved. The service is paperless and eliminates visits to a bank branch. It's similar to a traditional bank offering a linked savings account to an existing checking or current account.

To access the service, all an M-Pesa customer needs to do is update their M-Pesa menu with a simple click, and they have a savings account. Movement of money between M-Pesa and the savings account is at no charge, no ledger fees are applicable, and savings balances can be as little as Ksh1.[50]

M-Pesa's success in Kenya did more than just make money transfer convenient. Before M-Pesa's launch, there were plenty of banks in Kenya, but

---

49   http://www. kcbbankgroup. com/ke/index. php?option=com_content&task=view&id =460&Itemid=1

50   http://www.mobilepaymentstoday.com/blog/9469/Kenyan-Banks-vs-M-PESA-the-gloves-come-off

few branches outside the major cities. Before M-Pesa, the banks consistently focused on marketing to, and supporting, about three million people in Kenya. These were the richest people at the top of the pyramid. So while decades of traditional banking served the rich, it left out most people. M-Pesa is broadly distributed, lower cost, simple, secure, and has solved an important pain point for the customers. So began exponential growth in the adoption of nontraditional banking.

But what happened next was equally important. The same banks that were slow to change are now moving quickly to adopt new services. In addition, mobile carriers (in Kenya, all of which have similar offerings) and banks are all aggressively innovative, and it has created a vibrant, innovative "ecosystem" for new financial services products and services. These financial services enable a stronger, more innovative online commerce market to develop in Kenya—after all, more than twenty million people buying online is a bigger market than three million. In addition, they are fully plugged into the more global online commerce market.

Everyone wins. And our bet is that just like GDP growth has been tied to increased telecom access (a doubling of mobile data use leads to an increase in the GDP per capita growth rate of 0.5 percentage points[51]), so will the history books tie incremental GDP growth to increased banking access. M-Pesa broke through and showed the world what was possible.

THE TAKEAWAY

Besides being an outstanding example of a breakthrough in financial inclusion, M-Pesa demonstrates these additional pieces of the financial inclusion puzzle:

- Importance of a frequent compelling initial use case. For Kenya, that was domestic money transfer, since so many young people worked in Nairobi but frequently sent money home to rural family members.

- Role of a uniform identification system to lower the barriers to signing up for a new account and provide enhanced security. All banking regulators

---

51   A doubling of mobile data use leads to an increase in the GDP per capita growth rate of 0.5 percentage points. A report for the GSM Association November 2012

require KYC to be done in a complete fashion. Universal ID systems are key to low-cost, easy-to-do sign ups.

- Benefit of interoperability and ubiquity. M-Pesa achieves this because they were everywhere; most countries in the world will require inter-company cooperation to make this happen. But the longer they wait, the slower the adoption will be. What are they pretending not to know? Ubiquity and interoperability will be critical steppingstones to broad adoption, especially for domestic money transfer.

- Simple is better than complex. M-Pesa's success can be credited in part to its simplicity. Simple, easy to use, a few compelling use cases. Other more elaborate solutions have failed. Less is more.

- Agent network size and effectiveness is key. The bigger the network, the better trained, the better the motivations of the agents, the bigger the success. M-Pesa did this, and while few countries have been able to come close to their success, many have learned from them.

- Success means competition. Now other banks and telcos are working hard to compete in Kenya. This is driving innovation and choice for the users.

CHAPTER 6:

Kopo Kopo

M-Pesa is a hugely successful system by which individuals, using only their mobile phones, can informally send money to each other. M-Pesa accounts are personal. They are issued to individuals.

But what about payments to merchants? A shop owner who has two or more employees cannot open a standard M-Pesa company account for the store, and he or she can't very well ask the individual clerks to use their personal accounts for store sales.

In Kenya, the next step in mobile payments was therefore a system that could be used by merchants.

Enter Ben Lyon, Dylan Higgins, and Tom Bostelmann, who founded Kopo Kopo in August 2010. Having direct experience in microfinance, they originally envisioned mobile payments as a way to make lending organizations more efficient at disbursing and collecting funds from borrowers. They felt this extra efficiency could go a long way to making the credit lower priced for the recipient.

Once founded, Kopo Kopo moved quickly to refine their strategy before relocating to Nairobi, Kenya. (These pivots are increasingly typical for a fast-moving tech start-up.) Although their aspiration was to have a global impact, they quickly realized that despite all the press and promise, mobile payments were not scaled in most places in the world. Since they wanted to go where the clients were already using mobile money, the obvious choice was Kenya. Kenya has rapidly progressed from a typical African country of over eighty percent unbanked to having seventy percent of adults being active users of the most popular mobile wallet, M-Pesa. It's been one of the fastest disseminations of technology relative to an entire population in history. The company's move to Kenya was an acknowledgment that Kenya has become the "Silicon Valley of banking," especially for the poor.

In Kenya, there was a huge percentage of money circulating digitally among individuals, but no easy way to use it to pay for things at stores. The founders of Kopo Kopo realized that the emerging system used by the mobile credit card payments system Square could be the template for a similar system in Kenya, with one significant difference: they would eliminate debit cards.

Square works on just about any iPhone, iPad or Android device. First, the merchant downloads the free Square Register app through either the iTunes App Store or Google Play. Then the merchant signs up for Square Register at the Square website. Once the merchant is registered, Square ships them a free card reader—that small square device that plugs into the headphone jack of the smartphone. The merchant can also buy the card readers at a wide variety of outlets ranging from Starbucks to Wal-Mart, and receive a credit for the cost for later use with Square.

Next, the merchant enters the store's bank account information into the app so that credit card payments can be deposited into the store's account. Most payments are deposited overnight.

When a customer makes a purchase, the merchant swipes the card through the reader or enters the card number manually. Square charges the merchant a fee of 2.75% per swiped transaction, and a bit more for manually entered credit card numbers.

Square Register works just like a conventional point-of-sale terminal at a restaurant or clothing store. It lets the merchant create entries for everything that in the store, complete with pictures and prices. To make a sale, the cashier simply taps the items to be purchased. The app even will add appropriate taxes and tips.

Kopo Kopo adapted the Square approach—but without credit cards or swipers, just phones. Merchants can access the interface via SMS/USSD, the web (via Desktop), or Android. Although the company prefers "mobile first," they also accommodate PC users. A unique six-digit merchant number is assigned to the merchant. Customers pay for goods the same way they'd buy more airtime or send money to a loved one: they take out their own mobile phones and send their money to the six-digit code assigned to the merchant. The merchant sees the funds appear and the sale is closed.

Kopo Kopo is not a bank; it is a payment service provider. Here's how the company fits in: In the world of payments, the consumer has a relationship with an *issuer*. In US terms, the issuer could be your bank, which issues you a Visa or MasterCard. These providers are handling the role of issuing you a payment instrument. In Kenya, the biggest issuer by far is Safaricom, Kenya's massive mobile provider, and the product is not a card with a VISA or MasterCard logo. Instead it is an account tied to your mobile phone number, and branded M-Pesa.

On the flip side of the equation are the *acquirers*—the merchants who accept the payment methods held by their customers. Before Kopo Kopo, a minuscule number of merchants in Kenya were set up as acquirers that would accept mobile payments. What this meant was that seventy percent of Kenyans were walking around with the ability to make mobile payments, but there were very few merchants who would accept them.

Kopo Kopo stepped into this gap.

To create their system, Kopo Kopo needed to work with Safaricom. Kopo Kopo convinced Safaricom to adapt M-Pesa for use as a *merchant* payment system. This was necessary because M-Pesa had always worked as a consumer remittance system. Just like Western Union, the person sending the money was the one who paid the fee. And then the merchant and recipient would both have to pay an additional fee to withdraw the money.

"So if a customer wanted to pay a shop owner for a coffee with mobile money," says Ben Lyon, "the shop owner would have to ask the customer to add a fee to cover what the merchant had to pay to withdraw the cash. So the customer would be paying two fees. From a psychological perspective, for the customer this is a non-starter. We went to Safaricom and said, 'If you want consumers to use this service, it has to be free to them. And if you want merchants to accept it, and pay the fee, it has to be a small percentage. Your benchmark needs to be how much a credit card company is charging, and undercut it.'"

In the world of customers making payments to merchants, in order to offer the convenience of paying digitally, the standard is for the one taking the payment—the merchant—to absorb the fees. Kopo Kopo managed to convince Safaricom to remove the fee to the customer in these cases but to charge the merchant a single fixed fee of what is now one percent.

In addition, when Kopo Kopo launched the service in 2012, Safaricom wanted a percentage fee plus a fixed minimum. "If a merchant collected less than 670 shillings," says Lyon, "We would have to pay Safaricom ten shillings because they had a fixed floor that they wanted to recover immediately. But we would charge the merchant only 1.5 percent. So for small transactions—which were thirty percent of our business—we were taking a loss because we wanted one simple price. Eventually Safaricom saw that this was inefficient, and waived the fixed payment. This was the first time that this had been done for merchant payments in emerging markets."

Another challenge to adapting the M-Pesa system for merchant payments was that there existed an informal practice of reversal on demand by the money sender. "Say you sent money to your brother," says Lyon. "But then your mother gets sick. You could call the service and say, 'I need to cancel the transfer because my mother is sick. ' If your brother hadn't collected the money, the transfer could be canceled. No problem. But for merchant payments, this could not be allowed to happen. You cannot buy a coffee, pay with mobile money, walk out of the store with your coffee, and then call and have the transaction cancelled. Merchants knew about this, and, for this reason, many refused to accept informal mobile money payments. We solved that problem by managing the merchant 'till numbers' assigned by Safaricom. A transaction could only be reversed with the consent of the merchant."

So while Square was breaking new ground in the US getting large number of merchants to accept credit cards via smartphones, Kopo Kopo was breaking new ground in Kenya getting large numbers of merchants to accept mobile money without using a card. Their business models are in fact similar: Square aggregated lots of small merchants for the payment provider (Chase Paymentech), while Kopo Kopo aggregates and serves small- and medium-size merchants in Kenya, and Safaricom (owner of M-Pesa) is the payment processor.

Kopo Kopo is responsible for doing everything for their merchant clients: recruiting, training, customer support, providing the platform, reconciliation, and value-added services. All the customer needs to know is that M-Pesa is accepted at the store. Like a back-end credit card processor, Kopo Kopo is known to the merchant but is not a brand the consumer knows or even cares about. All the customer knows is that now they can go to the corner store and pay for groceries using the M-Pesa app on their SIM card.

Their shift from microfinance to merchant services was an acknowledgment that the second big frontier for mobile payments in Kenya was for small- and medium-size businesses to accept mobile money. This was a huge opportunity that would help the businesses (some of who were customers of microfinance organizations) in many different ways. It increases sales, lowers costs of back-office accounting, and improves their customer experience, since now the customers could use the money on their phone instead of having cash in their pockets.

This is really important to SMEs in general, but especially in emerging markets like Kenya since there is so much opportunity to give them tools for both their front-of-store and back-office operations. They have traditionally been very manual and cash oriented. Kopo Kopo focuses on the needs of these merchants and gives them added productivity, sales, and improved service.

One of Kopo Kopo's customers is Nairobi Java House, the local chain similar to our Starbucks. When you walk into the coffee house, you see a sign in Swahili that says, "Pay here with M-Pesa." And there is a five- or six-digit number on the sign. When a customer is ready to pay, they simply open their phone, open the M-Pesa SIM card application, and enter that number, their pin, payment amount, and other details. The phone sends a secure message in the background, the payment happens, and a confirmation message is sent to the merchant and the customer.

"It's a 'push' transaction," says Lyon. "It's initiated by the customer. The interface the customer uses is provided by the telecom operator. We're not visible. Once the merchant receives payment, that's where we come in."

It's relatively low-tech, using basic messaging and a very simple application on the phone SIM toolkit, USSD based. Not anywhere as fancy as our smartphone applications. But what is great is that it works on all phones, and it's secure.

One exciting thing about this low-tech solution is that by the nature of the technology and the consumer pushing the payments, there is little possibility of a Target-like security breach, with criminals getting peoples' payment information and using it to steal. The company has seen fraud attempts on its network, but nothing like the scale of what has happened in the United States with magnetic-stripe credit card and POS systems.

"Our primary selling points were low fees and payment security—the inability of the customer to reverse the transfer," says Lyon. "There was also a third benefit—increased revenue security. In Kenya, as in many places, a problem for merchants is 'internal leakage.' That's a nice way of saying 'employee theft.' With digital payments, internal leakage is vastly reduced because people aren't handling as much cash. And ordinary theft is reduced too. In insecure communities, you don't need armed guards to carry bags of cash to the bank. Your revenue never sees the light of day—it goes straight into your bank account. For many of our customers, that was a big selling point."

To date, Kopo Kopo has twelve thousand merchant customers and fifty million dollars a year in payments. But it is growing. There are only three in emerging markets that have this kind of success—Kopo Kopo in Kenya, Telesom in Somaliland, and EcoCash in Zimbabwe. Don't be fooled by all the press releases; these are early days for merchant acceptance of electronic payments. Most countries are still dominated by cash payments. The change is very fundamental but powerful; transitioning from money in your pocket or mattress, businesses operating on cash with little electronic record keeping, people paying only in person in cash.

This is an important transition, but also requires so much to change. Without these changes, businesses and people will be sidelined from participation in global e-commerce. With the change, the world reshapes and starts to become a world of opportunities where even small companies and entrepreneurs around the world can participate.

Kopo Kopo is part of the second wave of modernization in Kenya. The first was led by consumers opting into using mobile money. The second is all about the merchants. We in the developed countries might miss the distinction because it is all about mobile, but we may take it all for granted because we went through both stages a long time ago when we started to use banks, cards, internet payments. We had gone through all this before mobile phones entered our lives.

Also, we might think our capabilities are all because of one company—our bank, like Citibank, or our card brand VISA, or our internet wallet PayPal. But the truth is that this is just the brand we associate with the payment. The actual payment is orchestrated by a number of actors working in concert to make secure, 24/7 payments, universally accepted.

So Kenya made an amazing thing happen. It got seventy percent of the people of Kenya to move almost overnight from cash to electronic payments for a couple of use cases; the most popular was money transfer between friends and family members. At the same time, a few merchants started to use that same P2P to take payments from their customers, but this was small because it wasn't easy and didn't fit the needs of the merchant.

It took another actor to enter the scene to increase the fit and provide services around M-Pesa to make it work for the business. Kopo Kopo is a true pioneer, and their platform is tailored to the needs of SMEs and retailers in emerging markets. This is different than the needs of a major retailer like Tesco or Wal-Mart.

Not only did they build the technology solution, break new ground with Safaricom, and do "heavy lifting" with the individual merchants, they also helped the merchants upsell this capability and encourage their customers to use it.

"Our goal for global growth and to service global demand," says Lyon, "is to take our technology and everything that we've built for ourselves and for our merchants, and to offer it as a white-label service to a bank, mobile operator, or other third party. This will allow them to leverage their existing distribution network to launch a merchant payment strategy quickly, as opposed to going through the same learning curve that we needed to. We want to bring merchant payment services to countries like India, Bangladesh, and Pakistan.

"We want to reach the bottom of the pyramid. For our customers—especially small businesses—we've found that the lower-income business owner tends to be the most risk-averse. They may be challenged by seasonality, or employee theft, or other problems. They're not thinking about growth; they're thinking about survival. He or she is less willing to adapt to new technology. Therefore part of our task is educational, and to reach these millions of very small businesses and convince them that this is a positive asset for them. Trust is the foundation. Offering the payment system is the introduction; we hope to advance into additional products such as cash advances for small businesses, an accounting package, automated tax filings—we'll see."

The task of supporting all aspects of electronic payments and banking is really like an orchestra, with different instruments working together to make great music. Our developed market solutions do that, but the instruments are different, and the number of sections are all from one industry. This orchestra that is forming around the world has modern instruments and a lot more diversity of contributors. The music will reach more people and serve more diverse needs, but the preproduction is very complicated due to all the different companies, technologies, and solutions that need to be brought together.

THE TAKEAWAY

The puzzle expands:

- Financial services are not a solo act. With all the success of M-Pesa, there is a need for a larger community of actors to realize the broad potential of financial services. Merchants need services to specifically address their needs, and Kopo Kopo emerging means this larger community is emerging. Because it gives them additional utility, this benefits both merchants and consumers.

- Actors like Safaricom can encourage these actors to enter the market and add value by offering their service as a platform with APIs. This makes it easy for a rich set of supporting actors to emerge.

- Business models will need to be refined to meet the needs of the different actors. If we try to take the model for merchant payments from VISA, MC, and Amex transactions and force-fit them into the rest of the world, it will be painful and probably not successful. Kopo Kopo is doing groundbreaking work with Safaricom to sort through the specific pricing that will work. This will be iterative for a while.

CHAPTER 7:
CHAPTER 7:

Bangladesh and bKash

More than seventy percent of the population of Bangladesh live in rural areas where access to formal financial services is difficult. Yet these are the people who are in most need of such services, either for receiving funds from family members in distant locations or to access financial tools to improve their economic condition.

While less than fifteen percent of Bangladeshis are connected to the formal banking system, nearly seventy percent have mobile phones.

A BRAC Bank subsidiary, bKash was conceived primarily to utilize these mobile devices and the omnipresent telecom networks to extend financial services in a secure manner to the underserved remote population of Bangladesh. The company is headed by Kamal S. Quadir, a Bangladeshi-American entrepreneur and artist best known as the creator of CellBazaar, a mobile-phone-based electronic marketplace which, after reaching four million users, was acquired by Norwegian telecommunications operator Telenor in 2010.

In 2011, mobile operator Robi Axiata Limited, the biggest telecom in Bangladesh, signed a partnership agreement with bKash to provide access to its services for Robi subscribers and extend the distribution of the service. At the launch ceremony, Bangladesh Bank Governor Dr. Atiur Rahman marked the occasion as a milestone event, not only for the advancement of Bangladesh but also to celebrate a true partnership between banking and telecom industries.

Launched in the second half of 2011, by the end of 2012 bKash had grown to two million accounts, by the end of 2013 the number of registered accounts had shot up to eleven million.[52]

In April 2013, International Finance Corporation (IFC), a member of the World Bank Group, became an equity partner, and in April 2014 the Bill & Melinda Gates Foundation became the equity investor of the company.

The ultimate objective of bKash is to ensure access to a broad range of financial services for the people of Bangladesh. It has a special focus to serve the low-income masses of the country to achieve broader financial inclusion by providing services that are convenient, affordable and reliable.

In addition to eliminating initial monetary costs involved in entering the banking system, bKash greatly minimizes opportunity costs such as time and effort required to access such services. The service charges are minimal and there are no hidden costs involved.

BKash's CEO Kamal Quadir said the company is growing rapidly in Bangladesh, a country with 95 million mobile phones, while noting that nothing similar has caught on in the developed world. "Fundamentally, bKash is designed for poor people," he said. "In the US, one of the reasons this kind of service hasn't kicked in yet is because we have so many alternatives."[53]

BKash oversees a network of 45,000 agents across the country who provide services to its customers. That way it avoids the overhead expenses that a traditional bank would have to pay. BKash uses middleware technology from Visa called Fundamo to store customers' transactional information.

How to Use bKash

Opening a bKash wallet is very easy, and it is absolutely free. A customer needs an Airtel, Banglalink, Grameenphone, or Robi phone service connection; a photo ID; and two portrait photos. The customer must also provide a thumbprint.

Here are the directions (as of September 2014) to open a bKash account: Go to any nearby bKash agent along with:

---

52   http://www.cgap.org/publications/bkash-bangladesh-fast-start-mobile-financial-services

53   http://allthingsd. com/20130416/bkash-offers-mobile-banking-for-bangladesh-a-country-with-few-bank-accounts/

a. Your mobile phone with Airtel, Banglalink, Grameenphone or Robi connection.

b. A copy of your photo ID (national ID/passport/driving license).

c. Two copies of passport-size photographs. Fill out the Wallet Opening Form. Print your thumbprint and signature properly. Please make sure that you have taken your copy (customer copy) from the agent and preserve it for future reference.

After the first stage of the wallet opening, the customer needs to activate their bKash mobile menu. He or she then follows the steps below to activate their mobile menu.

1. Go to bKash mobile menu by dialing *247#. Choose "activate mobile menu." Enter a 5-digit PIN for your bKash wallet. Re-enter the PIN to confirm.

After successfully following these steps, the customer's mobile number will become his or her bKash wallet number. The customer may immediately use "cash in" and "receive money" services in their new bKash wallet. Then, after their KYC form verification is completed (maximum three working days), the customer will be able to cash out, buy airtime, make payments, and use all other services of bKash. Once the wallet is fully active, the customer dials *247# to access bKash services twenty-four hours a day, seven days a week.

To deposit money into the bKash wallet:

- Go to any bKash agent.

- Let the agent know the amount you want to cash in.

- Write down your bKash wallet number and the cash-in amount in the agent's register.

- Pay the amount of money you want to cash in.

- In exchange, the agent will send the new balance to your bKash wallet. You and the agent will both get a confirmation message from bKash. Remember to sign the agent register before leaving the counter.

To send money from the bKash wallet to another bKash wallet:

- Go to your bKash mobile menu by dialing *247#.

- Choose "send money."

- Enter the bKash wallet number you want to send money to.

- Enter the amount you want to send.

- Enter a one-word reference about the transaction.

- Enter your bKash mobile menu PIN to confirm the transaction.

- Done! You and the receiver both will receive a confirmation message from bKash.[54]

Even though as of July 2014 Bangladesh's central bank had approved more than twenty licenses to offer mobile financial services, more than eighty percent of transactions were through bKash. Unlike large mobile money businesses in other countries, bKash is not a mobile network operator (MNO) and did not have an existing customer base to which it added mobile financial services. BKash is neither telco-led nor bank-led; it is a standalone company designed to provide mobile financial services.

In the words of Greg Chen and Stephen Rasmussen in CGAP, three factors have combined to drive bKash's fast start:

1. A specialized organization built to deliver mobile financial services;

2. A shared vision for scale among a diverse investor group;

3. An enabling and flexible regulatory environment.[55]

If we look closer at the scaled success of bKash, we see that although they did much of the heavy lifting, they were not alone. Their success is due to this hard work but can also be attributed to the efforts of BRAC Bank, which is a large successful microfinance bank, and Robi Axiata. Bangladesh's central bank

---

54   http://www. bkash. com/i-want-register/registration-agent-point-customer

55   http://www. cgap. org/publications/bkash-bangladesh-fast-start-mobile-financial-services

has been supportive in creating a regulatory environment flexible enough to allow a bank subsidiary like bKash to operate.

THE TAKEAWAY

- bKash is a great example of a new company emerging to meet the need of people at the bottom of the pyramid. They did a great job of identifying and servicing their users. The adoption and usage is a strong proof of this.

- Although independent, their success was not exclusively due to their own execution. Their partnership with BRAC Bank and Robi Axiata was, and continues to be, critical to their success.

- Regulations are key to enabling new actors and encouraging existing players to be supportive.

CHAPTER 8:

India – A Big Vision
for a Populous Nation

If Kenya, with a population of forty million people, a land area 224,081 square miles (580,367 km^2), and one dominant mobile provider, is a perfect laboratory for the incubation of progressive mobile banking solutions, then India is the land where such solutions would succeed or fail based on their scalability. With a population of 1.2 billion people and an area of 1.3 million square miles (3.3 million km^2), India represents a market that's thirty times as large as its African counterpart.

India has a long and rich tradition of commerce and institutional banking. From the Vedic period in ancient India (beginning 3250 BCE) there is evidence of loans being made. Later during the Maurya dynasty (321 to 185 BCE), an instrument called *adesha* was in use, which was an order to a banker requiring him to pay the amount of the note to a third person, which corresponds to the definition of today's bill of exchange. During the Buddhist period, there was considerable use of these instruments, and merchants in large towns gave letters of credit to one another.

Banking in India in the modern sense originated in the last decades of the eighteenth century. The first banks were Bank of Hindustan (1770 –1829) and The General Bank of India, established 1786 and since dissolved. The oldest bank still in existence in India is the State Bank of India, which originated in June 1806 as the Bank of Calcutta (which in 1809 became the Bank of Bengal). The East India Company established the Bank of Bengal, Bank of Bombay

(1840), and Bank of Madras (1843) as independent units and called them presidency banks. For nearly a century, the three presidency banks acted as quasi-central banks, as did their successors. In 1921, the three banks merged to form the Imperial Bank of India. In 1935, the establishment of the Reserve Bank of India (RBI) as the country's central bank ended the quasi-central banking role of the Imperial Bank.

Upon India's independence on August 14, 1947, the Imperial Bank of India was nationalized and became the State Bank of India. The government constituted the State Bank of India to act as the principal agent of the RBI and to handle banking transactions of the Union government and state governments all over the country. In 1959, seven banks owned by the princely states were nationalized and became subsidiaries of the State Bank of India. In 1969, fourteen commercial banks were nationalized, and in 1980 seven more banks were nationalized in 1980. With this, eighty percent of the banking sector in India came under government ownership.

TRADITIONAL SOLUTIONS

Much has been written about the poor state of financial inclusion in India.

India ranks fiftieth in the world for financial inclusion and has the second highest number of financially excluded households in the world after China. As of 2009, 51.4% of farmer households were financially excluded from both formal and informal sources (45.9 million out of 89.3 million). Seventy-three percent of all farmer households have no access to formal sources of credit. The extent of financial exclusion indicates the inefficiency of the existing financial inclusion models, which leads to high transaction costs. The huge number of underserved Indians illustrates the failures of the established banking systems and encourages those citizens to lose faith in the system.[56]

India has about 600,000 villages, but only 74,000 of those are banked, a difficult situation the government has to deal with as it endeavors to roll out direct cash transfers of benefits and subsidies. The government is working at full throttle to provide physically accessible basic banking facilities. It has already

---

56   "Banking the Unbanked: An Indian Perspective" http://tejas. iimb. ac. in/articles/72. php

started tapping the unbanked areas through expanded bank branches, banking correspondents, and common service centers (CSCs).

The IT revolution had a great impact in the Indian banking system. The use of computers had led to introduction of online banking in India, and the computerization of the banking sector of India has increased dramatically after the economic liberalization of 1991 as the country's banking sector has been exposed to the world's market. Without the use of advanced information technology and computers, Indian banks were finding it difficult to compete with the international banks in terms of customer service.[57]

The country today has about 98,000 bank branches, of which about 60,000 belong to public sector banks. Covering all 600,000 villages with bank branches won't be feasible. You just "can't get there from here," at least not fast enough.

One solution has been to boost India's network of ATMs, which (it is hoped) would drive down transaction costs. It's true that the cost of transactions at ATMs is much less compared to that of a branch; the cost incurred by a bank per transaction at a branch is Rs 40-50, whereas it is Rs 15-20 at an ATM.[58]

Another idea has been to boost the use of prepaid cards. In April 2013, the State Bank of India (SBI) launched a prepaid card using the Visa platform to bring financial services to the unbanked sector of India. The card, named the State Bank Smart Payout Card, allows employers to issue prepaid cards to those employees who may not qualify for bank accounts, such as contract laborers. The card can be used to pay salaries or other funds. Payees can withdraw cash from the prepaid card at any ATM, or use it for electronic or online payments.

Prepaid card holders do not need to open bank accounts, eliminating the need for paperwork that temporary or blue collar workers may not have. Each card is protected by a unique PIN number, just like an ATM or debit card.

The minimum amount that can be loaded on the card at a time is Rs 100 and the maximum is Rs 10,000. (As of this writing, one US dollar = 54 rupees. Therefore, the minimum amount you can load onto the card is about $1.86.) The limit for a single transaction is Rs 10,000 (US$185), and it has a monthly limit of Rs 25,000. The card, to be available at all SBI branches, can be used for

---

57   Business Standard, New Delhi http://www. business-standard. com/article/finance/ flipside-over-half-a-million-villages-remain-unbanked-in-india-113010100077_1. html

58   Business Standard, New Delhi http://www. business-standard. com/article/finance/ flipside-over-half-a-million-villages-remain-unbanked-in-india-113010100077_1. html

cash withdrawal at any ATM of SBI and its associate banks free and at other banks' ATMs for a nominal fee. It can also be used at point-of-sales (POS) terminals at merchant establishments and on websites accepting Visa cards for e-commerce transactions. It can also be used as an add-on card for existing account holders on the Visa network. At the time of the launch in April 2013, SBI had 75,000 POS terminals and planned to double the number in a year.

Existing Visa customers with bank accounts at SBI are also eligible for the prepaid card. These customers can top-up their card through online banking, while corporations issuing cards to employees without bank accounts will have to go to a physical bank branch to add value to the prepaid cards.[59]

These efforts, while admirable, require extensive physical ATM networks, and a prepaid card can't be used to make transactions as easily as a mobile app. Also, most Indians, even those with bank accounts, have never used an ATM or paid for goods and services with a card. So while the largest bank offering a simple prepaid card may sound compelling, it doesn't go far enough to address the needs of 700 million underserved Indians.

MOBILE BANKING

In 2009, the number of mobile users in India was 429.73 million. Early 2013 estimates from the Telecom Regulatory Authority of India (TRAI) put this number at 906.62 million. In a little over three years, the number of mobile phone users in India doubled to reach a figure that is greater than the entire population of the European Union and the United States combined.[60]

In June 2008, the Reserve Bank of India, Department of Payment and Settlement Systems, issued the draft of "Mobile Banking Transactions in India – Operative Guidelines for Banks." This document for the first time sought to specify operating guidelines on mobile payments in India.

RBI mandated that M-banking service must work on all mobile operators and use SMS as a medium for transactions. Although some day in the not-too-distant future, most Indians will have access to smart phones with data services, today it is all about voice and SMS for most of India. So the solutions

---

59   Asia Pacific FutureGov http://www. futuregov. asia/articles/2013/apr/29/prepaid-card-launched-unbanked-india/

60   http://www. jana. com/blog/india-mobile-users-experience/

that will be mass market need to accommodate. This SMS method means that the messages between the phone and the banking backends need to use SMS to communicate. That way they can reach more people, especially those who are underserved.

Many private banks offering M-banking had to improve their service to comply with the regulation. "Looking at the huge and diverse customer base of SBI, we have developed a solution which will work across mobile operators and support various methods of communication," said Spanco Telesystems vice president (technology) Kamal Maheshwari, the company that has developed the solution for SBI.[61]

With mobile phone penetration of over eighty percent, India has a huge potential for mobile banking. But on the global landscape, mobile payments still have a long way to go.

There's been some research into mobile readiness. The MasterCard Mobile Payments Readiness Index (MPRI) is, as the project website states, "a data-driven survey of the global mobile payments landscape. Using public and proprietary data, as well as original market research, the survey gauges the preparedness and receptivity of thirty-four countries for mobile payments of three varieties—person to person (P2P), mobile e-commerce (m-commerce), and mobile payments at the point of sale (POS)." The MPRI uses a scale of zero to 100, with 100 representing the complete replacement of plastic cards by mobile devices, an admittedly unlikely scenario. In MasterCard's judgment, the point of inflection—the stage at which mobile devices account for an appreciable share of the payments mix—is a Mobile Readiness score of 60. As of April 2014, the thirty-four countries in the current Index achieved an average score of 33.2. Singapore topped the Mobile Readiness chart with a score of 45.6, followed by Canada and the US with scores of 42 and 41.5, respectively. Coming in at number five with an impressive score of 40.4 was—you guessed it—Kenya.[62] The lowest score of 22.4 was posted by Argentina. No market reached a score of 50, indicating there is work to be done before mobile payments become mainstream.[63]

---

61   Times of India http://articles. timesofindia. indiatimes. com/2008-06-30/telecom/27763194_1_m-banking-mobile-banking-core-banking-solution

62   http://mobilereadiness.mastercard.com/the-index/

63   http://businesstoday.intoday.in/story/mobile-banking-on-the-rise-in-india/1/191851.html

According to MPRI, among the thirty-four surveyed countries India ranked twenty-first with the score of 31.5 on a scale of 100. As MPRI noted, "India's annual investment in telecommunications of $69.7 billion gives it a leading spot in infrastructure . . . Consumers in India have not yet fully embraced mobile payments . . . Fourteen percent of Indian consumers are familiar with both P2P and m-commerce transactions, and ten percent are familiar with POS transactions."

Thanks to its convenience and accessibility, mobile banking is becoming more and more prevalent in India. Month-on-month transactions carried out through mobile banking are surging both in volume and value terms. According to Reserve Bank of India (RBI) data, a total of 3.7 crore (30.7 million) mobile transactions took place between February and November 2012, jumping around 1.7 times in volume during this ten-month period. These transactions saw nearly a three-fold increase in value over the same period. Increasing smartphone adoption and initiatives such as media promotions and customer education programs for mobile banking have contributed to this uptrend.[64]

But these numbers fail to tell the whole story of India. There is a large, well-served banked segment of India that is contributing heavily to the success of mobile banking. However, for the underserved segment, change has been slower than anyone has wanted. These people live without the benefit of convenient banking, lack easy methods for deposit and withdraw of money, struggle to sign up for a bank account, and live without the convenience of electronic payments. It is a massive underserved population—and the mobile banking progress to date that improves services for the traditional bank customers falls short of addressing this critical problem.

CHALLENGES

India is not Kenya; it is roughly thirty Kenyas. There is no single dominant mobile banking services provider.

Indians have millions of mobile phones, but they have yet to use them for financial transactions. When asked in a recent survey which activities they conducted on their mobile phones, respondents provided an intriguing insight. The most popular activity among respondents was not SMS or email, but updating their Facebook accounts. Seventy-six percent of respondents use their

---

64   Source: RBI

mobile phones to update Facebook while only seventy-four percent and sixty-four percent use it for SMS and email respectively.[65]

On July 24, 2012, the Reserve Bank of India (RBI) deputy governor H. R. Khan warned that mobile banking had failed to develop adequately in India and called upon banks and mobile companies to work together for the benefit of their customers.

As of May 2012, nearly 3.34 million transactions were concluded for Rs 2.86 billion (about US$53 million) through mobile; just a year earlier the number was Rs 1.28 million transactions of Rs 0.91 billion. At a seminar in Bhubaneswar, Khan said that this growth rate in the value and the volume of mobile-based transactions was much lower compared to the number of bank accounts and number of mobile subscribers. This, he said, indicated that banks were yet to fully exploit this technology even for their existing customers. "This growth rate is low compared to the number of bank accounts and the vast mobile subscriber base of more than 900 million," said Khan.

Another perspective is provided by TM Bhasin, chairman and managing director, Indian Bank, and author of E-commerce in Indian Banks. "The shift during this period has been from branch to alternative delivery channels such as ATM, Internet and mobile," he says. "We are seeing more and more people shifting to alternative delivery channels, which account for thirty to forty percent of customers at present. Over the next few years, this is likely to go up to seventy or eighty percent."

Chanda Kochhar, MD and CEO of ICICI Bank, says only fifteen percent of transactions on average take place through the bank's 2,700 branches, while the rest are happening outside.

Global research firm Celent expects the number of ATMs in India to double by 2016, with more than fifty percent being set up in small towns. "Today, ATM provides more than cash withdrawal. Apart from fixed deposits, cheque book requests and balance inquiries, there are also enhanced banking services," says Shivaji Chatterjee, vice-president, Hughes Communications India, which helps banks create their ATM networks.

Though paper check is still the dominant mode of payment, during the past five years the value of check-based transactions has been on a gradual decline. The RBI has worked to promote paperless payments such as credit and debit

---

65   http://www.jana.com/blog/india-mobile-users-experience/

cards, electronic fund transfers, and mobile banking. During 2011–12, the volume of online fund transfers through NEFT (National Electronic Funds Transfer, used for low-value transactions) and RTGS (Real Time Gross Settlement, used for high-value transactions) grew by 71% and 11.7 %, respectively, according to RBI data.

In the fast-growing Indian economy, cash remains the preferred payment mode. "Currently, only two percent of the entire payments go through the electronic system in India," said Pralay Mondal, senior group president, Retail and Business Banking, Yes Bank.[66]

VERIFIABLE IDENTITY: KNOW YOUR CUSTOMER

As we have discussed, one of the foundations of banking is "know your customer." In India, with its vast numbers of migrant and rural workers, those who are illiterate, and those who are living outside the structure of civil government, knowing your customer can be a huge challenge when your customer doesn't have a birth certificate or any other item of verifiable identity. The lack of a standardized identity system has helped to keep millions of people walled off from participation in the economic life of the country and confined to the bottom of the pyramid.

To understand the importance of verifiable identity, let's look at the life of a common man in India:

Meet Raju Lingam, who is thirty-five years old—or thereabouts, he says. He doesn't know his exact age because he doesn't have a birth certificate. Raju was born at home, in a village in the state of Odisha. There was no written record made of his arrival into this world. The conditions of his birth were typical, and although it happened more than three decades ago, half of all births in India still occur at home, far from a primary health center or a hospital.[67]

"I didn't know what a birth certificate was until much later," says Raju.

A birth record is the first form of a verifiable identity for any person, and an institutional newborn delivery mechanism leads to the creation of such an

---

66   Business Today (4 May 2013) http://businesstoday. intoday. in/story/india-e-banking-mobile-banking-popular-branch-banking-stays/1/191073. html

67   Home birth attendants in low income countries: who are they and what do they do? http://www.biomedcentral.com/1471-2393/12/34

identification infrastructure. A birth record system matures into an identity verification system across geographies.

An integral aspect of a functioning society, verifiable identity facilitates interactions among individuals and between an individual and an organization. For an individual, the need for an identity begins from infancy as an objective record of his or her parental lineage, date of birth, and medical immunizations. As the individual grows, the identity is required for academic enrollment, to enter the workforce, and to get social services including banking, telecom, and welfare.

In the Indian context—and indeed in any developing country—a weak or the sheer absence of an institutional newborn delivery mechanism leads to a medieval culture in which identity is simply assumed by an individual and there's no way to verify someone's claim beyond the assertions of family and neighbors. According to the BBC, it is estimated that 300 million Indians lack adequate forms of official identification. That's twenty-five percent of the population, and a number nearly as great as the population of the United States. And, according to UN figures, with the Indian urban population expected to grow by another 497 million by 2050, this could be set to be an even bigger issue.[68]

When Raju was five years old, he could not enroll in the local school as most kids his age did. This was partly because his parents were unable to afford to send him to school, but also because they had no identity documents to send him to the free government-run school in their small village. The only solution was for Raju's guardian to resort to bribery to enable Raju to get enrolled in the government-run school.

As the years roll by, the story assumes a painfully familiar arc. Raju's lack of verifiable identity forces him to pay a bribe to get himself eligible for subsidized grain, energy, to open a bank account, apply for a scholarship, or participate in government employment guarantee scheme.

In such a reality, the constraint and impact put on Raju's ability to connect with the fabric of society make risk-mitigating financial products such as insurance or a pension as unrealistic for him as for you, dear reader, to consider the marvels of time travel or interstellar teleportation as seen in science fiction films.

A weak or non-existent identity infrastructure can be divisive. It creates hurdles and excludes a sizable population from accessing basic services and facilities. The problem becomes extreme for the economically poor, who end up

---

68   http://news. bbc. co. uk/2/hi/programmes/click_online/9722871. stm

paying a poverty premium to access some of these basics, which are otherwise available at a basic cost to those with a formal, recognized identity.

The market, regulatory, and infrastructure conditions for financial inclusion are critical to scaling. In Kenya, where M-Pesa scaled quickly, there was already in place a universal government issued ID that was used when people opened their M-Pesa accounts. Although Safaricom had to validate who the person was who had that account, this meant that signup was fast and efficient.

In addition, a weak identity system leads to the creation of a multiple, pseudo-identity system using various entitlement documents. In India, pseudo-identity documents that are frequently used are the ration card (a government-issued entitlement document for subsidized food grains), the voter ID card for registered voters above the age of eighteen, drivers' licenses, and others.

Another challenge is that a weak identity system creates ghosts and duplicates. Based on various studies and surveys, it would be fair to estimate that up to forty percent of beneficiaries in the above-mentioned systems (ration, voters, drivers) are ghosts or duplicates. These fraudulent recipients misuse the system and siphon assets that could be used to benefit others in need.

A universally accepted, robust identity mechanism is essential for the inclusion of all people regardless of their economic level, as well as to minimize the misuse of the system by ghost and duplicate entries. The absence of a robust identity mechanism means people will be harassed by authorities, denied service or welfare, and be forced to resort to retail corruption.

For service providers, a universally-accepted robust identity system is critical to efficiency and scale. It dramatically lowers the cost of sign-up (providers are required to do "know your customer"), removes friction for the customer during the sign-up process, and lowers ongoing fraud rates and cost of compliance. It results in ease of use for customers, the creation of safer systems, and it lowers costs of providing service.

THE AADHAAR PROGRAM

The Unique Identification Authority of India (UIDAI) is an agency of the government of India responsible for implementing the Aadhaar scheme, a nationwide personal identification project. (In Hindi, adhar means "foundation" or "cornerstone.") Established in February 2009, Aadhaar is a twelve-digit unique number that the UIDAI issues for all residents in India on a voluntary basis (at least for now).

The word "resident" is *very important*. For simplicity, Aadhaar has chosen to include any person who is physically on Indian soil in a verifiable manner for a certain duration of time. This approach enables the person to get an identity and get included in the various systems without the citizen/non-citizen debate.

The key is that the Aaadhaar number *does not entitle the bearer to do anything*. It's not like a driver's license or a passport. Its only purpose is to verify that you are who you say you are. Whether you happen to be a citizen of India is not relevant.

The Aadhaar numbers are stored in a centralized Unique Identification Number database and linked to basic demographic and biometric information, including a photograph, ten fingerprints, and an iris image of each individual. The number—and therefore the bearer's identity—is easily verifiable in an online, cost-effective way. It is intended to be unique and robust enough to eliminate the large number of duplicate and fake identities in government and private databases. The random Aadhaar number generated for each resident is devoid of any classification based on caste, creed, religion, or geography.

On September 29, 2010, UIDAI launched Aadhaar in the tribal village of Tembhli in Shahada, Nandurbar, Maharashtra. The program was ceremoniously inaugurated by Prime Minister Manmohan Singh along with UPA chairperson Sonia Gandhi. The first resident to receive an Aadhaar number was Ranjana Sonawane of Tembhli village.

Addressing the assembled dignitaries and townsfolk, the prime minister said the issuing of unique identity cards was the beginning of a big effort for the welfare of the common man. "The poor did not have any identity proof," he said. "Due to this shortcoming, they could not open bank accounts or get ration cards. They could not avail the benefits of government welfare programs because of this and many times, these benefits were pocketed by others." He said those who are economically and socially backward will be the biggest beneficiaries of this program. "We will give every opportunity to live a dignified life to our poor, scheduled castes and scheduled tribes people."[69]

---

69   The Indian Express http://www. indianexpress. com/news/aadhar-takes-off-pm-sonia-launch-uid-in-tribal-village/689953/

For Indians who lack other forms of identification, Aadhaar could become the single source of identity verification. Residents will be spared the hassle of repeatedly providing supporting identity documents each time they wish to access services such as obtaining a bank account, passport, or driver's license. By providing a clear proof of identity, the UID will also facilitate entry for poor and underprivileged residents into the formal banking system and the opportunity to avail services provided by the government. It will also give migrants mobility of identity, and financial inclusion with deeper penetration of banks, insurance, and easy distribution of benefits of government schemes.

Aadhaar enrollment began in September 2010. By December 31, 2011, there were 36,000 active enrollment stations in thirty-two states and union territories. In February 2012, enrollment reached the originally approved target of 200 million. Enrollment commenced in the middle of April 2012 for 400 million residents being enrolled through the multi-registrar model. NPR (National Population Register project) continues to enroll in its assigned territory.

According to the Press Information Bureau, Government of India, Planning Commission, as of January 2014 "the Unique Identification Authority of India (UIDAI) has completed issuance of 56 crore [560 million] Aadhaar Numbers. With generation of about 13 – 14 lakhs [1.3 million – 1.4 million] Aadhaar Numbers every day, the flagship programme appears all set to complete its mandate of covering 60 crore population in the next few weeks.

"With an increased capacity of Aadhaar generation, UIDAI is currently generating more than three crore Aadhaar numbers per month and has the capacity to process 15 – 16 lakh enrollment packets every day leading to generation of 13 – 14 lakhs Aadhaar numbers per day."[70]

Verifiable identification is critical to closing the banking gap in India. Without a better identification system, just signing up the 700 million unbanked people will cost an estimated $31 billion US. With Aadhaar, that cost will be under one billion dollars. And more importantly, it eliminates the embarrassing process of people interrogating people about their identity when they go to open an account.

Verifiable identifications will make many transactions safer and faster. For money transfer, it will be an easy way to be sure the money is given to the

---

70   http://pib. nic. in/newsite/PrintRelease. aspx?relid=102540

intended person. For government disbursements, it will aid in more transparency and verification.

How Aadhaar Works

To create the vast national identity database, Aadhaar collects four basic pieces of demographic information from residents: name, gender, date of birth, and postal address. The email address and mobile are optional information that is recorded where provided. In addition, to establish uniqueness, Aadhaar collects biometrics on ten fingerprints and both iris images. These biometric images are used in the de-duplication process, and establish that one individual gets one Aadhaar, and there are no duplicates or ghosts in the system.

Unlike a birth certificate issued as proof of a child being born in a hospital, Aadhaar needs to rely on other systems to establish an individual's identity. To enable this verification and to be inclusive, Aadhaar has adopted three methods to enable individuals to get into the system. These are:

- Paper-based identification, where a resident can bring an existing identity document (ration card, driver's license, election card) to establish their demographic information.

- Introducer-based identification. People such as civil society workers and government employees who routinely interact with members of a community lacking identification can function as introducer and vouch for people who do not have identity documents.

- Head of family-based introducer system. Often the head of a family has individual identity documents, while the other family members do not have independent identity documents. In such cases, the head of the family can introduce his or her family members into the system.

The ethos of inclusion are strongly ingrained in the policy and process of Aadhaar, and is reflected in the fact that gender in the Aadhaar system can be male, female, or transgender. In addition, people who have one or more fingers missing, an iris missing, or have deformed fingerprints can be processed using a separate handling system.

Upon successful collection of demographic and biometric information, the information is processed for quality and uniqueness, and then the random twelve-digit number is generated. This random number is called the Aadhaar number of the individual. This number is communicated to the individual. Each number is allocated to an individual only once for life, with no-reuse thereafter.

Because it's a new system built from scratch, India and Aadhaar have had the luxury to use the latest in technology currently available. In today's mobile age, UIDAI has chosen to create an online identity that is verifiable on the cloud. This choice has allowed India to take a leap in the identity infrastructure rollout. While most developed countries still have a card/token-based identity infrastructure, India has leapfrogged and moved from a crippling no-identity reality to an advanced online-verifiable, platform-based identity reality.

Aadhaar and the Emotional Value of Social Inclusion

Identity, and the need to be formally recognized by a larger system, has much deeper meaning to an individual who in daily life is economically invisible. In India, elections are one of the most inclusive activities in the country. It has long been observed that on the day of an election, it's the economically poor who turn out in the largest numbers, dressed in their best attire, to participate and cast their votes, even if it means they have to stand in line for hours in the scorching sun. Interviews with voters reveal that it may not necessarily be in the support of a particular political party, candidate or policy that such toil is undertaken. For the voters, it's the fact that society formally recognizes their existence that provides the impetus to vote.

Keeping this emotional context in mind, the relevance and importance of inclusion in an identity program needs to be fully appreciated.

Inclusion has been one of the major cornerstones of Aadhaar; this is reflected in the fact that as part of its enumeration process Aadhaar has "transgender" as the third officially-recognized gender. Aadhaar is given to children of all ages, and in the case of children below the age of five years where capturing of biometrics is difficult, they are linked to their guardian until they attain the age of five years.

Aadhaar Acceptance

While Aadhaar provides the identity to the individual, a requirement for successfully closing the loop on recognized identity is the acceptance of the

Aadhaar by gatekeeper institutions. The regulators of the country for the various services such as the RBI for banking, SEBI for non-banking financial services, IRDA for insurance, Indian Railways for train travel, and TRAI for telecom have accepted Aadhaar as an acceptable proof, meeting their "know your customer" requirements for delivering services at a national level. In addition, various state governments and departments have also started accepting Aadhaar as a sufficient proof of identity of the individual to deliver their specific services. Thus slowly and steadily, the Aadhaar project of providing identity to each resident is enabling the inclusion of these residents who were earlier left out of political, economic, and social systems.

Some ministries are creating punitive incentives to residents to get their Aadhaar number. In January 2014, the *New Indian Express* reported that domestic LPG users in the City of Bangalore "have to soon get their Aadhaar numbers linked with their LPG gas connections to get supply at subsidized rates. With hardly fifteen days left for the deadline of January 31, only twenty percent of consumers in most areas in the city have completed the procedure."

The Union Ministry for Petroleum and Natural Gas sent out a notification on December 31, 2013, stating that the Direct Benefit Transfer (DBT) for LPG Scheme has been rolled out in twelve districts in Karnataka. Under the scheme, subsidy on LPG cylinders is provided directly to customers to their Aadhaar linked bank accounts. According to the ministry's notification, "At the end of the grace period of each phase, LPG cylinders will be sold to all domestic LPG consumers at market price. However, subsidy will be transferred to only those who have linked Aadhaar number to LPG consumer number . . ."

But residents are confused. While the lack of awareness among people on how to get their Aadhaar numbers registered with the banks and gas agencies is one of the major reasons for the confusion, the paper reported that many who registered with the Unique Identification Authority of India (UIDAI) had yet to get their numbers.

Devadas, age sixty, a cab driver, told the paper, "I am paying `423.50 per cylinder and I still do not have my Aadhaar number. Yesterday, I received an SMS from the gas agency saying I need to submit my Aadhaar number to my distributor and bank to avail subsidy on LPG. There is very little time left and it looks like I cannot benefit from it immediately."[71]

---

71   http://www. newindianexpress. com/cities/bangalore/LPG-Aadhaar-Many-Still-
       Confused-About-the-Connection/2014/01/13/article1997814. ece#. UxZ8Yt3Dx50

Online Authentication and Electronic Know Your Customer (e-KYC)

The Aadhaar system has been designed as an online identity system with the capability to perform online authentication. A person having an Aadhaar number can verify for a third party their demographic and/or biometric information that is kept with UIDAI, thus establishing identity before delivery of service. In addition, the resident with his active consent can even direct UIDAI to release their demographic information in a secure manner to an authorized third party.

Traditionally, a person who is starting any new service, opening a new account in a bank, buying an insurance policy, or getting a new SIM for mobile would be required to submit a paper copy of their identity and address proof to enable meeting the regulatory KYC norms. The paper trail approach to establish KYC is a very inefficient, expensive, insecure process. The paper trail is expensive due to the cost of handling and storing photocopies, and insecure due to the ease with which an illegitimate copy of the identity proof can be made without any audit trail.

However, in the absence of any alternative process, this has been the only process.

In this reality, the UIDAI's e-KYC service is a boon for both individuals and service provider agencies. In the UIDAI's e-KYC service, the service provider agencies (banks, insurance, telecom, etc.) become partners of UIDAI to enable the electronic integration of the e-KYC service.

Here's how it works: The customer approaches a service delivery point—say a bank branch—with no physical ID proof except for the knowledge of his or her Aadhaar number. The resident enters their Aadhaar number and provides their biometric (i.e., fingerprint or iris image) on the proper equipment. This information instantly travels to the UIDAI in a secure electronic manner through the e-KYC service. UIDAI recognizes the e-KYC request, performs a biometric match to establish the resident's consent for release of information. On a successful match, the resident demographic information with UIDAI travels electronically from UIDAI to the partner in a secure manner. The entire process takes a few seconds with the complete audit trail.

The service delivery partner agency now has the necessary information for KYC and has met the regulatory compliance for KYC without any paper trail but with complete electronic audit trail at a fraction of the cost. The customer has a near-instantaneous experience of an account opening or service delivery, obviating all the challenges that would have excluded them from using the service.

Aadhaar Enabled Payment System

Here's how Aadhaar is providing an end-to-end service for financial inclusion:

An individual typically wanting to use a basic banking service usually wants to perform two services within the banking infrastructure. First, he or she wants to conveniently receive money in their bank account from another person or organization; and secondly, make withdraws and deposits into the bank. Thus, including the account-opening KYC need, there are three requirements for an individual with no bank account to become a fully functional bank account holder.

Banks link the resident's Aadhaar number with his or her bank account number. Inter-bank payment processing organizations such as National Payment Corporation of India (NPCI), VISA, etc., are creating a mapper called Aadhaar Payment Bridge (APB), which holds the bank account details and Aadhaar of an individual, making Aadhaar a financial address of the individual, which is linked at the backend to a proper bank account. When a person or an organization wants to transfer money to a person, all they need to know is their Aadhaar number and the money reaches the addressee.

To meet the challenges of inter-bank payments, residents can conveniently change their bank accounts without the need to inform the various entities about the change and continue to receive the funds. This is a big convenience for an individual who would otherwise need to manage multiple bank accounts or update their banking information at multiple places if the bank account were changed.

The utility of a bank account in a largely cash-based retail economy depends on the convenience with which you can withdraw and deposit cash from the account. The traditional bricks-and-mortar bank-branch model cannot be a profitable service delivery model in rural areas, and has thus not penetrated sufficiently in their service offering. To reduce the cost of service delivery, the business correspondent (BC) model for extending retail banking and taking it to the end consumer's doorstep was developed.

A business correspondent, according to the Reserve Bank of India, may be any individual or organization that meets a set of criteria. In the words of the Reserve Bank, qualified BCs may be: Individuals like retired bank employees, retired teachers, retired government employees and ex-servicemen, individual owners of kirana/medical/Fair Price shops, individual Public Call Office (PCO) operators, agents of Small Savings schemes of Government of India/Insurance Companies, individuals who own Petrol Pumps, authorized functionaries of well -run Self Help Groups (SHGs) which are linked to banks, any other individual including those operating Common Service Centres (CSCs);NGOs/ MFIs set up under Societies/Trust Acts and Section 25 Companies; Cooperative Societies registered under Mutually Aided Cooperative Societies Acts/Cooperative Societies Acts of States/Multi State Cooperative Societies Act; Post Offices; and companies registered under the Indian Companies Act, 1956, with large and widespread retail outlets, excluding Non-Banking Financial Companies (NBFCs).[72]

Since BCs are an extension of individual bank branches in a particular geography, they provide only intra-bank service. In addition, due to the intra-bank nature of service offering, the BC model is constrained by the limited number of customers. In addition, the BC model requires the bank to deploy a pin/OTP/card-based verification mechanism at the last mile to correctly identify the customer.

This reality gave birth to the Aadhaar enabled payment system (AEPS).

In the AEPS, the BC (individual or storefront) carries a hand-held micro ATM with a biometric sensor. At the transacting point, the customer is asked to enter their Aadhaar number and biometric to access their bank account. Upon successful authentication by UIDAI, and back-end linking between the Aadhaar and bank account, the customer can access their account in any bank via any BC and complete the transaction. In addition, the authentication service provided by UIDAI obviates the need for banks to deploy any special authentication service, further reducing the cost of service delivery. Because the BC now services customers from across banks, it has a larger number of transactions to make the business viable.

Aadhaar has facilitated the creation of an infrastructure to solve the financial inclusion challenge from no-identity status to a complete service delivery in

---

72   http://www.rbi.org.in/scripts/NotificationUser.aspx?Mode=0&Id=6017

partnership with the existing players, creating a win-win situation for resident and all partners involved.

Aadhaar: Protecting Resident Privacy

Common concerns about any national identity program are privacy rights and privacy violations of people in the database. The Aadhaar program has some features that help to alleviate these concerns.

Aadhaar is a voluntary program, created to provide a convenient and universal identity for inclusion. It collects ubiquitous demographic information—name, gender, address and date of birth—which is often available in several publicly available registers like the election rolls. There is no information collected to profile a person on the basis of caste, religion, ethnicity, or economic status.

In an authentication request from a UIDAI partner, UIDAI responds only with a match/no-match response, and does not provide any additional information.

In the e-KYC service of UIDAI, an active consent in the form a biometric authentication or OTP authentication is required before data can be released from UIDAI to the partner at every release. This data would have been shared for compliance with the partner to start the service delivery, and e-KYC merely makes process secure, efficient, and auditable, thereby improving the privacy protection of the customer.

Publicly Funded Electronic Platforms and Their Impact on Society

Aadhaar is one of the first (and definitely the largest) online biometric identity verification systems in the world. This is of immense importance in developing countries, where weak birth delivery mechanisms have created vacuums in the identity systems of the country. To add to this need fulfillment and the leapfrogging done by UIDAI, Aadhaar has been created like a public platform. Public platforms have historically had a positive impact on the host societies, and often lead to applications that are rarely envisaged at the time the platform is created. For example, when the Internet platform was first created, applications such as Twitter or Facebook were not envisaged. The GPS satellite system was created to enable the guidance of missiles. Once GPS was put in public domain, the location-based services industry blossomed. Turn-by-turn directions and even driverless vehicles, once the stuff of science fiction, are now possible because of GPS.

Similarly, the application of Aadhaar as an online biometric verification platform will move to dimensions beyond attendance, enabling KYC and Aadhaar as a financial address to areas beyond our current imagination creating new services and products.

India will be the first large country in the world to take benefit of this infrastructure. It will be the first country that will leverage this infrastructure to significantly reduce the cost of performing a transaction (where identity verification is essential), create new services and products, and have a new kind of utility which will make rapid inclusion possible among developing countries.

The scope and vision for Aadhaar take my breath away.

THE TAKEAWAY

- Infrastructure is the starting point—it can propel you forward or hold you back. Identity systems are a critical infrastructure to banking the masses. Without them, we can't get there from here.

- We can't underestimate the role of government. While too much government involvement can be counterproductive, the right government involvement can propel things forward. India is striking the right balance here, and we believe the next five years will bear this out.

- Although not detailed in this chapter, but evident for those involved, India is working hard on many fronts, including new government-sponsored payment switch, regulations allowing new actors and new roles, and government disbursements initiatives. These efforts are all moving India from being a poster child of financial exclusion to one of modern technology with a vibrant ecosystem and showcase of financial inclusion. It is a work in progress—but one that will be fascinating to watch.

CHAPTER 9:

Two Approaches
to Branchless SME Banking

India, with its population of 1.2 billion and an annual increase of newborns equivalent to the entire population of Australia, is an ancient yet tenuous patchwork of a nation. It has twenty-two different official languages and twice as many unofficial ones. It has its fair share of millionaires as well as hundreds of millions of residents who earn less than two dollars a day.

The population of India tends to be much more fluid than in Western industrialized countries. There's both seasonal and traditional migration, in which people from rural India travel to urban locations in search of a better livelihood and to utilize their skills for employment. In India, according to the 2001 Census and based on place of last residence, 309 million persons were classified as migrants, which constitutes about thirty percent of the total population of the country. This is an increase of thirty-seven percent over the previous census of 1991.[73]

In contrast, in the United States, the U. S. Census Bureau reports that 35.9 million US residents, or 11.7% of all Americans, moved between 2012 and 2013. "Relatively few of these movers traveled long distances," said David Ihrke, a demographer with the Census Bureau's Journey-to-Work and Migration Statistics Branch. "In fact, nearly two-thirds stayed in the same county."

---

73   http://censusindia.gov.in/Data_Products/Data_Highlights/Data_Highlights_link/
      data_highlights_D1D2D3.pdf

Even those who did leave their county didn't move very far: 40.2% of inter-country movers relocated less than fifty miles from their original home. Only 24.7% moved five hundred or more miles to their new location.[74]

Compared to their Indian counterparts, American households move less often and have a higher rate of banking. The FDIC's National Survey of Unbanked and Underbanked Households of 2011 found that 97.8% of US households have some sort of bank account. About two-thirds of US households have both checking and savings accounts.[75] With a rate of bank accounts per household, that's much higher than in India, many US movers either kept their current bank account or simply opened a new one in their new hometown.

In India, the high percentage of migrants who do not have bank accounts means domestic wage remittance is both a challenge and a large market opportunity. Because many Indian migrants do not have identification or official residency, saving money is difficult, and having access to other services like money transfer to villages back home through banks is available to only a fraction of the migrants. Instead, to send money home, most migrants must rely on informal networks like friends, families, hawala agents, couriers, or even bus drivers, making transfers both risky and expensive.

While the banking sector has advanced over the last few decades in India, it has yet to reach the majority at the bottom of the pyramid. The Reserve Bank of India reports that in rural areas there are only 270 bank accounts per thousand people, and in urban areas 483 per thousand. These figures are almost certainly overstated because they count dormant and non-transactional accounts. This is a national concern, and thus financial inclusion is now an important part of India's national policy.

For anyone who attempts to design a banking solution for the subcontinent, the sheer breadth of demographics in India can be overwhelming. The solution design for India must necessarily be inclusive. To be truly inclusive, strategies must address the wider segments of the financial pyramid. Providing a low-cost and scalable solution via technology and effective distribution could create the same result we have seen in Kenya—a tipping point in bringing people into the formal financial system.

---

74   http://www.census.gov/newsroom/releases/archives/mobility_of_the_population/cb13-192.html

75   http://www.fdic.gov/householdsurvey/

MOBILE PHONES ARE A POTENT SOLUTION

India may have relatively few bank accounts per household, but it's got lots of mobile phones. As of this writing, India has close to 876 million mobile phone users—roughly seventy-three percent of the population—permeating every social segment. In less than five years, digital communications have achieved mass-market success and nearly universal reach. Ninety-five percent prepaid, mobile is distributed through retail. Without these retail "last mile" solutions, the majority of Indians would still be excluded.

To do banking, you often need a physical presence in a town or community, but you don't need to build a big, expensive branch. Branchless banking technologies include the Internet, automated teller machines (ATMs), point of sale (POS) devices, electronic funds transfer at point of sale (EFTPOS) devices, and mobile phones.

A key component to India's national financial inclusion strategy is to enable last-mile reach through business correspondents, or BCs. In 2006, the Reserve Bank of India introduced a regulation allowing banks to use the services of third-party, non-bank agents to extend their services right to people's doorsteps. A BC is any entity that acts as a teller for the bank and carries out a range of transactions on behalf of the bank. The BC earns a commission for services provided. BCs promote accessible branchless banking and the financial inclusion of a country's poorest citizens, and are typically grassroots entrepreneurs who enroll and serve customers on behalf of the bank. Like the prepaid top-up retail locations that were key to bringing communication to the masses, BC agent networks are key to bringing banking to the masses.

By being people of the same community they serve, they take banking to the people rather than taking people to the banks. BCs address a key challenge by not only establishing agent networks but also ensuring the viability and sustained interest of the agents. A capable network of agents invariably results in happy customers. This is a tough job, so it is not surprising that the most successful BCs are not only entrepreneurs but successful technology innovators.

According to CGAP. org, as of September 2012, the Reserve Bank of India says there are 221,341 BCs employed by banks to help get services to people at the bottom of the income pyramid.[76]

---

76   http://www. cgap. org/blog/financial-inclusion-20-india's-business-correspondents

One of the leading forces for financial inclusion, and an early nominee for our own Global Financial Inclusion Pioneer Award, is Delhi-based BC and technology innovator Eko.

EKO INDIA FINANCIAL SERVICES

The basic challenges of financial inclusion and providing banking services to the poor are that the amounts and transactions involved in the segment are often very low in value. The operational structure of major banks is not designed to cater to these segments in such low increments. In addition, migrants and many of the unbanked do not have the official records as required by the banks in order to open a bank account.

Eko India Financial Services Pvt. Ltd. aims to tackle these twin obstacles. Established in 2007 by brothers Abhishek and Abhinav Sinha and two other founders who left after a year, Eko provides no-frills bank accounts as well as deposit, withdrawal, and remittance services through mobile banking. Eko is a business correspondent (BC) service for State Bank of India (SBI) and ICICI Bank, which are India's two largest banks, as well as the new Yes Bank. Eko feeds all transactions directly into the computerized banking platform of these major banks, where their automated systems can process the transactions at negligible costs. Eko's platform essentially replaces the bank's high-cost manual processes with its low-cost processes.

Eko allows low-wage migrant workers in urban areas of India to remit money to their homes using mobile phones. Nearly eighty percent of its customers are migrants or among the unbanked section of the population.

The use of mobile phones for money transfer requires specialized technology. The first chairman of Eko, Sanjay Bhargava, spearheaded a security method that enabled a low-end mobile phone to be used to initiate secure transactions. Its technology platform is called SimpliBank because that is what it aims to transform banking into—simple and accessible banking for everyone. SimpliBank is designed with the mobile phone as its primary transaction interface.

Eko aims at being a comprehensive financial services provider, especially for people at the bottom of the pyramid using the mobile phone as the enabling tool. It provides a low-cost infrastructure powered by innovation and technology to enable instant, secure and convenient financial transactions.

To extend branchless banking services to the everyday Indian, Eko leverages existing retail shops, telecom connectivity, and banking infrastructure. In order to keep its costs low, Eko has enlisted neighborhood retailers, more widely known in India as "kirana stores," as its business correspondents. These retailers are conveniently located in the communities where they sell a wide range of products and services to local people, from household groceries to mobile recharges. These retailers have information about the various residents of the communities, and may sell goods at credit to the residents and, therefore, have an understanding of the credit history of the residents. The lack of official records pertaining to the customer can be replaced by the informal insights that the BC retailer has about the customer. Therefore, these retailers are performing the necessary "know your customer" functions at a reduced cost. These BCs collect the information of the customers and receive deposits and disburse money.

Eko also partners with institutions to offer payment, cash collection and disbursal services. Customers can walk into any Eko counter (retail outlet) to open a savings account, deposit and withdraw cash from the account, send money to any part of the country, receive money from any part of the world, buy mobile talk-time, or pay for a host of services. A low-cost mobile phone acts as the transaction device for retailers and customers.

The service works across all phones—the simplest to the most sophisticated handsets—through a multi-modal (USSD, SMS, IVR and Application) approach. Eko also uses a two-factor-strong authentication to complete the transaction. It has created and patented a low-cost One Time Password (OTP) generator called "OkeKey." It's a simple lookup table that transforms the user PIN into something else for every transaction. The transformed PIN is simply dialed in as a part of the transaction. Thus, the customer's PIN never travels in clear text, and only the server knows how to decipher the original PIN from the transformed PIN. Performing a transaction only requires numeric literacy for number dialing.

What makes Eko different is in the way it enables even a basic mobile phone to be able to initiate a secure financial transaction using just number dialing. It does not require any additional device purchase, application download, provisioning, menu navigation or knowledge of any language for this. It thus caters to the millions in India who may not be literate, who may own an ultra-low-cost-handset, and who may not have data services enabled.

Eko has already processed over a billion dollars in transactions and serves 350,000 customers every month. Eko uses existing shopkeepers as banking agents. So the trusted next-door mom-and-pop store, chemist, grocery, or the mobile recharge shop turns into a bank counter and the shopkeeper becomes a bank teller. Eko is today present in around 2,500 such shops spread across Delhi, Haryana, Punjab, Uttar Pradesh, Maharashtra, Andhra Pradesh and Bihar.

The most widely used service of Eko today is domestic remittance. The most popular path is cash-to-account, meaning the sender has cash and makes a deposit into the receiver's bank account. The money is then available for use at home through their local bank. Regulations don't yet allow universal cash out at BC agents, but it is estimated that regulation change will allow this to happen in the near future. When it does, Eko plans at expanding to allow cash-to-cash transfers similar to Western Union in the US and mPesa in Kenya.

In addition to payment innovation, Eko uses data analytics to appoint or select its agents, and uses unique processes to manage the cash inventory as it flows through the agent network and to monitor a growing network of agents. This technology-centric approach allows Eko to scale their agent network in a cost-efficient manner.

Eko recently opened up its technology platform and it is being used by other affiliate BCs and microfinance organizations. This has resulted in better network utilization and cross-network services like P2P remittances to be offered. Eko is releasing a comprehensive set of APIs which would enable even more participants to plug and play and not only bring their own networks but also to be able to leverage each other's networks.

Eko believes that financial inclusion must stay away from what they call a "poverty perception trap." People often casually equate the poor as being always "less than" the privileged others. This is reflected in the way financial inclusion policies and solutions seem to treat the poor as beneficiaries of charity rather than as paying customers. Financial inclusion tends to get overshadowed by benefit transfer schemes that evoke images of the benevolent few doling out benefits to the miserable poor. Reducing BoP customers into mere beneficiaries subverts the financial inclusion challenge. The long-term effects of such a perception bias could be just as detrimental as financial exclusion itself. A good solution must give a sense of empowerment to these customers and treat them with the same dignity as the financially included customers. Eko is using their innovative technology platform to do just that.

Still Much Work to Be Done

The sad part of the India business correspondent (BC) sector is that in 2012 government involvement increased significantly. The unintended consequence has been that since then, there has been not a single investment in the sector by venture capital or private equity. Although the current prime minister advocates for "minimum government," this isn't the case for the BC sector, which has put a hard ceiling on the growth of BCs like Eko. For Eko and others to reach their potential, they absolutely need outside capital sources that are not available to them today.

But maybe the money is correct not to enter, since there are other underlying obstacles to overcome—the biggest of which is the banks' discriminatory approach towards low-income and rural customers. This manifests in multiple ways; no bank has invested in creating the right products, and even the marketing of existing products uses words and language that have a discriminatory undertone. Similarly, the banks view BC business as a cost center and not as a profit center. This is unfortunate because when bank priorities change, BC businesses are frequently impacted negatively. This makes it even hard to create scale and innovation in an area that desperately needs both.

But Eko CEO Abhishek isn't giving up. "Financial inclusion is meaningless without customer centricity and customer protection. We will push until regulators, policy makers, and financial actors ensure this. Eko is pursuing banks to make a full portfolio of services available to all customers and allow interoperability among banks. Moreover, the discriminatory mindset of the financial sector towards its customers needs to change, most visibly in their communication (stop using words such as 'poor' and 'beneficiaries') and how they envisage products and their pricing. Last but not the least of the issues are legislations, regulations, licenses, and culture of doing business is not favorable towards the BCs and hinders them from realizing their potential towards making banking truly universal."

By not working with the BC sector to address these issues, the banks in India are shortsided. BCs offer a great way to extend the assets of the bank to reach the mass market. If this isn't addressed, then the next phase of development in India will continue to see limited BC growth.

GLOBOKAS PERU

In November 2006, Gino O. Picasso completed his role as CEO of Mobile 365 by selling the world's largest processor of text messages (SMS) to a larger company, Sybase. This was not Picasso's first CEO job; he had also previously been the CEO of Iridium Satellite. Clearly an accomplished executive, he wanted to apply his skills to make a more direct impact on the poor.

Two experiences influenced what Picasso did next.

First was his exposure to the impact of the work and the needs of Opportunity International. This is one of the largest non-profits focused on spreading microfinance (banking for the poor). There he saw the power of providing financial services to those who were financial nomads, whether by choice or circumstance. This was 2006, and microfinance had spread to many countries but was still primarily "high concept" and "low tech." As a business-man, he closely identified with the creative power that is unleashed when an entrepreneur receives capital at the right time.

Second, in his years as a telecom executive, he had learned that in remote areas of the globe there existed a whole world of people and business. Most people think that in remote places, people have no money and nothing is hap-pening. But Iridium was in the business of communications in very remote places, and Picasso saw firsthand there was a vibrant world of commerce and "action" beyond the traditional communication grid. Some of the world's largest industries operate in these remote areas (energy, mining, fishing). And in these communities there were also people living with less money while raising their families, running their small businesses, and participating in a greater community.

So Picasso, who is always in search of a challenge, started GTV GloboKasNet to help solve one of the most vexing problems for microfinance and businesses in general: how to help people manage cash in remote, unbanked locations. The company, headquartered in Chevy Chase, Maryland, aimed to leverage technology in microfinance and to help scale financial services to communities and people whom the banks were not reaching. Picasso was excited about the reports from the Philippines about Smart and GCash, and thought the idea had potential beyond Asia; but to make these concepts work, there had to be a robust, well-functioning network of cash-in/cash-out points, i.e., a sort of on-ramp to the financial electronic highway.

Picasso and his partner, Michael Deutschman, did an exhaustive macro-analysis of the best environments to test their concepts out, and Latin America, where the microfinance sector was having increased success, came to the top of the list.

Latin America is like many emerging regions of the world. Over seventy-five percent of the population have traditionally lived without the benefit of institutional financial services. Brazil was a notable exception, due primarily to the ambitious initiative of a large Brazilian bank, Bradesco.

One of the countries that stood out in Latin America was Peru, a country with a stable economy, opening up to the global economy through free trade agreements, with an influx of foreign direct investment, but with marked economic and social inequalities. In 2005, Peru had about fifty percent of its people living below the line of poverty, two-thirds of the economy was informal, and three-fourths did not have access to financial products. Poverty numbers have since improved, but the other indicators have not moved much.

All of this provided a good environment for the development of microfinance. Peru was (and still is) considered one of the most attractive economies for microfinance in the world.

Nonetheless, like much of the world, microfinance in Peru had developed without much use of technology. The market was ripe for the innovation that GloboKasNet would bring with the launch of its services in the country.

The company's focus is on providing a "human ATM" network of business correspondents (BCs). Picasso knew from his Iridium days that in many areas in the world, it didn't make economic sense to put up bank branches and install physical ATMs. But he had a different idea, one that was being tried in other parts of the world with mixed results and wasn't yet established in most Latin American countries.

Picasso was prescient to describe this agent network as a human ATM network, because the big banks already understood the business model for ATMs; he merely plugged into that existing framework and made it make sense for the banks. It was a more cost-effective way for the banks to reach their customers.

Since he thought of it as an extension of a bank's physical footprint, he developed a business model that matched that of shared ATM networks. He decided he would build a network of qualified mom-and-pop shops in urban and rural locations. In addition to providing a lower cost per transaction, the individual shopkeeper offered a great benefit over an ATM: members of the local community generally trusted the local shopkeeper, which would overcome one of the most vexing problems for ATMs, which is cash-in. Globokas equipped the stores with a standard point of sale (POS) terminal that allowed the shopkeeper to provide banking services that a teller could provide at a bank window.

The shopkeeper BCs are called KasNet agents. The network of KasNet agents allow:

Banking access, through the sole rural service coverage in Peru, with the possibility of choosing locations among more than 200,000 localities at the national level and also through additional urban and semi-urban service coverage in the entire country.

Distribution channel enhancement by expanding coverage to new localities, with lower service time in its collections and distribution routes, eliminating cash, generating purchase orders and permitting the preliminary prospection of clients or consumers.

Data spread, by permitting the spreading of sectorial information at the national level.

Types of KasNet agents include:

- Traditional Agents—Business establishments serving outside the coverage of the bank branches, which may be found in urban and rural areas in general.

- Peripheral Agents—Business establishments facilitating payments for services in high traffic peripheral areas, such as markets, bus stops, etc.

- Mobile Agents—Trained and instructed individuals operating in a booth in bank offices or branches to help end users become familiar with the concept and help bank branches reduce lines.

- The types of transactions that KasNet agents can provide include:

- Bill payments.

- Deposits and withdrawals from accounts.

- Bank transfers.

- Credit fees payment.

- Balance inquiries.

- Bank account transaction history.

- Credit card payments.

- Currency exchange consultation.

- Individual loan payment using national ID.

- Group loan payments.[77]

Globokas aligned closely with microfinance organizations like MiBanco, one of the leading microfinance banks in the world, before getting large banks on board. BBVA Continental, a subsidiary of the Spanish bank BBVA and the second largest bank in Peru, was the first big bank to agree to participate in their network.

Unlike many other BC networks, KasNet agents are shared between multiple banks. In Peru, Globokas is the only banking agents network operating with Mibanco, BBVA Banco Continental, Scotiabank, BanBif, Banco Financiero, Financiera Confianza, Financiera CrediScotia, Caja Sullana, Caja Trujillo, Financiera TFC and Caja Huancayo, and others in the process of integration. With a network of banks, the individual KasNet agent can be more productive. The typical KasNet agent does about five hundred transactions a month. This is only possible if the agent can be bank-agnostic, meaning they can support customers of major financial institutions in Peru representing a combined sixty percent of the banking sector.

The company's KasNet agent network in Peru is impressive, boasting over 2,500 agents—forty percent in Lima, sixty percent in the rest of Peru. Their focus is not just on having a lot of agents, but on quality agents. They see

---

77   http://www. globokas. net/

many BC networks in other parts of the world experiencing high expenses and poor profits.

Globokas selects agents carefully, trains them, lends them the POS hardware, and gets them productive and, as a result, they're now reporting ninety-seven percent of their locations as active and productive by their internal metrics. Most importantly, everyone in the value chain wins, including the banks and the shopkeepers. Each store receives two benefits: commissions paid by Globokas for transactions, and an increase in foot traffic that drives growth in their traditional retail business.

Selecting, training and working closely with agents is critical to the success of any retail distribution, but it is particularly important for branchless banking agent networks. The consumer must trust that their money is safe and, when transferred, reaches the ultimate destination. The bank, MFI or other enterprise, must trust that agent to handle the transaction properly and provide a good customer experience. Running out of cash is not an option. Dirty environments reflect poorly on the brands of the banks being served, which need to be very closely associated with the agents to instill consumer confidence. This all requires a great deal of attention to every aspect of the supply chain. The idea of having a large number of agents is attractive, but never at the expense of the quality of service. GKN is achieving scale, but only after identifying in systematizing the processes and IT that make up good agents.

The best KasNet agents are trusted members of their community. They are successful entrepreneurs who know how to handle money. They are required to put up their own capital to fund the e-float and cash on hand required to perform financial transactions, and they cannot run out. They must have security practices because many operate in communities where theft is high. A single robbery can wipe out all the profits that they make from being an agent. The successful agent works closely with Globokas field personnel to approach other businesses and people in their community to incorporate into the eco-system (e.g., encourage them to open bank accounts and transact through these accounts). All of these elements require a great deal of attention and close monitoring.

The experience of banking is simple. The shop keeper has a reliable and secure POS device that allows the customer to swipe their bank card and receive a number of services including deposit, withdrawal, top up, bill pay—basically any type of transaction that they could perform at a bank teller window, as securely as if they were in the bank. The added convenience of being able to do banking right in their community and not have to travel several hours to the nearest bank branch only to wait in long lines encourages people to open bank accounts. The consumer who is not banked also benefits. In most countries outside of US and Western Europe, consumers must do all of their business at banks, from paying their utilities to school bills to receiving their pay or government benefits. Globokas allows these consumers to perform these same transactions right in their local community, at the store they usually shop in, without having to wait in long lines.

The business model works well. The banks pay a transaction fee for transactions performed by the BC. But the fee is less than they would pay if they had to have real ATMs or branches.

Building on seven years of experience as pioneers of the multibank model, Globokas has developed and fine-tuned a methodology that is now applying to accelerate growth. Globokas doubled in size during 2013 to 1,500 active agents and plans to double in size again during 2014.

There are about 220,000 mom-and-pop *bodega* stores in Peru. Therefore, there is still tremendous potential for growth. Estimates surrounding an electronic wallet initiative by the Association of Banks of Peru state that the Peruvian market requires at least 40,000 cash in/out agents for such a solution to be viable.

One of the keys to success over the years is the multidisciplinary team that Globokas has assembled with experts in regulation, transaction processing technologies, project management, bank channel management, fraud mitigation, and field operations, among others. The Peruvian team has been led from the beginning by the former Superintendent of Banking and Insurance in Peru. His network of contacts in the financial services industry has been instrumental to the success of the company.

In addition to growing the number of agents, another dimension of growth for Globokas is expanding and creating new services. Starting with the view that moving cash is very expensive and cash never has to leave a community, Globokas seeks ways in which technology can be used to reduce the need for physical cash transport, much the same way that the telegraph eliminated the need to transport cash via stagecoaches in the Old West. The reason that cash is still so widely used is because it's convenient. The question is how to make electronic services even better. Globokas knows that most consumers do not buy technology, but solutions, and the company's efforts are focused on solving real consumer problems.

Working very closely with the end consumer, they try to understand their needs and wants. They are not tethered to any "form factor" or technology. Today it is card and POS, but tomorrow it could be mobile-to-mobile or other ways to allow secure transactions. Paper receipts are still used because they're a good way for customers to have a record of what they did; that could go away eventually, but traditional receipts are important to consumers now. Globokas recognizes that consumers anywhere are slow to change habits unless there is a compelling value proposition.

In a pilot project partly funded by a grant from the Inter-American Development Bank, Globokas recently achieved its greatest proof that its services can truly increase banking penetration. Working with BBVA Continental and a distributor of consumer goods, Globokas selected 1,017 bodega owners in three small cities south of Lima. Only five of the bodegas had ever held a bank account. By using collection of payments owed to the delivery truck as a catalyst, Globokas was able to bank fifty percent of those targeted with high-transaction accounts. This program is now being planned to be rolled out nationally in Peru.

Some of the success factors for the pilot project included:

- Carrying out focus groups to understand the dynamics of the local economy, and the willingness to adopt new technologies.

- Aligning interests between the distributor (large producer of consumer goods) and the small mom and pop shops, with the bank and Globokas as intermediaries. The corporation has an interest in reducing the use of cash, and the bodega owner has an interest in improving security with less cash around, and organizing his/her finances with records of transactions made.

- Emphasizing efforts to inform, educate and promote the new service with bodega owners. As with any new service, potential users had many doubts and questions before making a decision to sign up.

- Zero-fee bank accounts. One of the salient themes during the focus groups were that they would consider signing up only if the bank accounts had zero fees. BBVA Continental obliged with a zero-fee savings account.

Globokas has a model that allows them to run a profitable, successful business that can scale up and reach even more people. They have learned that it is better to closely manage the agent network and aren't yet comfortable with two-tiered distribution to the agents. They want a more intimate involvement with the agents than this will allow.

Currently, they are exploring expansion to other Latin American countries, with a particular interest in Mexico and Colombia. They have documented all the methodologies currently being applied in Peru, but their design has built-in flexibility as other countries have different regulation and local customs that need to be taken into account.

Here are two case studies that illustrate the success of Globokas:

Salary Payments in Espinar, Cusco

Espinar is a rural area about three hours outside of the city of Cusco, where one of the main activities is mining. Prior to the arrival of KasNet to the area, workers from the mine would get paid via direct deposit into their bank account, and they would have to travel to the city of Cusco in order to withdraw money from branches or ATMs. The Globokas supervisor in Cusco learned about this situation, visited Espinar, and enlisted local shops so they could become "human ATMs" for the workers. Now, the workers save time and money getting paid, and the local shops have increased business from increased spending on top of earning commissions from withdrawals.

Servicios Matíaz in Villa Maria del Triunfo, Lima

This agency is operated by a stay-at-home mom in one of the peripheral neighborhoods of Lima. When asked how she became BC, she describes that she had seen agents in other parts of the city and saw an opportunity to be the local banker in her neighborhood. She called various banks, as well as Globokas, and they all stated that one of the requirements was to have some sort of business with a municipal license. The problem was that she did not have a business. So she went ahead and set up a gift shop with the sole intent of becoming a business correspondent for the banks. Today, she is an agent for Globokas, as well as for other banks that have their own networks. She has become the local banker in her neighborhood. Given that she is alone with her child during the day, in order to manage the cash she gets from bill payments so that it can be deposited at the bank daily, she has enlisted her mother-in-law and a relative's gas distribution business a few houses down the street.

Both EKO and Globokas Peru demonstrate the power of new entrants extending the core assets of the banks to the bottom of the pyramid. These innovators are key to reaching the underserved. If regulators get the rules governing financial services right, there will be a tsunami of new services in the area, and the best ones will be adopted and scale.

One rule the regulators in all countries need to get right is the one to let nonbanks offer financial services and to allow responsible non-bank actors like EKO and Globokas Peru provide financial services. Some of the new entrants will be innovators like them, others will be retailers, telcos, and online companies. They should be able to be licensed to provide various financial activities including load/unload cash, move money, hold funds in trust for others, electronically pay, and lend. Many of these non-banks are not only innovative—they have great assets like trust, new technology, and distribution which can be effectively leveraged to reach and serve customers.

This is not a one-size-fits-all world. What works in India may not be the right model, technology, or go-to-market approach that works in Peru or Mexico. Local differences matter a lot in developing solutions. So the best way for this to happen globally is not for one solution—say the Google of banking—to emerge. Instead, we need to foster innovation through investment and good regulations, and expect that local actors will emerge that will scale from meeting the needs of the local market.

THE TAKEAWAY

- Eko and Globokas demonstrate once more the power of new innovative companies dedicated to leveraging technology and serving the Bottom of the Pyramid. It is so important to foster this type of entrepreneurship globally.

- Eko and Globokas tackle similar challenges but have developed locally-appropriate solutions. It is not a one-size-fits-all world.

- We are beginning to see the huge benefits when regulators get the rules right for financial inclusion. It is important to accelerate the global spread of regulations that promote financial inclusion.

CHAPTER 10:

Richard Leftley and MicroEnsure

As the world's first microinsurance intermediary, MicroEnsure provides protection against the many risks faced by those living in poverty. Innovative products cover policyholders with crop, health, and life insurance, offering clients a safety net when an unexpected hardship or disaster occurs. With average premiums of about $1.50 per month for a family of five, MicroEnsure is making affordable life insurance available for the first time, exclusively to low- and middle-income families. Other innovations include policies covering persons infected with HIV/AIDS, weather-indexed crop insurance for rural farmers, insurance against political violence, and affordable health insurance for the economically marginalized.

CEO Richard Leftley began working in microinsurance in January 2002 after leaving Benfield Greig, a leading reinsurance intermediary, where he worked as a reinsurance broker responsible for the African account and with a team covering the Middle East and South East Asia.

Leftley pioneered the introduction of insurance products within the Opportunity Network, which led to the establishment of the Micro Insurance Agency, which in 2008 became MicroEnsure. An industry expert in the field of microinsurance, Leftley also served on the steering committee of the ILO "Micro Insurance Innovation Fund," a $35 million fund supported by the Bill & Melinda Gates Foundation.

The MicroEnsure story began when Leftley became fascinated by the question of why poor people didn't buy insurance. Statistics indicated that only about one percent of people in Africa and Asia purchase insurance. For high-income families, most of that buying activity is mandatory because they own a car or a motorbike and the government requires that they have insurance. But in terms of the risks they face, quite often low- and middle-income families face the greatest risks of any people living on the earth today.

It was clear to Leftley that traditional insurance was not meeting the needs of vast numbers of people. He was living in London, and he took a two-week voluntary service trip to Zambia. He found himself living with a rural family who led a very simple life and had very few possessions. He was surprised to learn that they had once lived in a nice apartment block in the city. They had regular jobs and had owned things like a car and other middle-class items. Then the family had suffered a series of disasters. They described what had happened to them as being like a real-life game of Chutes and Ladders. Ironically, in their tiny home the children had an actual Chutes and Ladders game board, and the mother pointed to it and said, "It's like this—we were trying to get out of poverty, but we kept suffering setbacks. In the city, my husband caught HIV, and he eventually died. We spent every penny we had trying to keep him alive." In Zambia, funerals are very elaborate, so the rest of the family's money was spent on the funeral, and the family had to move to the village.

At that moment, Leftley realized that insurance is like a safety net that moves underneath us, and helps us as we rise from poverty up through the middle class and higher. Insurance can't keep bad things from happening, but it shields us from the effects of negative events and keeps us from falling back to the bottom of the pyramid.

He left his job and started working in microfinance for Opportunity International, based in Chicago. Through them, very basic life insurance products were provided to about a million people. After three or four years, they realized they were limited in what they could do within a microfinance organization, and that the company needed to reach many more clients with more products. In 2005, Micro Insurance Agency was set up as a standalone company, and in 2007 the organization received a significant grant from the Bill & Melinda Gates Foundation.

Three years later, the company, now called MicroEnsure, started working with mobile phone companies, which allowed the company to rapidly scale up its efforts. In 2013, the company went from being a non-profit to being a for-profit company funded by investors.

As opposed to selling insurance an industrialized economy, what MicroEnsure does for microinsurance in the microfinance space is not just taking a standard insurance policy and knocking off some benefits and lowering the premium—they're fundamentally redesigning the product and making it extremely simple. MicroEnsure sells some life insurance products that have absolutely no exclusions. They do not demand to know about pre-existing conditions. They do not consider cause of death, whether it be disease, civil war, or suicide. All of these things are normally excluded under a policy that a rich person would buy. With microinsurance, if you die, MicroEnsure pays—no questions asked.

The company tries to work around the fact that in many developing countries, people do not know how old they are. In the US or the UK, many policies have age restrictions—you can't be over sixty-five or seventy, or whatever age is specified. MicroEnsure strives to avoid that because many customers, especially older ones, don't have birth certificates and have no way of verifying their age.

SHAPING THE CONCEPT TO FIT THE MARKET

The business is expanding rapidly. As of this writing, MicroEnsure has about ten million customers who are spread across sixteen different countries in Africa and Asia, and adds 60,000 new clients every day. In terms of gender, as recently as 2013 their clients were eighty percent women and twenty percent men; this reflected the fact that microfinance organizations interacted primarily with women and made loans to women. But as they've started to work with mobile phone companies, the balance has shifted to being closer to fifty-fifty, simply because both men and women use phones.

MicroEnsure starts by talking to their potential customers. As Richard Leftley said in an exclusive interview, "If you sit down with a family in Africa and you ask them to describe the things that happen to them that are unforeseen—not school fees or rent payments, but unexpected expenses—they will say medical emergencies, funerals, fires, natural disasters. Their business may be in an unregulated marketplace, in a makeshift structure; and if there's a fire at one end of the market it sweeps right through and everyone is wiped out.

In rural areas there's the risk of death of livestock from disease or drought, or crop failure.

"Something that we've learned—it's become a mantra in the company—is that no one wakes up in the morning and says, 'Today, I want to buy insurance.' This is especially true if you're low income, because you're concerned about getting to work on the public bus, and about feeding your children and putting clothes on their backs. Those are the things that worry you today. Insurance is about paying for some future abstract problem that may or may not occur.

"But you *do* wake up in the morning and wonder what will happen if your spouse dies. You wonder what will happen if your kids get sick. You wonder what will happen if the rains don't come, or if there's a natural disaster or a fire."

MicroEnsure wanted to use this customer behavior to sell into this market. The company also knew that they didn't have time to build up their own brand identity. It would have taken forever. So they went to consumers and asked them whom they trusted. Was it banks, insurance companies, or telecos—the mobile phone companies? They learned that the first answer was the telecos. This is because telecos have become ubiquitous. They're like Google, which has said that it wants to be like your toothbrush—something you use every day without thinking about it. In Africa and Asia, people are topping up their phones, on average, once a day. They're spending money on airtime, and they're seeing that it works. The telecos are brands that they're used to and that work: they pay money and they get immediate service, and can call people and send text messages.

In contrast, if they had an insurance company, they would only interact with it once or twice a year. MicroEnsure learned that instead of building their own brand, it would be far better to use existing channels to reach the market.

The company can't do it alone. They're marketing products that have a current top line revenue to MicroEnsure of twenty-three cents. That's just enough money for the company to administer the policy. To mass market insurance into the low-income market, there are three key players that need to be involved. A risk carrier. This is typically a big insurance company. A distributor. They need to have a strong brand, points of sale that are accessible to the low-income market, and they need to have the ability to transact cash. A back office, which is what MicroEnsure does.

MicroEnsure targets and corrects four big deficiencies with the existing market:

1. Conventional products are too complex. Clients don't understand the products, and when it's time for the insurance company to pay a claim, the lengthy verification process often costs more than the claim itself.

2. The company needs to educate the local consumer.

3. The company needs to do it on a massive scale. If you're making twenty-three cents per policy, you need a huge number of policies to break even. You need a really robust IT platform because the insurance companies don't have it.

4. The company needs to pay claims quickly. MicroEnsure targets paying claims within seventy-two hours. As Leftley said, "I think our record—from the time we were notified of the claim to the time we were in the woman's house with a check—is six hours. This isn't about taking weeks or months; this is about really fast turnaround."

USING MOBILE NETWORKS TO SELL INSURANCE

With all of this in mind, MicroEnsure went to the telcos and told them that they wanted to provide insurance to their client base.

Here's how it works: In developing countries, everyone has multiple SIM cards. You can go to any street corner and get one free of charge for every network. They do this because it's cheaper to call your friends and family on a network-to-network basis. Plus, networks often offer promotions. It's very common and very easy for people to switch the SIM card in their mobile phone. Some phones have the ability to carry two or three SIM cards in the back of the phone. Consequently, mobile phone companies suffer from disloyal clients. They each have only a share of overall expenditure on prepaid airtime.

So MicroEnsure proposed to the telcos that they offer free insurance. Say a customer spends two dollars on mobile top-up in one month. Then he or she might qualify for two hundred dollars' worth of insurance the next month. Spend four dollars and they get more free insurance. It gives the consumer a reason to spend more of their airtime with this network than with another network. They're still going to be switching their SIM cards, but they'll have more of an incentive to put the company's card in their phone.

MicroEnsure said to the telcos, "Spend three percent of your call time revenues on insurance, and we will increase those revenues by ten percent." It works. The telcos are going out into the market and saying, "Give us your business, and we'll give you free insurance." Consumers who either don't want to or can't afford to buy insurance see it as a real value because they're genuinely worried about their futures.

It's all about adding value. For example, if a company spends a dollar to put its logo on a baseball cap, it does little to change consumer behavior. Instead, the company spends that dollar buying insurance for a customer. Now the customer sees value. They think that the insurance is worth fifty or a hundred dollars. It gives them an easy justification to become insured.

To achieve scale, the company aligns itself with big players—willing partners who are trusted and who already have these systems in place. In Asia, they have a relationship with Telenor, the Norwegian-based company that has operations in five countries in Asia. In Africa, they have a relationship with Airtel, which is based in India and has operations in seventeen countries in Africa. MicroEnsure works with six or seven telcos, but these are the biggest.

To market the offers to consumers, the company uses a wide variety of traditional low-tech methods. These include TV adverts, radio slots, billboards, and banners beside the road. They do SMS blasts that reach millions; they have IVR, a static phone line; and for old phones that can't accept apps, they have USSD menus that create a real-time connection to a server. (USSD means unstructured supplementary service data, and is commonly used by prepaid GSM cellular phones to query the available balance.) The company has paper forms at centers, and they have agents in the field. Probably the most successful are the end-of-call messages that are played when a customer uses their phone to make a balance inquiry. When the balance message is relayed to them, they also hear a message about the insurance offer. When the company uses end-of-call notifications, they see fifteen to twenty thousand people sign up every day.

PARTNERING WITH BANKS

MicroEnsure also went to the banks. The problem faced by banks is that they have a large number of depositors, but the balances are very low. When a family has money, they'll put a small amount in the bank. They'll also buy a sheep or a goat, buy some gold jewelry, and perhaps make a loan to a friend or relative. They spread their savings so they don't have all their eggs in one basket.

Most people in the low-income market don't care about the interest; it's not enough to make a savings account attractive. For savings accounts, the banks offer eight or ten percent interest, but if the rate of inflation is fifteen percent, the customer is actually losing money. To stimulate savings, MicroEnsure went to the banks and said, "Why don't you offer free insurance? If a customer puts in fifty dollars, give them five hundred dollars' worth of insurance the following month. For sixty dollars, make it six hundred dollars' worth of insurance."

The banking partners saw a two-hundred-percent rise in deposits. This was measurable because people started depositing exactly fifty-one dollars, which was more than they had done previously and just enough to qualify for insurance. This is because the insurance promotion added value to the savings account.

This is exactly the same kind of rational consumer behavior that's exhibited in wealthy countries. When poor people spread their cash around, it's no different from a Wall Street investor who has a diversified portfolio. As another example, consider the business traveler who is one flight away from reaching the next highest level on his or her frequent flyer miles. They'll always take a flight before the expiration period because the perceived value of the extra points is more than the price of the flight. Poor people have just as much brand loyalty as anyone else, and they reward fair treatment and good value.

PRODUCT DIVERSIFICATION

The first insurance product offered by MicroEnsure was very simple—life insurance. You die, and the company pays. Then the company quickly found out that what people really wanted was medical insurance. They'd say to the field reps, "I only die once, and it's not my problem! But my kids get sick all the time. And if I get sick, I need to get better. It's not just their problem, it's my problem." So the company came up with the Hospital Cash product. It's very simple. The company doesn't try to figure out the cost of treatment. They don't care what type of hospital the customer goes to. They simply say, "OK, for every night you're in the hospital, we're going to pay you a fixed amount," which is something like five or ten dollars. Administratively it's very simple. Across an entire country with millions of low-income people, the last thing any insurer wants to do is start verifying individual medical bills.

It costs roughly a dollar a month for a family, and it's easily scalable. In just six months in a country like Ghana, MicroEnsure sold 650,000 of these plans.

MicroEnsure does not invest all of its time in product development, as many insurance companies do. Their products are ubiquitous. Instead, what they focus on is the process, and in particular on three elements of the process:

First, why people buy insurance, how they feel about it, and under what circumstances they'd be willing to make the investment and enroll in a way that they understand.

Secondly, how the company answers their questions about the product.

And thirdly, how quickly the company pays them what they've said they're going to pay.

If these issues and processes can be worked out, then the product takes care of itself. MicroEnsure has found a way to operate in alignment with these big companies that have strong brands. What they do benefits their core businesses, whether those are selling more airtime or opening more bank accounts. As Leftley said, "We could be selling potato chips, but we're selling insurance because we've found out that it really affects customer loyalty. Our 'secret sauce' is in knowing how to design the product and the process around the mass market in Africa and Asia."

The company has two sets of customers. Their first customer is the chief marketing officer of the telco or the bank. They have to convince that person that this is not just craziness, but that this is something that they should actually do. Leftley's pitch is, "This does involve a leap of faith. We've got a product that, if you give it away for free, will change customer loyalty. But since you can measure it month by month, the exit ramp is only a month away. If you don't see that it enhances customer loyalty, then you can stop the program immediately. But if it works, you'll have millions of customers who now have insurance and to whom you can cross-sell or upsell."

The second customer is the individual or family consumer in Africa and Asia. MicroEnsure has to convince them to be more loyal to their bank or telecom provider. MicroEnsure needs to convince the consumer that the company can be trusted, and that they'll pay when they say they will. If they don't do this, the CMO of MicroEnsure's provider partner will shut off the tap.

If MicroEnsure can do this, then six months later the company can go back to the customer and say, "If you like the product, and it does what you expect, then for a dollar a month you can keep it—and we'll also cover your spouse."

As Leftley said, "It's a marketing scheme not unlike the one used by Candy Crush. The mobile phone game sounds like a crazy idea, so you give it away for free. People try it and they like it. Then you tell them that if they want to keep playing at a higher level, they need to pay ninety-nine cents. And they do! We're careful to make it very easy. We don't say, 'Please pay us a dollar.' We say, 'If you want to continue with your insurance, press number one on your phone, and send us an SMS text. We'll deduct your dollar in increments from your air time.' As we know, buying airtime is something that people do every day. It's a familiar transaction. So they can stay insured very painlessly."

Six months later, the company goes back to them and says, "Since you're happy with your life insurance, how about health insurance?" MicroEnsure takes these basic lessons from the internet economy and applies them to the bottom-of-the-pyramid market in Africa and Asia to sell people something that's good for them and helps to provide stability in their lives; in doing so, they're finding out that these low-income consumers behave the same way as people in developed countries. They may be less literate than Western consumers, and the company needs to take the time to understand them, but in many ways they're just like middle-class customers.

In Pakistan, the company worked with kids to find out how they buy ringtones. They used that information to approach the problem of buying insurance, and they said, "OK, how can buying insurance be made as simple as buying a ringtone?" So the company made both the product and the process as simple as possible. They realized that knowing their customer—crucial in both banking and insurance—was easier than they thought because the telco already had the customer information. They already had the customer's name and national ID number. To start the signup process, MicroEnsure didn't need to know anything else. So the company ran a TV advert that said, "If you want free insurance, send an SMS to *123#500." That was all. The customer didn't even have to provide their name. Then MicroEnsure sent them texts telling them in more detail how the product worked, and what number to call if they wanted to change something or if they had a question. The company got a hundred signups per minute.

THE FUTURE

Looking ahead, Leftley sees continued rapid growth. The company is currently serving over ten million people, and by the end of 2014 it could be fifteen million. While profitability is a goal, so is continued growth. Sanlam Emerging Markets and AXA have made significant investments, and the company plans to expand into North Africa and the Middle East. Since they've proven that the concept works with telecom companies and banks, he'd like to see if it will work in other areas too. They'd like to explore working with money transfer organizations such as Western Union, and explore partnering with consumer goods. For example, Leftley noted that Coke and Pepsi are global competitors in the fast-moving consumer goods (FMCG) category. It may be possible to use insurance to incentivize the last-mile distribution of these kinds of FMCG products into these markets. He's interested to see where it goes.

At the end of the day, it's the personal narratives that matter. "There is a story that illustrates what this is all about for me," said Leftley. "A few years ago I was in Bangladesh. I visited a family of twelve in the small shack where they lived. I could not see how they all went to sleep at night at the same time—in this tiny shack there was not enough room for them all to lie down. The mother told me that once one of her children got sick. She took the child to the government hospital, where there were supposed to be doctors and medicines. For a day she waited there with her child, who was getting sicker. No one treated the child. So the mother takes her child down the street to a private non-profit clinic. They had doctors and medicines. They could treat the child, but the cost would be three dollars, payable in advance. The mother had no money, so she hurried home to look for things that she could sell. She sold her few belongings—things like pots and pans that the family needed for cooking—before rushing back to the hospital. She arrived with her three dollars only to discover that her child had died."

Leftley had heard variations of this story many times before, and at a certain point he just said, "I cannot go on without trying to do *something* about this." It's that fire in the belly that motivates everyone in the company, and it's the impulse that can be found in nearly everyone who is a part of the effort for financial inclusion.

THE TAKEAWAY

- We can learn a lot from MicroEnsure's Success. They worked hard to work through many tough challenges.

- Design the product to meet the needs of the bottom of the pyramid. They would have failed if they tried to create an entry-level traditional insurance product. Instead, they started with the needs of the people and designed a product to meet their needs.

- Most people don't think about design principles when they're wrapping their heads around the problem of financial inclusion. Recent research by Anke Schwittay and Paul Braund of the Institute for Money, Technology and Financial Inclusion (IMTFI) analyzed the principles of good design and how it can make financial inclusion achievable specifically in Latin America. They developed ten design principles and emphasized the importance of great design for inclusion.

- Now, new innovative financial services companies like Juntos Finanzas are being started by CEOs who are well trained in design. Ben Knelman, CEO of Juntos, got his masters in engineering at Stanford, which included courses from Stanford's prestigious Design Institute (d. school). Juntos's product success is part technology and part design. This is especially important for financial inclusion because the traditional banking products just don't fit. The Chapter 17 will tell more about Juntos.

- The second big lesson from MicroEnsure is that scale will come from distribution and marketing that overcomes the lack of familiarity issue. Most customers never had insurance, and may not really understand what it is. The company knew that many of their customers would be new to insurance. They didn't take anything for granted. They also knew they needed to stay close to the customer to be sure they could easily get the benefits. They removed the complexity from being a first-time customer using an insurance product.

CHAPTER 11:

WIZZIT–Creating Economic Citizens

WIZZIT Payments (Pty) Ltd is a provider of basic branchless banking services for the unbanked and underbanked in South Africa. Its services are based on the use of mobile phones for accessing bank accounts and conducting transactions, in addition to a Maestro debit card that is issued to all customers upon registration. Its company slogan is, "Pioneers in financial inclusion through cellphone technology." Launched in 2004, Wizzit is formally a division of the South African Bank of Athens but its brand is owned and its operations are run by a group of independent entrepreneurs.

"We started Wizzit," says founding director and CEO Brian Richardson, "after we talked to many people who were unbanked, and we asked them a simple question: 'Why don't you have a bank account?' The answers all came down to the same three things: affordability, accessibility, and availability. We call them the 'three A's.' Take affordability: rightly or wrongly, banks are perceived as expensive and elitist. Our customers know that if they put one hundred dollars under the mattress, in a year they'll still have a hundred dollars. But if they put that hundred dollars in a traditional bank, the bank will eat it up in fees. Whether or not the customer makes even a single transaction, by the end of the year a significant chunk of that hundred dollars will be gone. We aimed to change that."

Accessibility is a problem. Traditional banks are centered in urban areas. Once you go to the countryside, there are very few branches. If you live in a village, the nearest branch may be twenty-five kilometers away. Few rural people have the time or the means to travel long distances for routine bank business. It's just a huge waste of time.

Availability? According to Richardson, banks in South Africa still maintain what in the old days was charitably called "banker's hours." Business hours are from nine in the morning to three-thirty in the afternoon. At banks he visited in Cairo, Egypt, the hours were from eight-thirty until two o'clock. "There's an obvious disconnect," says Richardson, "between when most people have to work and when the banks are open to serve them."

The answer was technology. But it was not internet banking, which would not work for customers at the bottom of the pyramid. Most low-income people don't have computers, but most of them have basic mobile phones.

"Our philosophy," says Richardson, "was that a person could be a legal citizen of a country, but he or she could never be an *economic* citizen without access to a basic bank account. It's almost a birthright. There is no reason why everyone should not have the opportunity to have a bank account."

The key to inclusive banking in developing areas is to be in alignment with the technology and infrastructure *that are already in place*. What may work in one country may not work in another. The technological resources of the local market will dictate the bank's business plan, not the other way around.

For example, in the rural South African market served by Wizzit, it would have been pointless to offer debit cards, which are ubiquitous in industrial societies. You could issue every account holder a debit card, but the problem is that there are few *acquirers*: those merchants who have point-of-sale terminals where consumers can use the cards. The technology between consumer and merchant would not be in alignment.

But if mobile phones are ubiquitous, you design your bank around mobile phones. And not just smartphones; you need to be able to leverage ordinary phones too. The only demand that you place upon the customer is to insert a new SIM card, which everyone knows how to do.

Wizzit has partnered with the Absa Group and the South African Post Office, which act as banking agents and allow Wizzit's customers to deposit funds at any Absa or post office branch. Similarly, Wizzit customers can pay for purchases and withdraw funds using their debit card at any point of sale (POS) or ATM-accepting Maestro cards. Wizzit has also partnered with Dunns, a fashion retailer focusing on lower to middle-income customer segments, that acts as an agent for opening accounts.

The company pursues a unique corporate vision that reflects its commitment to serving those at the bottom of the pyramid. For staffing, it maintains a policy of only recruiting unemployed people, which it has integrated into its promotion strategy. For marketing, Wizzit does not use mass media advertisements but relies instead on what it calls WIZZkids, who are previously unemployed individuals that the company certifies to become sales agents. The WIZZkids are typically young, low-income individuals living in the communities from which they recruit their customers. Besides the commission on sales, WIZZkids receive annuity income based on the transaction level of account holders, which motivates them to train customers to use their accounts.

According to Brian Richardson, as of this writing, Wizzit has an estimated six million customers. The company has expanded into Namibia, Botswana, Zambia, Tanzania, and Rwanda. Outside of Africa, the bank is entering Romania, Honduras, and potentially Brazil.[78]

Wizzit aims at partnering with either existing banks or microfinance institutions (MFIs) in the countries it intends to expand to, a strategy it has been testing with Beehive, a South African MFI. Wizzit has acquired merchants as agents in South Africa's rural areas, where the majority of its potential customers reside and where there is only an underdeveloped payments infrastructure available, such as ATMs and POS devices. If successful, merchants will offer customers the ability to deposit money to and withdraw money from their Wizzit bank accounts, as well as to pay for purchases by using their mobile phones.

"Banking is about trust," says Richardson. "It's about money, which is serious business. We want our low-income customers to trust the programs we're offering to them. We also must earn the trust of our bank partners. They need to know that the technology is totally reliable, and that by working with us their reputations will not only not be damaged, but will be enhanced."

Wizzit believes that people will not go through the hassle of opening a bank account simply to be able to make mobile payments. They'll open a bank account to keep their money safe and to build up a track record so that they can access loans when they might need them. Financial inclusion runs the gamut from access to banking to insurance, loans, and credit.

---

78   Interview with Brian Richardson.

"Of course our customers are apprehensive," says Richardson. "They say, 'What happens if I push the wrong button?' Or, 'Can I get my money when I need it?' But then they see that there's an audit, and they get statements that track every transaction. They start using it, and they see that it works the way they expect. It's like learning to ride a bicycle. It may seem scary at first, but once you get the hang of it, it becomes second nature."

Using Wizzit South Africa as a test and reference site, Wizzit has taken its mobile banking and branchless banking model to leading banks in emerging markets. As of September 2014, Wizzit has been implemented in:

- StanbicIBTC in Nigeria

- Banco Occidente in Honduras

- Bank Windhoek in Namibia

- Bank Gaberone in Botswana

- BPR in Rwanda

- NMB in Tanzania

- Sure Bank in South Africa

- Zanaco in Zambia

- BCR in Romania

The goal is to get the Wizzit technology and model implemented in fifty countries.

Each of Wizzit's bank partners shares the company's passion for financial inclusion and empowerment, and through the implementation have met—and in most instances exceeded—their strategic and financial objectives. It has given them the ability to be leaders in their respective countries, and in a very cost-effective way get to a market (the unbanked) that previously was not only difficult but very expensive to get to.

While the banks use their state-of-the-art technology for their existing customers, Wizzit's focus remains on making economic citizens of those who have been previously excluded. The attraction to the banks is the very quick implementation cycle (around twelve weeks) and integration into their core banking system with minimal disruption to their already stretched IT resources; the cost-effectiveness of the investment; the instant account opening that is fully compliant with in country regulation; the ten-year practical and hands-on track record; and the ability to share information and learnings with other banks in non-competing territories.

Wizzit's vision still remains to "bank the unbanked of the world using mobile technology."

THE TAKEAWAY

- Partnering with existing banks can work, and Wizzit has developed a repeatable model to do just that. The key to success is for bank partners to share a passion to serve this traditionally underserved user while delivering financial services that empower the user's life and work.

- Scale beyond borders is achievable. Wizzit has spent over a decade developing their platform and execution capability to achieve ten country implementations and to be in a position to achieve their aspiration to have fifty countries. Entrepreneurs aspiring to follow their lead would be well served to mature their platform and execution in one (possibly two) countries before attempting this type of larger scale.

CHAPTER 12:
Simpa Networks:
Solar Power On Microcredit

There are many ways to promote greater financial inclusion for the billions of people living at the bottom of the pyramid. Common solutions involve re-inventing financial services such as bank accounts, or expanding the use of mobile money. There are other ways too. Simpa Networks attacks the problem from the perspective of energy and shows how a company can improve human lives by changing the energy industry's business model.

Headquartered near Delhi, Simpa Networks is a venture-backed technology company with a bold mission: to make modern energy simple, affordable, and accessible for everyone. The company has designed a for-profit business model that attracts mainstream capital to address a vexing social problem: lack of access to modern energy.

To fulfill its mission, Simpa created an innovative business model called Progressive Purchase that strives to make sustainable energy choices "radically affordable" to the world's 1.5 billion BoP consumers who currently lack any access to electricity. In addition to these 1.5 billion people, one billion people live with brownouts—they may have a connection, but the power is on only a few hours a day. In rural India, you see the power lines, but power is delivered sporadically. In many rural areas, when the sun goes down, it gets *dark*. There are no lights anywhere.

The solution is not based on new technology, but on a new business model. "There are many different ways to affect financial inclusion," says Simpa's president and co-founder Paul Needham. "Most people immediately think of things like microloans, bank accounts, and credit cards. But we saw a need to create a financial product that's designed for the energy-poor, a financial solution that can help make clean, reliable electricity affordable for the mass market. To expand access to energy, we needed to expand access to finance."

The company, which has a US office in Seattle, Washington, launched in India in 2011. After about two years of piloting and improving its model, the company launched in northern India. At the time of writing, the company's sales area covered eight districts of western Uttar Pradesh, India's most populous state, and one which contains the most numbers of un-electrified. Simpa sells in rural villages where the economy is primarily agricultural. According to the Indian Government 2011 census, only 36.8 % of households in Uttar Pradesh use electricity as their primary source for lighting. Without electricity, the most common lighting solution remains the humble kerosene lantern, which burns a form of oil and emits toxic fumes.

Even urban dwellers in Uttar Pradesh suffer from the abysmal power supply situation. A typical report on conditions in Uttar Pradesh is this one, from the *Times of India* in May 2012: "Unscheduled power cuts in Noida, Greater Noida, and Ghaziabad in the NCR [National Capital Region] have thrown life out of gear for residents. While residents have to bear the sweltering heat in the absence of air conditioners and coolers, excessive use of diesel generators has also burnt a hole in their pockets owing to the high cost of fuel. Power cuts have not only affected studies of school children, but absence of continuous supply has had an adverse impact on industries as they have failed to attain desired outputs and fallen short of targets.

"Residents allege that their complaints to the top brass of the power department have not yielded any results despite all sectors of Noida being hit by the crisis. Entrepreneurs allege that industries are in particularly bad shape due to the crisis despite the government declaring the region as a 'no power-cut zone.'"[79]

While city folk and industrialists complain about inadequate and erratic power supply, most people in rural India go without entirely. The consequences

---

79   http://timesofindia. indiatimes. com/city/noida/Power-cuts-throw-life-out-of-gear-in-Uttar-Pradesh/articleshow/13367754. cms

of poor access to clean energy are economic stagnation, diminished security, lack of social mobility, restricted education, and lower quality health services.

THE POWER OF A SOLAR PANEL

Simpa's president and co-founder Paul Needham saw an opportunity and acted upon it. A veteran IT entrepreneur, in 1999 he quit the economics Ph.D. program at Cambridge University to co-found an Internet startup. He eventually wound up at Microsoft, with responsibility for launching the software giant's online advertising network business in Canada. He left Microsoft to co-found Simpa Networks. Needham is also on the board of directors of CAMFED USA (Campaign for Female Education), a not-for-profit organization that tackles poverty and HIV/AIDS by investing in the education of girls in Africa.

"It was on a trip to Tanzania that I saw solar energy being used in some very interesting ways," says Needham. "I met with a group of young women entrepreneurs who had received micro loans to expand their businesses. Some were raising chickens, some were raising pigs, many were growing and selling crops. I remember meeting one woman farmer who was growing tomatoes. Yet despite her investment to expand her land holdings, she was really struggling to make a living. She was ultimately subject to the weather. Last year had been bad, she said, and her crop yield was poor. Not enough tomatoes. Even when the weather conditions were good, she explained, it's hard to make a living because there is over-supply. Then there is the problem of too many tomatoes and with all the other farmers also having bumper crops. Prices get pushed down and her tomato crop spoils. It felt quite hopeless for tomato growers in this area.

"That woman introduced me to another local entrepreneur, a solar entrepreneur. The second woman had purchased a solar panel and was using it to make money. The panel wasn't very big—maybe a square meter. Keep in mind that this was in a rural area, far off the electrical grid. Lots of people had cell phones but nowhere to charge them. This young woman was using her solar panel to charge peoples' mobile phones, and she was making a healthy income. I was struck by the contrast, and struck by the economic value of solar energy. One woman was capturing sunlight to grow tomatoes, the other was capturing sunlight to make electricity. In one case, it took two acres of land, and in the other case it took only a square meter of solar panel. They were using different technologies to convert sunlight into something valuable, and it was clear to me then that selling electricity was the better business model. At that moment I resolved to leave my position at Microsoft and seriously explore the economic potential of solar energy in rural areas."

At that time in North America, very few people were switching to solar. It was primarily a matter of scale and expense. To power the typical North American home required twenty thousand dollars' worth of solar equipment. In rural areas of undeveloped countries, people live much simpler lives. Their power requirements are much less; they need light, power for their mobile phone, and in hot weather they need a fan to break the heat and keep off the mosquitoes at night. These basic home energy needs can be met with energy-efficient LED lights, a solar panel, and a battery.

Simpa sells small-scale solar home systems. A typical system includes one forty-watt solar panel, plus two or three energy efficient LED lights, plus an electric fan, and a mobile phone charger. The panel looks small—only about the size of a fully-opened copy of a daily newspaper. But with that small patch of sunshine, a family can light several rooms using high-quality LED lights from Schneider Electric.

The fan is a big selling point in western Uttar Pradesh where Simpa is operating. Summer temperatures can climb to forty-eight degrees Celsius—nearly 118 degrees Fahrenheit. Fans provide relief from the heat and mosquito control at night. But the fan uses five times as much energy as an LED light, so the system has to be large enough and powerful enough to meet the customers' demands. That, of course, increases the costs.

Despite their simplicity, even these small systems cost between two hundred and four hundred dollars, which is too expensive for most of Simpa's customers to buy on a cash basis. "The energy-poor," says Needham, "tend to be among the poorest people in their own countries. They cannot afford the high up-front costs of a quality solar energy system, but they are ready and willing to pay for the energy service. We saw the opportunity, and we introduced a financial innovation, a rooftop solar leasing model made appropriate for energy-poor customers in rural areas."

Here's how Simpa's innovative pricing model works:

1. The customer makes a small initial down payment of roughly two thousand rupees, or forty US dollars. The customer does not need a bank account or credit card, just the cash and a mobile phone.

2. Simpa technicians install the rooftop panel and make sure that the house is wired correctly. The system also includes a digital pre-pay meter about the size of an ordinary keypad.

3. The customer goes to an authorized agent and makes a payment, just like he or she would make a payment to top up their mobile phone airtime.

4. The agent manages the payment on his or her mobile phone.

5. The agent sends an SMS message to the customer's mobile phone. The SMS message consists of a numerical code.

6. The customer enters the numerical code into the digital pre-pay meter, and the solar system is activated for a set amount of usage.

7. When the prepaid usage has been used up, the solar system shuts down until the customer makes another "top-up" payment and receives a new activation code.

PROGRESSIVE PURCHASE

This is a similar system to the ones used by the mobile phone companies when they provide microloans for purchases of new phones, which is also available from many mobile operators focused on the budget-minded consumer, like MetroPCS in the US in partnership with Better Finance, which provides the credit.

Instead of expensive monthly billing for set amounts, the customer tops up the solar energy account based on how much they can afford. They manage their own consumption. Customers can buy enough time to operate the solar system for five days, a week, or more.

"We find most customers in Uttar Pradesh are buying a month at a time," says Needham. "The meter shows them how many days they have left. For the meter, we use encryption technology. The code that is typed in by the customer is one that only their meter can read. The software in the meter recognizes the code and adds the appropriate amount of usage."

The meter itself is not connected to the mobile phone network, because this would be impractical. As is the case anywhere in the world, you don't always get good mobile phone service in your home. You can get it when you're out and about, but not necessarily in your home.

In this rent-to-own arrangement, each payment for energy adds towards the final purchase price. Once fully paid—typically after two years—for a small additional fee the system unlocks permanently. The consumer owns the system, which produces energy, free and clear. If the customer wants to keep paying, they can upgrade their system, and they can get access to new credit for the upgrade if they need it. They can grow their use over time, and in affordable increments to their families.

BUILDING THE DISTRIBUTION NETWORK

Like all good things, the Simpa initiative is starting small. Over the first couple years, the company piloted and improved its offering, so progress was slow. But once the company was ready it re-launched under a new sales model and sales started to really pick up. It took the company two years to reach its first 500 customers, four months to reach its next 500 customers, and then only two months to reach its next 500 customers. At the time of writing, Simpa was adding 500 customers every two weeks and still accelerating. As of August 2014, Simpa had over 4,800 customers and was adding at a rate of at least 1,000 per month. Building the sales and distribution channels—marketing, installations, payments, servicing—is no small task. By definition, their rural customers are underserved, and for a very good reason: they're spread out in small, low-income villages. The company has built an effective team that includes people from other sectors—insurance, microfinance, and mobile phones. These are industries that have successfully reached out into rural India. The company's VP of sales was hired precisely because he has spent his career building sales channels in rural India.

"We've discovered special challenges in the rural Indian market," says Needham. "For example, the solar system is installed by our technicians. It turns out that monkeys, which are ubiquitous in these areas, love the rooftop panels.

Perhaps this is because the panels are shiny and look interesting. The monkeys try to take them off—to steal them and take them home, I suppose. So we have to bolt them down very securely."

Rural customers usually hear about the opportunity from a local person—a neighbor or sales agent. In alignment with this reality, when Simpa decides on a territory it wants to develop, they go in and hire local people to be sales agents. The company isn't trying to create entrepreneurs; it looks for people who already *are* entrepreneurs. The new hire may be operating a shop, or involved in agriculture. "I recently met a guy," says Needham, "who makes money selling mobile airtime. He's also a banking correspondent for India's largest bank. His neighbor, whom we also signed up, makes money by transporting fresh milk for local farmers. Every morning he makes his rounds and takes the milk to a collection point, where it's chilled and sent to market in the cities. These are people who are already successful entrepreneurs, and we try to win them over by showing them this new business opportunity. They can make money by signing up new customers and by servicing those customers."

THE WIDER ECONOMIC RAMIFICATIONS

The benefits provided by clean energy are more than monetary. Users of kerosene complain of headaches. The lanterns get knocked over by children and cause fires. Switching to solar energy provides immediate environmental benefits in the home or shop.

"We recently met a customer who explained the profound impact electricity can provide," says Needham. "He had been using the solar system for about a week, and we wanted to make sure everything was okay. We asked the man how it was working for him. Through the interpreter, he replied that it was fine, and his only wish was that he had been given this opportunity five years earlier. 'Why five years?' we asked. He replied that five years ago, his wife, the mother of his three children, had gone into the kitchen one night to get some milk for their baby. It was dark. Although they had a connection to the grid, there had been no power for days, and the kitchen was very dark. As she fumbled in the dark to reach for the milk container, she felt a sharp bite on her wrist. She had been bitten by a snake. They couldn't get her to a hospital in time, and she died that night. 'If you had been here five years ago,' said the man, 'my children would still have their mother.'"

Basic lighting is essential for safety and security. It also can generate positive income generation opportunities for farmers and entrepreneurs. In his research into the underserved economy, Needham started thinking about the wider impact of affordable energy. Having a light in your house is a very good thing, but the possibilities for change can run much deeper.

Needham remembered the woman who was growing tomatoes in Tanzania. Could affordable, clean energy help her? On one visit, Needham asked her how business had been that year.

Her answer was that it had been terrible. The rains didn't come when they were supposed to, and her crop was not very good.

"How about the year before?" asked Needham. "How was the rainfall?" During the previous year, the rainfall had been fine. Did the woman make any money?

No. That year, because of the abundant rain, everyone had lots of tomatoes—too many tomatoes, and no way to get them into the markets in the city. Consequently, many of them rotted on the vine.

Needham realized that the two women—one with an acre of tomatoes, and the other with her single solar panel—were both trying to convert sunlight into a commodity. In one case it was tomatoes; in the other case it was cellphone charging. The woman with the solar panel was making money. The woman trying to grow tomatoes was never able to make much money.

As an economist, Needham asked himself if there were other ways to make money with a solar panel. There were capital costs, but couldn't there be other solar entrepreneurs? Could you light a school? Could you light a house, or keep your shop lit so it didn't have to close at sunset?

For the woman who grows tomatoes, a partial solution—at least for dry periods—might be solar-powered irrigation. "We're not doing that yet," says Needham, "But I can see that our customers are asking for more powerful systems. They're asking for systems that can power a pump for irrigation. Many people are asking for a system just big enough to power a television set. One benefit of the solar system is that you can scale it up. Once you've paid off your first solar panel, you can get another one, or a bigger one. I can see customers going up the 'energy ladder.' At first, what they want to do is get rid of their kerosene lantern. They just want clean lighting. Then they start to see and imagine more possibilities. They start asking for upgrades."

Many of Simpa's customers own cattle, which they milk in the morning. The milking has to be done very early, so when the collection truck comes around the milk is ready to be delivered. Every one of these customers has installed a light outside. This is so they can work with the cattle in the evening and the early morning, as well as for safety and security. These cattle are their livelihood and a source of stored wealth. Lights deter cattle thieves and provide a real security benefit.

One Simpa customer has a roadside tea stall. Crammed into this tiny stall are the goods that truck drivers want—tea, strong coffee, cigarettes. He's got a light installed outside so that the truckers can see it in the distance and get ready to apply the brakes. His battery allows him to keep the light on all night. (Customers use the solar system in different ways; if you don't use the fan, for example, you can operate the light for a much longer period of time—even twenty-four hours a day.) Two months after the initial installation, Needham returned to visit the roadside tea stall. The owner had installed a brand-new counter. He reported that since he was now able to stay open late at night, he was making more money. His tea stall was one of the few along the highway that had an electric light, and business was booming.

"Most people will not be satisfied with only basic levels of energy," says Needham. "Most people will want more power. More power to run TVs, refrigerators, coolers, water pumps, computers, power tools, and other machines. Energy is opportunity, and opportunity cannot be denied."

Conventional dry-cell batteries are expensive. "Look at a D-cell battery—those large flashlight batteries, which are very common in India," he continues. "If you analyze the cost of the electricity you get, you're paying about *fifty dollars* per kilowatt hour. In contrast, American households pay an average of *twenty cents* per kilowatt hour. It's very expensive energy, and people use these batteries in flashlights and radios. Many of our customers are already spending ten dollars a month for this type of old-fashioned technology. This includes things like kerosene for their lamps. These customers can take that same ten dollars a month and spend it with Simpa, and they get multi-room lighting, mobile phone charging, and a fan. You can't power a fan with kerosene!"

Many Simpa customers can switch from kerosene and pay the same amount per month for their energy. By switching they get much better quality energy. Eventually, they own their system, and their electricity is essentially free.

Human beings have harnessed electricity. We use it to power our homes and appliances. We use it for irrigation. We use it for communication. It helps us do what we want, and it helps us educate ourselves. Without access to electricity, life can be very stunted, and even more dangerous.

LEAPFROGGING

Looking towards the future, Needham anticipates a growth trajectory for solar power that will be analogous to the growth of mobile phones. "At the turn of the twenty-first century," he says, "there were probably five million people in India who had a mobile phone. Today there are a billion people in India with mobile phones. What happened? There's been a tremendous transformation based on an innovative pricing model. The customer makes a small investment in the phone itself. Then, you just pay for it when you want to use it. You can pay as little or as much as you want. And the phone company doesn't have to chase after you with a bill. You never get a bill! This is how many rural people buy things. You buy one cigarette at a time. You buy soap or shampoo in small packets. In India, this is called 'sachet marketing.' It's named after the introduction of shampoo sachets in India by Hindustan Levers. The shampoo sachets were created to specifically target the 'bottom of the pyramid' market. To better suit the income and cash flow of individuals in the marketplace, the products are available in smaller quantities than traditional shampoo bottles. The concept allows consumers to have access to affordable products at a small scale more suited to their levels of daily income."

The mobile operators allow their customers to purchase the product in very small increments, while the company still makes a profit.

There's also a leapfrog opportunity. The billion people who have become phone subscribers in India don't have landlines. To run phone lines to rural areas would be impossibly expensive. These billion consumers are using the latest technology. They've leapfrogged from no phone to mobile phone. The potential exists for the same to happen with electricity. The traditional model used in developed countries is to have a centralized power producer with a distribution system that radiates from it to each community and household. Back in the early twentieth century, this was the most efficient solution, and allowed millions of homes to get rid of their dangerous gas lights. Times have changed, and so has technology. There's little reason to construct a massive power grid when you can deploy a billion individual solar panels that each generate enough electricity to power a house or a shop.

Even in developed countries, the use of landline telephones is declining as more consumers switch to mobile. "I think that what we'll see in a decade," says Needham, "is a similar shift in electricity delivery. The revolution is happening in rural areas. The adoption of solar technology will happen there, where it is most economically viable, and spread backward, so to speak, into developed countries."

THE TAKEAWAY

- We need to think about financial inclusion as much bigger than just about bank accounts and online payments. Financial inclusion is about all sorts of services that support life and work.

- Simpa shows us the power of looking at financial inclusion and energy inclusion together. This enables the development of powerful new models.

- Instead of trying to fit BoP into rich people's models, Simpa is a great example of leveraging technology to fit into BoP's lifestyle. This should be applauded and mimicked.

CHAPTER 13:

Wing

During the past thirty-five years, Cambodia has struggled to establish a solid and stable economy, but the path has not been easy. During the period under the rule of the Khmer Rouge, most of its professionals and educated elite were slaughtered. Pol Pot, the leader of the Khmer Rouge, also abolished money, markets, and private property. In pursuit of these policies, he ordered the destruction of the Central Bank. Between 1975 and 1980, the country had no monetary system.

In April 1980, the national currency—the riel—was re-instituted. But this currency never gained complete public acceptance, with most Cambodians preferring foreign currency. The UN peacekeeping operation of 1993 injected a large quantity of US dollars into the local economy, and the dollar became the country's common currency.

While the reissued Cambodian riel is in wide circulation today, many Cambodians remain distrustful of it and regularly convert their riel into gold, jewelry, or US dollars. This practice of "dollarization" perpetuates the ineffectiveness of Cambodia's financial institutions, banking systems, and regulatory agencies.

In rural areas, the riel is commonly used; however, roughly ninety percent of the money in circulation in Cambodia is US dollars with heavy usage in urban Cambodia and tourist areas. Thus Cambodia has in effect a two-currency system. Having a funds transfer service operating only in one currency means customers have to pay exchange rates when doing day-to-day transactions.

This was just one of the many challenges facing Wing, a mobile payment service provider launched in January 2009 that allows their individual and business customers to transfer, deposit, and withdraw money between each other and with anyone in Cambodia, via any mobile phone, at low cost. As the leading mobile payment provider, Wing allows customers to make payments like bill pay and phone top-up at their convenience.

Wing recognized the importance of giving their customers a choice of currencies, and in July 2010 the company began operating in both currencies. This was a big challenge; Wing is the only m-banking company in the world needing to work in two currencies. Its multi-currency model is customer-driven, reflecting the way the country already operates, and giving their customers the choice to make transactions in the way that works for them.

Operating in two currencies has had a huge impact on the business. Before multi-currency, Wing was focused on individual customers storing and moving money, and airtime mobile phone top-up. The company was not able to serve businesses. Multi-currency allowed Wing to introduce payroll, B2B, billing, and bulk payments to its ever-growing list of services.

When opening a Wing account, the customer chooses whether they prefer the account in dollars or in riels. It's possible to transfer money from a dollar account to a riel account, and vice versa. A daily change rate will apply. (As of this writing, roughly 4,000 riels equals one US dollar.) At any time, the customer can decide to change the currency of the account by accessing their account settings using their mobile phone, or simply calling the Wing Care Center. For customers in need of transacting regularly both in riels and dollars, it's possible to own two accounts in the two different currencies.

Customers access their money via any mobile phone and their funds are stored in a regulated bank. With their Wing Cards, customers can cash-in and cash-out their accounts in any physical Wing Cash Xpress outlet, and cash-out from all ANZ-Royal ATMs. Transactions including sending and receiving money, phone top-up, or bill payments are done from any mobile phone, and secured by a personal four-digit pin code.

There is no monthly fee charged for holding an account with Wing, nor any minimum balance.

It's Simple to Send Money

The company says that sending money to another Wing account is the easiest and cheapest way of sending money in Cambodia. The money is instantly transferred from the sender's account to the receiver's account.

It sounds simple enough—here are the seven steps:

1. Dial *989#

2. Enter your Wing number xxxxxxxx

3. Enter 2 [WING-2-WING]

4. Enter 1 (or [Enter pre-saved contact number] which then skips step 5 below)

5. Enter Receiver's Wing number xxxxxxxx

6. Enter amount xxxx

7. Enter PIN xxxx

A receipt is sent by SMS to both sides, indicating the amount of money transferred, the transaction reference ID, and the new balance.

A customer can also send money to somebody who does not have a Wing account by generating an eight-digit passcode along with the recipient's phone number, which once communicated to the receiver can be used to withdraw the money at any Wing Cash Xpress. For security, the Wing Cash Xpress operator verifies the passcode and the recipient's phone number before providing the person access to the money.

Business Services

Wing also offers easy and scalable business solutions, including payroll and disbursements, electronic money collection (billing), and petty cash. Depending on the company's needs, Wing staff can open Wing accounts for a company's employees or beneficiaries, train their employees or beneficiaries on how to withdraw cash, and perform payments, reconciliations, and settlements.

Wing Balance Advance

Wing makes "nano-loans" to its customers. With Balance Advance, the customer can borrow funds ranging from $0.50 to $2 depending on the customer's credit history, determined from historical top-up records. This nano-loan allows the customer to top up a mobile phone number even if the customer doesn't have enough balance in their account. The interest fee is fifteen percent and is deducted automatically when the customer receives sufficient funds to their Wing account. This provides a safety net for mobile phone minutes, which can help keep the phone supporting their business or family needs between the time they run out of minute credits until they can top up.

THE CULTURE OF CAMBODIA

Aside from currency issues, a significant challenge to building the network in Cambodia was cultural. "In Cambodia," said CEO Anthony Perkins, "there's a tradition of having someone else do everyday tasks for you. There'd be a guy in the village to whom you'd go, and he'd do things like pay your electricity bill or send money to a family member. People weren't used to doing these things themselves.

"This story is typical. Once while we were up in the north near the border of Laos, I was at a Wing Cash Xpress when a local guy pulled up in a Range Rover. He was obviously wealthy. He talked to someone on his mobile phone in English. I became curious—why is this wealthy man using Wing? And if he can speak English, why doesn't he do his own transactions? So I went up to him and asked him why he was using Wing Cash Xpress to send money—I think it was something like two hundred dollars to a family member. He said, 'I know a guy who takes care of all of this stuff. I give him the money and he does everything for me. I don't have to worry about the technology. If something goes wrong, I can talk to my guy. I don't have to contact Wing; I have a human interaction. Whatever the problem is, he can fix it.' So even though he was perfectly capable of making his own transactions, he still did things the old way."

In Cambodia, Wing takes great pains to provide excellent customer service at every Wing Cash Xpress outlet. If an agent isn't professional, he or she will be replaced.

Wing takes precautions against scammers. "We've done public TV and radio slots where representatives are interviewed and explain scams," Perkins said in an interview for *The Cambodia Daily*.[80] "We've posted online and at Wing Cash Xpress outlets a campaign telling customers not to send money to people you don't know. Wing Cash Xpress agents also are trained how to ask customers about their transactions and track criminal activity. The Xpress outlets also have CCTV cameras." Perkins added that of the three million transactions Wing does a month, one or two are logged as possible fraud cases. He said the fraud cases tend to range between ten dollars to less than two thousand dollars.

A Fast Roll-Out

When Wing was launched, the company didn't take the route of slowly growing organically out of Phnom Penh. The Wing leadership wanted to establish Wing as a big and trustworthy company as quickly as possible. To make it look like Wing was everywhere, the company signed up agents all over the country as quickly as possible. Once Wing was up and running they went back and put much more focus on quality and training.

"It also helped that we were affiliated with ANZ Royal Bank," said Perkins. "As a joint venture between local conglomerate the Royal Group, and Australia and New Zealand Banking Group Limited (ANZ), one of the largest banks in the world, everyday Cambodians trusted it more than their locally-owned banks. They trusted that we would not run off with their money."

In addition, because of Wing's affiliation with ANZ, the National Bank of Cambodia was willing to let Wing get established even though the customary federal regulations were not yet fully in place. It's a bit of advice that Perkins would give to other Southeast Asia countries, such as Laos or Myanmar. "If they wait until all the regulations are in place, people will have lost interest," said Perkins. "It's far better to just let a reputable player get on with it whilst drawing up regulations in parallel."

That's part of the Wing strategy: get new products to the marketplace quickly and let consumers test them. Listen to consumer feedback, and then fine-tune the products. For Wing, this agile approach is better than spending

---

80   http://www. cambodiadaily. com/news/phone-scam-promises-govt-positions-for-cash-61196/

years trying to perfect a product in the lab before rolling it out. To cut development time even further, in the past few years Wing has brought its technology platform in-house.

Wing partners with the seven major mobile networks in the country. They include GSM operators Cellcard, Metfone, Smart, Beeline and QB, along with CDMA carriers Excell and Cootel. Its customers can access their Wing account via any of the GSM operators, independently from their phone number or handset. In some countries, customers need to subscribe to a particular mobile phone network in order to use their mobile money solution or even to use the m-banking from their bank. But Wing recognized that many Cambodians subscribe to more than one mobile phone operator. They wanted to offer Cambodians their choice of networks. These networks cover one hundred percent of Cambodia's geography and population. Virtually everyone, no matter where they are, can access Wing.

Money transfer—domestic remittance—is a big part of the business. "In May 2014," said Perkins, "we processed $250 million dollars for our customers. In 2013, we processed just over $1.2 billion. It's a phenomenal amount when you consider the GDP of the country, which is about $14 billion US dollars."

A critical part of the Wing strategy is to make its Cash Xpress agents highly visible. The company wants its agents to have more than just a sign on their shop, or an umbrella with a logo. Wing has discovered that when an investment is made in upgrading the appearance of a Cash Xpress outlet, the volume of transactions increases dramatically. It's all about appearing to be stable and trustworthy—and then living up to that image.

The network of 1,600 Wing Cash Xpress outlets nationwide cooperate with each other and give each other advice. They're willing to listen to other agents because the agents are not employees of Wing. In fact, one of the first agents who upgraded his storefront spread the word among the other agents that for an investment of a thousand dollars in marketing materials from Wing and a store upgrade, they could expect to have their investment repaid with higher sales in just two or three months. Wing now offers a catalogue with marketing materials that they sell to the agents at cost. Because the Wing agents own their signage, they also take much better care of it and keep it well maintained, a very real problem in locations along dusty main roads.

Wing also takes top agents on management trips to visit other agents, and to share their experiences and insights.

The Future

"What we've done here has just scratched the surface," said Perkins. "International remittance and expanded government payments are on the table. Tax collection is another one. The retail market in Phnom Penh needs to be developed. The pricing for credit cards is an obstacle because the merchants don't want to pay the fees; they'd rather just take cash. As a result, building the market for card payments has been very difficult for the big banks.

"Beyond our sixteen hundred mobile money agents, we also have six thousand top-up dealers who only do prepaid top-up. Every single one of those outlets has a post device that can accept card payments. We're trying to put together the half-million cards we've got with these outlets, and build a retail proposition and get card payments off the ground. In Cambodia, there are no big retail chains—no Wal-Mart or 7-11. It all has to be done shop by shop, but with the right partners we can expand into retail card payments.

"We've got an online API that works pretty much the same as PayPal. The customer gets switched from the retail website to our secure payment gateway. A Wing customer can pay for goods on the Internet. It's a tiny market now, but over the next five or ten years I see it as becoming a massive part of our business.

"We hope to make money fair and provide as many financial services as possible to every Cambodian, rich or poor."

Wing is a great example of a pioneer working in adverse environment—eight mobile operators, lack of trust of local banks, little personal financial history available, dusty roads, regulatory uncertainty, and on and on. All this adds up to significant challenges in a country where the majority are underserved. Despite all this, they are succeeding in breaking through and building momentum.

In the last section we are going to look at ways countries can foster innovation in financial inclusion, which will benefit existing providers like Wing and provide productive ground for new entrants.

THE TAKEAWAY

- Wing's success followed the approach we saw work so well in Kenya. Roll out quickly and focus on building relevance and trust. Be bold! Momentum matters.

- Very small loans may seem unnecessary to many people in the world, but can be hugely valuable to support the underserved.

- Once again, we see a young, dedicated organization overcoming obstacles and delivering results in an adverse and challenging environment. The world should take notice and be impressed with their success.

CHAPTER 14:

Activehours Provides Access to Earnings

In the United States today there are over seventy-five million hourly workers. They work at entry-level jobs: cashiers, cooks, sales associates, burger flippers, drivers. Unlike salaried employees, hourly workers punch in and out on time clocks. They only get paid when they actually show up for work.

Typically, these employees are paid through their employer's payroll company. They receive a paycheck weekly or biweekly. For a biweekly worker who gets paid every other Friday, by the time Thursday rolls around, they've been working for nine days without receiving a paycheck. And typically there's a lag of at least a week between the days they've worked and the paycheck they receive.

For example, say a cashier starts work on Monday, June 1. Mary works for two weeks until Friday, June 12. On that day, the payroll company electronically deposits her two-week paycheck into her bank account. But the *pay period* of the check is always at least a week behind. Mary won't get paid for the work she did June 1 through June 12. She will be paid for the two-week period from May 25 to June 6.

So on June 12, Mary gets paid for the work she did from May 25 to June 6.

If Mary is an hourly worker, chances are her wages put her near the bottom of the economic pyramid, which means that she lives "paycheck to paycheck" with little or no savings.

Here's a sample of the pay rate for selected hourly employees at some of America's biggest companies:

Company	Hourly Pay Rate	Annual (35 Hrs Week X 50 Weeks)
Starbucks barista	$8.80	$15,400
Wal-Mart sales associate	$8.85	$15,487
McDonald's crew	$7.77	$13,597
Taco Bell cashier	$7.63	$13,352
Domino's delivery driver	$6.94	$12,145
Disney Parks & Resorts cast member	$8.79	$15,382
Hilton Hotels front desk agent	$11.38	$19,915
Old Navy sales associate	$8.37	$14,647
SOURCE: GLASSDOOR. COM / June 2014		

If you're making less than $20,000 a year in America and you're single, you're not technically considered to living below the federal poverty line; but if you have a family to support, you are, according to the United States Department of Health and Human Services (HHS) figures for poverty in 2014:

Persons in Family Unit	48 Contiguous States and D. C.	Alaska	Hawaii
1	$11,670	$14,580	$13,420
2	$15,730	$19,660	$18,090
3	$19,790	$24,730	$22,760
4	$23,850	$29,820	$27,430
5	$27,910	$34,900	$32,100
6	$31,970	$39,980	$36,770
7	$36,030	$45,060	$41,440
8	$40,090	$50,140	$46,110
Each additional person adds	$4,060	$5,080	$4,670

When people who are living without savings need cash against their earnings, they turn to very expensive solutions. They risk overdraft fees, use credit cards, or take out payday loans or car title loans. We discussed payday loans in an earlier chapter; suffice it to say that the rates are usurious. For a seven-day payday loan of $600 you might pay a fee of ninety dollars. That translates into a whopping annual percentage rate (APR) of 782%.

IT'S NOT A CONVENTIONAL LOAN

In the United States, collectively the hourly wage workforce earns three trillion dollars a year. Of that, over a trillion dollars is subject to an average time delay of two weeks while the workers' pay sits in the employers' accounts as unpaid wages until paychecks are cut. It's a huge cash float that is very expensive for the individual worker. The system hasn't changed in hundreds of years.

Ram Palaniappan, the founder and CEO of Activehours, saw an opportunity to provide relief for millions of hourly workers. Ram was a top-level executive at a leading prepaid card company. He was very good at reaching and serving underserved people with prepaid cards. He had a large team of hourly workers who reported to him. He noticed that there were times when his employees were very anxious because they ran out of money before their paycheck was issued. He knew how many hours they had worked, so to help his employees he started to "give them access" to their paycheck, but only the portion that he knew they had already earned. It was good for business because they were less anxious, more productive, and happier in their jobs. He also knew when they got paid, and he asked for repayment on their payday. In many ways, he was a personal banker to his employees.

He realized that if his employees had this problem, others did too—and he had the solution. The idea was simple and had three features that made it very different from expensive payday loans.

1. In a conventional loan, you typically borrow against your future earnings. Ram's system was simply to provide access to money that you had already earned and which you could prove you were going to receive. It was like a same-day payroll, and you pay yourself for "active hours" you have already worked.

2. No high-priced roll-overs. The transaction is settled on the employer's regular payroll date.

3. No fees! The first customers were his friends and he didn't want to make money off of them. Instead, Ram said, "Tip me whatever amount you can."

Ram decided he would leave his position in his company and start a company dedicated to this idea.

The result is Activehours, a San Francisco-based for-profit company that markets a free app for iPhone and Android systems. Released on May 21, 2014, the Activehours app seeks to make accessible to the individual hourly worker the money they've earned and is due to be paid to them. The company does not make loans against *future* earnings. The money it provides is money that the customer *already owns* but hasn't received yet.

For example, if Mary has worked from May 25 to June 6, she's earned her pay. But her company may not release her money to her until June 12. Because she's a low-end hourly worker, Mary lives at the bottom of the financial pyramid with no reserve savings. Let's say that on June 7 her car breaks down. To get it fixed, she would normally be forced to borrow against her future paycheck—and for people at BoP, borrowing is horrendously expensive.

Activehours fills the gap. Acting as a middleman, on June 7 Activehours provides Mary the unpaid income she has already earned. When she gets paid on June 12, Activehours automatically repays itself from her bank account after her pay has posted.

The service works completely on her smart phone.

Activehours exists to help hourly workers get paid early when they need it. If a person works a job tracked by the hour and uses an electronic clock-in/clock-out system, that person can sign up. From there they enter their hours and provide their bank account information. Once Activehours verifies their information, they can get their next paycheck deposited directly into their bank account early. If they don't want all of it up front, they can select a specific number of hours for early payment instead. When their paycheck gets deposited into their account on payday, Activehours will remove only the forwarded money.

Activehours is not a bank and doesn't need to be regulated like a bank. While it's physically based in California, it services customers throughout the United States.

How Activehours Works

Anyone can sign up for Activehours. A customer can use the service immediately if they are:

- Using an iPhone or Android.

- Paid hourly.

- Paid by direct deposit into their bank account.

- Using computer or online timesheets at work.

- A US resident.

Activehours uses the customer's bank information so it can deposit money directly to their account. This information also allows Activehours to confirm their employment information, including their pay cycle and hourly rate. The customer's bank information is secured with 256-bit encryption.

After the customer opens an account, their timesheets are usually verified and available in the account within a few hours. Depending on the time of day and workload it could take longer. Activehours is not able to verify paper timesheets, where the worker manually writes in their hours.

Activehours determines the customer's "take home" hourly rate, which is after taxes and deductions.

Once the account is set up, the customer signs in and sees a screen display.

The screen shows the customer a conventional monthly calendar. On the upper left is a field that says, "Available: XXX hours = $XXX." In the language of loans, this is the customer's credit limit, or how much the customer can access. But because it's not a loan, Activehours uses the term "activate." Below this it says, "Choose the number of hours you wish to activate. XXX hours = $XXX." The calendar graphic shows the customer the number of hours they have already worked during the week, such as eight hours on Friday. The hours that have been "activated" (used as collateral for a pay advance) are shown in orange.

Their Activehours timesheet will only display hours that have not yet been paid out. If the customer submits hours from a previous pay period (or even the hours that the customer plans to work in the future), they will not appear.

On payday, after the customer pay is electronically transferred into their bank account from their employer, Activehours removes the amount they owe.

The customer can cash in as many available hours as they want up to certain limits. A customer's limits can increase over time as they use Activehours.

The service strives to be prompt. According to the Activehours website, if the customer cashes in hours before 4:00pm PT (7:00pm ET), the money will always reach their bank the next business morning. Transactions requested on Friday after 4:00pm PT (7:00pm ET) are sent Monday, so the money will reach their bank Tuesday morning.

Activehours offers various tools and functions through the sites (the "services") that can assess the value of virtual assets such as accrued pay, benefits, and rewards programs (the "virtual assets") and allow the customer to:

a. View the value of their virtual assets, or

b. Use the value for monetary transactions, by assigning to Activehours the complete right, title, and interest in those virtual assets ("activating").

When the customer's virtual assets have been activated, for valuable consideration, the customer sells and transfers to Activehours, all right, title, and interest in and to those virtual assets. The customer warrants that the virtual assets are just and due and that they have not received payment for the virtual assets or any part of the virtual assets. The customer further warrants that if they receive payment for the assigned virtual asset, including by their employer, they will transfer those payments, or permit those payments to be transferred to Activehours.

By activating virtual assets—that is, by accepting money from Activehours that is due to them from their employer—the customer authorizes Activehours to charge their bank account for all payments due to the company. The customer agrees to maintain a balance that is sufficient to fund all payments they initiate. Activehours reserves the right to charge the customer's bank account at any time after the paycheck associated with virtual assets the customer has activated and has been deposited into their account.

"The solution works without the employer needing to be a part of it," said Ram (he goes by his first name because many people find his family name difficult to pronounce). "We market directly to the consumer. If they want to get paid for hours they've already worked, all they have to do is download the app and set up their account. We get the customer the money, and we collect it as soon as the paycheck is deposited."

Prior to its release, the company had employees from over a hundred companies testing the service. Since the release, the response has been tremendous. When people first try the app, they may not believe that it really works the way the company says it works. Then they see the money actually appear in their bank account, and they're convinced. Not being tied down to the rigidity of a biweekly paycheck is something very new. Once they get over the familiarity curve, they quickly become used to the idea of managing their own payroll and accessing their own unpaid wages.

"As consumers acquire more power and get better technology," said Ram, "we're seeing a movement towards financial services that actually help the individual. Smartphones give consumers a lot of computing power in their hand, and they're going to choose apps that help them. Every hourly employee should have the Activehours app on their iPhone or Android phone. There's no reason not to. It can save them from exorbitant overdraft fees and from paying bills late. By tapping into their unpaid wages, anyone can save on overdraft fees."

The Activehours Revenue Strategy

How does the company make money? Activehours has an unconventional revenue strategy: the company does not charge any fees or interest. They believe that bank overdraft fees are unfair. They're supported by voluntary "tips" from their users and they ask that the customer tip them what they think is fair.

"We're supported by our consumers," said Ram. "We ask our consumers to pay us what they think is fair. So far, it's worked really well." One of the reasons is the cost structure of Activehours. The system is completely smartphone-based. Without physical branches or ATMs, its operating costs are very low.

The tip model, or "pay what you want" (PWYW) system, allows customers to pay what they want for a given service. Donations can usually be made anytime. Such business models were never very popular until 2007, when the British rock band Radiohead implemented PWYW for their album *In Rainbows*. Radiohead's experiment with PWYW worked, and the scheme exploded. Today there are many services that use the model, though most tend to be charity oriented.

"When you're doing a tip model you're having a really strong relationship with your customer," Ram added. "It sets a very different tone with your relationship with your customer."

Panera Bread has tried the PWYW model. Co-CEO Ron Shaich told National Public Radio that in most of the stores, the idea paid for itself.[81] And though the estimates are rough, the Panera Cares program claims sixty percent

---

81   http://www.npr.org/blogs/thesalt/2012/09/07/160685977/panera-sandwich-chain-
      explores-pay-what-you-want-concept

of their customers give the suggested amount, with another twenty percent contributing *more* than requested. Another business using the PWYW revenue model is Humble Bundle, a game company providing PC and Android.

A 2011 study published by the Proceedings of the National Academy of Sciences found that PWYW can work as a business model.[82] Through a series of experiments, researchers found consumers are willing to pay a fair price when asked to do so—even more so, in fact, than when prices are set by a business.

From Ram's experience, that's fairly accurate. He said some customers may not be able to give immediately, but they usually come back and contribute when they can. Donations, too, he said, scale with the size of the transaction: bigger advances, for example, nets bigger tips. The result, he said, is a mutual feeling of accomplishment.

"We found this by accident, but we really, really like it," he said. "It feels like we're all on the same side. We're a for-profit company, but we're not for obscene profits. Take bank overdraft fees, for example. The typical overdraft fee is thirty-five dollars. The actual cost to the bank is three-tenths of one cent. So that's a ten-thousand-percent markup. The only reason customers pay it is because they have no choice. It's probably the most hated fee in the country. With Activehours, customers are voluntarily paying us for a service that they love."

What do the big banks think of this? "I don't know what the banks think," said Ram, "But I know that many bank employees love the service because they use it."

The company has not disclosed the amount that it receives in tips or what the average tip amount is. Ram has only said that the company's revenues are sufficient to make it sustainable as it grows.

According to Ram, what started out as a banking experiment is becoming a more practical business. Activehours's customers now include employees from Apple, Bank of America, Target, Staples, Home Depot, Lowe's, Best Buy, Nordstrom, Starbucks, Chase, Wal-Mart, Walgreens, Pizza Hut, Sprint, AT&T, Chipotle, Whole Foods, Urban Outfitters, and many more.

Activehours is just one more way that bold entrepreneurs are closing the gaps in our financial system and making life a little bit better for the many hard-working people who live at the bottom of the financial pyramid.

---

82   http://www.pnas.org/content/early/2012/04/17/1120893109.abstract

THE TAKEAWAY

- People need access to short-term loans to help with emergencies and difficult situations. Today their options are most likely very limited, expensive, and can lead to a downward cycle.

- The answer is to foster innovation in how we serve the short-term financial needs of the underserved. Activehours is doing this, and there are others with this same "out of the box" approach.

- Regulators and concerned groups should figure out how best to encourage more of this. In trying to control the predatory payday lending industry, regulators often hamper this type of innovation.

CHAPTER 15:

G-Xchange and Government Payments in the Philippines

Mobile money is being established in countries across the globe, and we have already seen consumer and business applications leveraging it. If we think of mobile money systems as platforms, then the same infrastructure can also be used by governments to modernize how payments are disbursed and revenues collected.

This is significant because it creates an opportunity to change how government transactions are made. This opportunity is multi-dimensional, including government-to-person payments (G2P, such as government salaries and social services payments), person-to-government payments (P2G, taxes, fees, utilities payments), as well as similar payments made from government to business (G2B) and business to government (B2G).

When we look at payments between individuals and the government, they are normally characterized by a very large number of people making transactions of relatively small value. This is a perfect fit for mobile money. In addition, increased government use of mobile money adds to the overall success of the mobile money ecosystem by creating key use cases and lowering the cost of funds transfer.

Within the past century, governments in developed nations have moved from taking and sending payments by paper check to the increased use of electronic funds transfer and debit cards. For example, beginning on March 1, 2013, to cut costs the US government stopped sending paper checks for Social

Security, disability, and other benefits. Instead, the Treasury Department now distributes funds electronically, either via direct deposit or on a prepaid "Direct Express" card. At the time of the cessation of paper checks, over ninety percent of recipients were already receiving their payments electronically, but five million checks were still being mailed each month, according to CNN Money. Paper checks were costing the government about $4.6 million per month. Over the following decade, the total cost to taxpayers would have added up to one billion dollars.

For government transactions, mobile money is the next frontier, especially in countries with low percentages of bank account holders and the lack of reach of the physical infrastructure of ATMs, POS terminals, and bank branches. Mobile has a special role in helping governments evolve G2P payments to reduce the use of cash, checks, and other paper-based payment methods. The payments landscape is being transformed by mobile money, which doesn't rely on this traditional infrastructure.

Much of the infrastructure being built by mobile network operators (MNOs) and banks for mobile money applies to government payments such as disbursements, collections, business transactions, and intra-government payments.

The challenges are many but the benefits are great. Here's a good example of eliminating a traditional cash disbursement method and replacing it with a mobile powered method.

GLOBE GCASH IN THE PHILIPPINES

Much global attention for mobile money is focused on Kenya, no doubt because nowhere else in the world do we see the scale of usage and speed of adoption. But from the beginning of mobile money, the Philippines has been the pioneer.

Any discussion of banking in the Philippines must begin with a brief overview of geography. The Philippines is a nation of islands. The Philippines archipelago comprises 7,107 islands, of which about 2,000 are inhabited. The islands are clustered into the three major island groups of Luzon, Visayas, and Mindanao. Among all the nations, at approximately 300,000 square kilometers (115,831 sq mi) in area the Philippines ranks at number sixty-four. With a population of approximately 99 million people, the Philippines is the seventh most populated country in Asia and the twelfth most populated country in the world.

To reach some remote island villages takes several days by boat, and some settlements are not even visible on the map.

It is a geography that is daunting for traditional branch-based banking, but which is ideal for mobile banking.

As early as 2001, telecoms were rolling out innovative functionality to promote mobile online commerce. So it is not surprising that one of the best examples of government application using mobile money can be found there.

In the Philippines, there are two leading mobile network operators: Smart Communications and Globe Telecom. Both offer mobile money solutions that include complex behind-the-scenes cooperation between banks and mobile network operators.

Paolo Baltao is the President of G-Xchange, Inc. (GXI), a wholly-owned subsidiary of Globe Telecom. GXI pioneered the revolutionary model in cardless and cashless mobile commerce service called GCASH, which was launched in the Philippines in October 2004. At the time, Globe Telecom surveys suggested that only twenty percent of Filipinos were either banked or bankable; the other eighty percent were unbanked.

Today, of the total Globe's telecom customer base of forty-five million subscribers, GCASH has over one million users. "The Philippine regulators were very progressive in helping us to craft regulations that would spur the growth of mobile money," said Baltao. "The government created a category called e-money, or electronic money issuer. That's how GXI is categorized."

By 2010, GCASH claimed 18,000 outlets nationwide, making the company the widest remittance network in the Philippines. Its network of outlets is comprised of rural banks, pawnshops, other financial institutions, as well as neighborhood or community establishments such as airtime loading stations, cellular phone shops, mini grocery stores, and hardware stores. These outlets are located not only in city centers but also deep in the residential *barangays* (the smallest administrative division in the Philippines).

Today GXI is at the forefront of a new government disbursement application.

The company's first foray into doing disbursements for the government was the World Food Programme's Food for Assets project (also known as Food for Work), which pays workers with food in exchange for work. Community members are given food in exchange for work on vital new infrastructure or for time spent learning new skills that will increase the food security of households or communities.

This gave them some experience before they tackled their government disbursement challenge.

Since the late 1990s, Conditional Cash Transfer (CCT) programs have spread rapidly. Funded in part by World Bank loans to national governments, "first generation" CCT programs originated in Brazil and Mexico; CCT programs now be found across a wide range of countries and contexts.

CCT programs have dual objectives. One is social assistance, which aims to provide cash assistance to the poor to alleviate their immediate needs (short-term poverty alleviation); the second is social development, which intends to break the intergenerational poverty cycle through investments in human capital.

The payments are conditional upon the recipient meeting a set of objectives, such as keeping children in school, attending regular health check-ups, and vaccinating their children.

The national government of the Philippines wanted to improve its CCT program (known locally as Pantawid Pamilyang Pilipino Program, or 4Ps) that provides cash grants to extremely poor households to improve their health, nutrition and education, particularly of children from birth to age fourteen.

The target population is poor households in 140 of the poorest municipalities and ten cities. Beneficiaries are families with children less than five years old and/or pregnant women. Education grants go to poor households with children aged six to fourteen years old. Support is PhP 500 (US$11) per household per month, for a period of twelve months per year, regardless of the number of children. The education transfer is of PhP 300 (US$7) per month for a period of ten months per year, up to a maximum of three children.

The CCT grants are traditionally distributed through the branch counters of Land Bank of the Philippines, a state-owned bank, or through its cash card. This worked adequately for recipients in urban areas or developed municipalities, but was problematic for those in remote island areas. The majority of Filipinos are unbanked; therefore, crediting to their account posed a problem for the government. In the Philippines, credit card penetration is nine percent, and only fifteen percent of the population have ATM or debit cards.

Previously, the government made distributions to these unbanked accounts with cash that had to be physically transported to remote villages. The government had to transport cash over water, and even by renting helicopters, to reach isolated areas. It was difficult for the national government to deliver cash grants on time. And it would take a month or longer to know how much had actually been distributed.

In addition, while a typical recipient received an average of 2,800 pesos (about US$65), in many cases that same recipient would have to *spend* 900 pesos in travel costs to pick up their cash.

When Globe worked with the government to tackle the challenge of improving rural disbursements, it was too ambitious to expect that all the recipients could have bank accounts, or even a mobile phone. The Globe team had already invested in assets in the rural areas that could be leveraged. Since they had rolled out mobile money, they had field agents in the rural areas who were trained and ready to do "know-your-customer" (KYC) diligence, cash liquidity management, and cash out. And Globe could already electronically distribute value to all their agents in a secure, transparent way. All the agents needed in the field was their mobile phone, and it could be a regular phone—no data services or smart phone required.

Globe worked with the national government to design a system where when the disbursements happened, Globe's GCASH team and their agents were mobilized to get all the rural recipients their funds in three days or less.

"The network that we've built," said Baltao, "has been adapted to deliver money to beneficiaries living in far-flung areas of the country. By participating in this program, GXI is given the opportunity to demonstrate the possibility of merging technology, business, and social responsibility in a program that not only assists the government but also extends services to the poorest of the poor."

Here's how it worked:

The government would notify ahead of time how much cash would be needed and where. The agents would travel to the local municipalities. While Globe already had cash liquidity methods worked out to ensure enough cash was on hand, this new application would test that system since so many payments were done in such a short period.

Since these payments went to the poorest of the poor in rural areas, it was unrealistic to require them to adopt mobile money to receive these payments. So most recipients used the Globe GCASH agent as a branchless banker who would distribute physical cash to them in their local municipality. The agent would be in a safe municipal building. The recipient would come, and social workers were also there to ensure they could receive their money by giving the recipient their one-time-use verification code. And all the money was distributed quickly.

Initially, it was tested in three rural areas first with 10,000 recipients. By the end of 2010 it was rolled out broadly. Within four months, 200,000 recipients received money this way. Now it is reaching 700,000. Talks are underway regarding using this method to supplement the urban system, which is primarily done via state bank branches. Once that is done, the potential is for the majority of the 1.8 million recipients to use this method.

Benefits include better tracking, on-time and faster disbursements, lower government cost, the elimination of political strong-arming of recipients by local governments, and lower travel costs for the recipients.

While challenges were there, using an existing working mobile money agent application and network gave them a head start. They added government specific reports, which were not a significant execution challenge but were very important to the government.

The know-your-customer process includes checking government-issued IDs and logging verification codes, and tracking in real time. And the people don't have to make big changes to use the system. They don't have to have a mobile phone, adopt a bank account, or use an ATM. Those things are available and will continue to be an option, but it is not a hurdle. Travel cost is now 100 pesos or less. All recipients have had ID cards already and they were able to continue to use them with this new approach.

Globe GCASH earns a fee, but it is significantly less than old government costs. People love it because it's faster, there's less travel, and no political pressure.

In addition to using the platform for disbursements, a user with the GCASH service on their phone is able to pay some government payments such as business permits and real estate property taxes. This is important, because by using mobile money, you are able to get the "fixers" out of the way. You are eliminating those people who want to make a fast buck by "facilitating"—those who say to the person who needs to pay a fee to the government, "Just give *me* the money and I'll take care of it for you."

On December 26, 2013, the service was launched in Quezon City. "We are happy to give Quezon City taxpayers the opportunity to pay for their real property tax using their mobile phones," said Baltao.[83]

Quezon City taxpayers simply register with GCASH by dialing *143#, select GCASH, then register, and provide the necessary information.

Payment of QC real property tax can be made by dialing *143# using Globe/ TM SIM. Then select Quezon City on the list of cities. Choose real property tax, input the tax declaration number, confirm tax declaration number for assessment, and choose which balance.

"By using Globe GCASH," said Baltao, "taxpayers will surely save time and enjoy fast and secure transactions without the need to fall in line or to travel all the way to Quezon City Hall with their payments on hand. We would also like to extend our gratitude to the local government for supporting us in providing an innovative mobile money system to the residents of Quezon City."

For the millions of unbanked citizens, GCASH enables them to make payments directly to the government, with no middleman, and to safely receive payments in a timely manner.

THE TAKEAWAY

In a nutshell, the Globe—GCASH initiative encompasses two missions:

1. Globe Telecom's GCASH division is a licensed provider of e-money services. This allows the service to leverage the vast distribution of the mobile operator to reach ninety-nine million people on the Philippines archipelago, which is comprised of 7,107 islands. Branch banking could never achieve this type of reach in a cost-effective manner.

2. Globe and GCASH have joined forces with national and local government agencies to help people receive government payments or pay taxes. In the former case, the adoption of GCASH as a service is not required; instead GCASH uses Globe's agent network and GCASH technology as a platform for the disbursements.

---

83   http://www. globe. com. ph/press-room/globe-gcash-powers-easy-payment#nav

All of this makes payments faster and more efficient. It saves governments money and individuals time. It removes corruption in the system, by both government employees and private "facilitators." These types of solutions will scale to most nations in the world in the next few years. Globe and GCash should be acknowledged for their groundbreaking work in such a challenging environment.

CHAPTER 16:

Traditional Companies Move Into Financial Inclusion

MasterCard, Visa, and American Express are global brands we associate with traditional financial services including credit cards and charge cards issued by big banks. But increasingly, these companies are looking at how their products and marketing can apply to the two and a half billion people who earn wages and support families who are cut off from the institutional services that the wealthy take for granted.

Two of the most visible giants—MasterCard and American Express—have evolved their corporate strategies from serving the world's elite to making an effort to reach the bottom of the pyramid. And while this may be purely coincidental, it's interesting to note that the CEOs of both companies are people of color.

MASTERCARD

Born into a Sikh family in Khadki outside Pune, Maharashtra, India, Ajaypal Singh Banga is the current president and chief executive officer of MasterCard. Charismatic, outgoing, visionary, when Ajay took over leadership he was well received by both employees and Wall Street. Through his work in Asia, and by seeing the rapid growth of mobile payments in emerging markets, he developed his big vision for MasterCard. He quickly made financial inclusion a board and top strategy issue for MasterCard.

He is a tireless advocate for business being a force for good for the world. As he said in his commencement address delivered at the NYU Stern School of Business in 2014, "Half the planet's adult population remains excluded from the financial mainstream. They don't have an identity. They don't have a basic way to participate in what we take for granted: pay a bill, save money for a rainy day, borrow on reasonable terms . . . There's never been a greater opportunity for business to be a force for good in the world. Yes, we provide jobs, pay taxes, and serve needs, but I am talking about more than that. Global companies like Unilever are working with the United Nations on issues like sustainability. The World Bank has set a goal of ending financial exclusion by 2020. The private sector role here is vital."[84]

This is reflected in how MasterCard operates its business and their innovation agenda. It's still in the early stages, but the commitment level is high, and the company is taking multiple initiatives.

At the moment, MC's revenue from financial inclusion is small, but its aspirations are big. MC has always been an innovator, and today their inclusion projects are expanding mobile and technology access for the traditionally underserved. Let's look at a few of those projects, and note that all involve partnerships with local innovators.

MasterCard-Airtel

In Kenya, Airtel is a new player. Manoj Kohli, chairman of Bharti Airtel International, left his super-successful role as head of Airtel India—that nation's leading provider of mobile prepaid and postpaid, broadband, and digital TV services—to make Airtel successful internationally, with a focus on Africa. No stranger to big challenges, Airtel started to operate in Kenya, a very tough market given the extreme dominance of Safaricom, which had over ninety percent of the market before they offered M-Pesa.

So Airtel Africa decided to not only compete head-to-head with Safaricom, but also offer functionality from mobile money that would allow it to be useful with merchants who already accepted MasterCard or Visa payments. They worked with MasterCard to add an instant "virtual card."

---

84   http://newsroom. mastercard. com/wp-content/uploads/2014/05/NYUStern-
      Commencement-Address-2014-As-Prepared-for-Delivery. pdf

Virtual cards are ideal for paying whenever a physical card is not required, like online purchases, phone orders, or mail-in payments. A virtual card works like a typical credit or debit card number, and has a CVC, card number, and expiration date. It is a reloadable prepaid card. There is no bill to pay at the end of the month and no late fees. The advantage of virtual cards is that they can only be charged up to the amount that the customer specifies, and cannot be reused once that limit is reached. This means the customer spends money in their mobile money account, but the merchant gets a MasterCard or Visa payment. It's a clever system that adds lots of new uses for the money in the wallet.

They also brought in Standard Chartered Bank Kenya Limited, who had many of the local merchant relationships. Established in 1911, Standard Chartered's first branch opened in Mombasa Treasury Square. Standard Chartered opened the first ATM in Kenya; today, Standard Chartered has ninety ATMs and thirty-three branches spread across the country.

At the 2011 press event for the virtual card, Manoj Kohli said, "Today's launch of the world's first virtual number on a mobile card marks a big milestone in mobile commerce. The 'Airtel 1time Shopping Card' is proof that Airtel will deliver innovative and relevant mobile solutions that will help consumers overcome the daily challenges in their lives. The solution will offer consumers a robust e-commerce solution that delivers security, accessibility, acceptance, ability and a global reach. Subsequent phases of the program will allow Airtel subscribers to make payment across the MasterCard network."[85]

It's still an uphill battle in Kenya, but this model of bridging the old world and the new in a seamless way has huge value. The first challenge of financial inclusion is to drive adoption and initial usage. The second wave of challenges involves adding more relevant use cases. This virtual card approach addresses the second wave and creates more utility.

Egypt: "Flous," EBC and Etisalat

Mastercard has a vast business across the globe, so the second project reflects a totally different approach than the effort in Kenya. In Egypt, the government decided they wanted to sponsor a common infrastructure that combined mobile and financial inclusion. Think of this project as intense heavy lifting

---

85   http://telecomtalk. info/airtel-launches-world-first-virtual-credit-card/56036/

to build a whole new technology and communication capability to make new things possible. It was a huge challenge, and they knew they needed help with the implementation of this ambitious advanced infrastructure.

The players include:

The National Bank of Egypt (NBE).

Egyptian Banks Company for Technological Advancement (EBC). Established in 1995, the mission of EBC is to provide and construct a comprehensive infrastructure for financial electronic payment solutions in Egypt. EBC provides the banking community in Egypt with a shared cash network commercially called "123," which links more than thirty Egyptian banks supporting more than 1,500 ATMs distributed all over Egypt. This network provides the banks' clients with direct access to their different accounts at any time and from anywhere through the ATMs carrying the 123 logo. The 123 network is a gateway to MasterCard, Diners Club, and American Express International networks. Moreover, it is linked to regional networks in the Persian Gulf states, NAPS in State of Qatar, Benefit in Kingdom of Bahrain and CSC in Lebanon.

Etisalat is a leading international telecom company operating in fifteen countries around the world. Egypt operations were launched in May 2007, with Etisalat's entry in the Egyptian market ushering in a new era for the telecom industry there. Today, Etisalat Misr's robust, high-quality 2G and 3G network covers and serves ninety-nine percent of the inhabited areas in Egypt. Etisalat Misr is also the first and only operator in Egypt with an exclusive international gateway, and its customers enjoy competitive international rates to all destinations around the globe.

Flous (the word means "money" in Arabic) is a new system spearheaded by the National Bank of Egypt and Egyptian Bank Company (EBC). It interconnects all banks with mobile money implementations that are being provided to users, so the relationship between the provider of mobile money and the banks is guaranteed.

This project involved working with the National Bank of Egypt's efforts to create an infrastructure for mobile payments that provides common services and interoperability. In June 2013, MasterCard and Etisalat teamed up to offer the first commercial implementation of Flous. As the third-largest MNO in Egypt, Etisalat brought to their Egypt's subscriber base payment services via mobile phones.

The intent here is for this to be the first Flous implementation, but that all participants will support interoperability, which is sometimes hard to achieve as we have seen in so many places around the world. The program represents the world's first interoperable Arabic mobile money program, and is the first implementation of the Mobile Payment Solution that MasterCard and Egyptian Banks Company (EBC) introduced to over ninety million mobile users in the Egyptian market.

South Africa and Net1

In South Africa, MasterCard worked closely with Net1 Group to create secure and highly-functional electronic disbursements for government social payments to over nine million South Africans.

The Net1 Group, MasterCard's partner, is headquartered in Johannesburg, South Africa, with subsidiaries in Austria, India, Russia, the USA, and affiliates all around the world. Net1 has a track record of twenty successful years in the payments industry resulting in an in-depth knowledge of developing, integrating, and upgrading financial transaction systems. A subsidiary, Net1 Mobile Solutions, offers an array of products and services that cater for the needs of the global market across numerous industries such as banking, mobile, prepaid vending, security, chip, SIM, VAS, and more.

They work on bridging the traditional high-tech card world with a low-cost solution that could work with unbanked people. Between March and July 2012, more than 2.5 million South African Social Security Agency (SASSA) Debit MasterCards have been issued to social grant recipients across South Africa. Net1 and Mastercard decided to add a new biometric payment card aimed to provide greater security and convenience, and which forms part of the social grants disbursements.

American Express

The third African-American to be named CEO of a Fortune 500 company, Kenneth Irvine Chenault is the CEO and chairman of American Express.

Amex talks publicly about their big decision to move from an exclusive brand to an inclusive brand. They're a great marketing company, so they probably understood what that meant and how the branding challenge was significant.

But they already had significant assets to bring to bear. Due to their traveler's checks business, Amex had already become a very big player in prepaid cards, a natural replacement for the old-style paper traveler's check. The new form had great advantages including reuse, reach to merchants, and ATM networks.

The prepaid card market is one of the fastest growing non-cash payments markets, with most of the growth and adoption of coming from the US "open loop" cards, which can be thought of as a prepaid-card-based money account. The value on the card is like value in your bank account; it can be transferred, loaded, unloaded, used for any purpose. American Express is one of the largest providers of prepaid cards to consumers.

According to Cap Gemini, prepaid open-loop volumes have grown by more than twenty percent during the past four years.[86] They're growing faster than the growth of regular debit cards. These payment methods are popular with underbanked customers because the risk of excessive bank fees is reduced and they also provide added spending control because "you can't spend what you don't have."

Already successful in prepaid consumer cards, Amex partnered with Wal-Mart to create a co-branded prepaid mobile solution designed to be a superset of a prepaid card. The Bluebird from American Express is a prepaid checking account/debit card. The customer can fund their Bluebird account with direct deposit, cash deposit refills at Wal-Mart, and also by buying Vanilla Reloads cards that some merchants including CVS, 7-11 and Walgreens allow you to purchase with points-earning credit cards.

Bluebird's motto is, "Loaded with features. Not fees." That includes no charges for opening an account online, overdraft, inactivity, card replacement, foreign transactions, and no annual or monthly fees.

To sign up for the card, customers visit the Bluebird site, click the button to "Register Now," and fill out a simple registration form. Customers can also buy a temporary Bluebird card starter kit at Wal-Mart for five dollars that they can fund with up to $500 using a debit card, and then register the card on Bluebird. com.

Since so many people use prepaid cards as lightweight bank accounts, this offering focused on making it all the things the consumers really wanted for this "lightweight" approach. Bluebird lowered the cost associated with prepaid

---

86   http://www.capgemini.com/resource-file-access/resource/pdf/wpr_2013.pdf

cards and increased the functionality, so that what rich people do with internet banking, Bluebird customers could do with these daily tasks from their mobile phone.

Now Amex is expanding this strategy. They are rumored to be moving Bluebird-like offerings to emerging markets and partnering with retailers in these markets for distribution.

But there is something else going on here that is more subtle but also more powerful. They are working hard to build awareness of the need to better serve the financially excluded. They understand that it's not easy to live outside the traditional financial system, and it's not cheap, either. For seventy million Americans, this has become a way of life that is dragging them deeper and deeper into debt and financial servitude. American Express's message is that we live in an era where technology can be harnessed to eliminate the barriers to financial inclusion, and it has never been more important to bring these barriers down.

SPENT: LOOKING FOR CHANGE

Not long ago, Amex asked Carol Realini, co-author of this book, to include her thoughts on financial inclusion in America for the film *Spent: Looking for Change*. Directed by Derek Doneen and narrated by Tyler Perry, with Academy Award-winning filmmaker Davis Guggenheim serving as the executive producer, this powerful documentary follows four American families as they struggle to make ends meet. The film highlights the financial problems many face on a daily basis, from paying bills to managing practically usurious interest charges. Their stories epitomize the struggles faced by millions of Americans.

From start to finish, the film highlights the financial problems and difficulties being faced by far too many American households. The film also presents a number of viable solutions that, if implemented, would go a long way towards stabilizing the economic foundation of our country. In turn, these solutions would create a future in which everyone has access to affordable financial services and the opportunities that such access provides.

You can view the full documentary for free on The Young Turks' YouTube channel, American Express's YouTube channel, and at SpentMovie.com. The producers invite you to share your thoughts on social media using #Spent or #LookingForChange.

One viewer of the film found it both informative and confusing. Amex is not mentioned in the movie as part of the solution, but is only mentioned in the credits as the funder of the money. This viewer asked why Amex, known as the charge card for the elite, had funded this movie. This comment says a lot about the marketing challenge Amex will have as they become more relevant to the underserved globally. But they are a great marketing company, so we think they are up for the challenge.

Besides that challenge, they also will have an innovation challenge. This is equally as tough. They will need to partner with innovators. We will have to wait and see how good they are at doing this.

It's hard for these companies; they have lots of assets but the changes are significant in product, distribution, and pricing. They partner with the innovators and sometimes acquire them. The potential is great, but it remains to be seen what their role will be. The process means spending a lot of time on businesses that represent a tiny part of their vast global operations, and it can be disruptive to their current businesses and large revenue. It will take true leadership and staying power.

MasterCard and Amex are the thought leaders, but many other large traditional players are stretching to be relevant. Other giants working on financial inclusion include:

Western Union's Money in Minutes Service allows customers to send money to over 200 countries worldwide. The customer calls a toll-free number, pays with a credit or debit card issued by a bank in the United States, and receives a tracking number.

Visa is constructively engaging the government of Rwanda to increase financial inclusion through electronic payments. The partnership has electronified Rwanda's economy and laid the foundations for financial inclusion. Its approach promises to reach millions of Rwandans with a full range of financial services over the coming years, in part through Visa's new mobile money service, mVISA.

Banamex, a Mexican subsidiary of Citi, is partnering with Telcel for mobile banking. Telcel is the leading provider of wireless communications services in Mexico.

Let's see how successful they will be. It will require partnering effectively with innovators, and in some cases acquiring innovators. But it will be extremely important as the payments market in electronic money will be very high growth, and mobile is becoming the most important form factor for online commerce and electronic payments.

According to a study by WorldPay, the UK-based payment service provider, mobile payments for online purchases will increase six-fold from $18 billion worldwide in 2012 to an estimated $117 billion in 2017. The WorldPay report, *Your Global Guide to Alternative Payments (Second Edition)*, estimates that mobile payments will make up three percent of the global e-commerce market in 2017, up from one percent in 2012.

The report notes that a large number of mobile wallet solutions were introduced in 2012. "Due to the infancy of many of these solutions, they predominantly only operate in their own local country or territory, with only a very small number demonstrating a truly global capability," the report reads. "DCB has become an important payment mechanism with the rise of smartphones and app stores, and aligns well with the purchase of digital goods and in-app payments. The process is quick and simple, and enables the shopper to remain relatively anonymous, only needing to provide their phone number to complete payment."[87]

THE TAKEAWAY

- Big players have to pay attention to this opportunity. The question is, what role should they play?

- Being relevant will require partnerships with innovators. Success may be tied to their effectiveness and forming and scaling these partnerships, including when they acquire them.

- Being OK with disruption will be key—a company can't be timid about this.

---

87   https://www. worldpay. com/global/forms/your-global-guide-alternative-payments-2nd-edition

- It's more than just about technology. Distribution, pricing, and branding will also be challenges.

CHAPTER 17:

Juntos Finanzas Connects
With the Newly Banked

Two and a half billion people do not have a traditional bank account, and many have never set foot in a bank branch. That means they don't have a relationship with a bank and do not understand how to use the services of a bank.

When they take the plunge and sign up for a service from a bank or other financial service provider, there's likely to be an information gap. The newly banked customer may not understand how to use the service or how to benefit from it.

The result? Talk to any company providing financial services to the under-served market and they will raise the issues of dormant accounts and accounts that use only a fraction of what the service has to offer.

When an unbanked person joins the ranks of the newly banked, the battle has just begun. For the newly banked person to become an active bank customer, they need to be empowered. They need to feel connected to their financial services provider. They need to believe that having an affordable bank account means a better future, and that this is within their grasp.

You would expect that a solution to this problem might come from Africa or India, since that is where the problem is massive in scale. But the most interesting innovator we found in this area has come from the design school at Stanford University.

During a class project in the d. school (as they call it), a group of students became aware of the financial struggles of low-income people working at

Stanford, so they reached out to a group of janitors. When Ben Knelman and his Stanford design teammates interviewed a woman named Karina, they asked her what she did with any money she had left over at the end of a week.

In response, she laughed incredulously. "That's impossible," she said. "I never have money left over."

A Mexican immigrant in her mid-twenties, Karina had come to the US about six years earlier. Working as a night-shift janitor, she earned $21,000 a year—much more than what she could make in her native Mexico. Most of her paycheck went to her basic living expenses, and of course she had to send some of the money home to her family in Mexico.

She had dreams, but financially couldn't make progress achieving them.

Working with Karina and other low-income people on campus, Ben finished the class project—a digital tool to help underserved people with their finances. They gave the tool to the people whom they had interviewed, got some positive initial feedback, and got a good grade on the project. At the completion of the class, they all went their own ways.

But Ben was haunted by what he learned in the project. It stayed with him and it felt unfinished.

A year later, he reached out to the immigrants who had been the focus of the project. To his surprise, Karina was excited to tell him that she had been using the tool and had saved $2,000 over the last twelve months. He saw a glow in her face he hadn't seen a year earlier. She was now on a path to pursue her aspirations, and it was a fundamental shift for her.

As Ben wrote on the Juntos Finanzas blog, "Seeing her face and what that meant to her, the changed sense of self that she felt, I knew without words that I had to work on it more—that there was something here that was deeply important and meaningful. That was the moment when the idea of Juntos was launched."

Financial inclusion was once considered to be simply a problem of access. Innovations in banking (including branchless banking) and the digitization of financial services (mobile money, mobile banking via USSD channels) mean that we're reaching people who had been previously excluded. Going deeper into rural areas and deeper into poverty is now possible. As we have seen from previous chapter examples, solutions are often provided by combining the reach of a telco, post office, or retailer with the capabilities of bank, insurer, or payment processor.

But even after that bit of heavy lifting is done, the customers don't always engage well with the service.

The data is striking: Between sixty and ninety percent of accounts opened by the newly banked fall dormant almost immediately, without a single dollar being deposited in the accounts or a transaction being done.[88]

A study by the GSMA showed that outbound call centers may improve activity rates in mobile money, but that isn't as scalable as what is really needed. What is needed is a warm relationship that is both affordable and is delivered through low-touch SMS or mobile application.

A broader problem that impacts not just financial inclusion is that digital financial services place customers at arm's length from the financial institutions that serve them. Someone may open an account and use it without ever interacting directly with a human being from that institution. New ways to connect with customers need to be developed in order to scale digital financial services while keeping costs low. Juntos is on the forefront of doing this, and the data from their implementations is confirming their value.

Inspired by Karina and propelled by principles of design thinking, Ben, and two colleagues formed Juntos Finanzas. They are:

Ben Knelman, who attended d. school at Stanford while earning his MS in engineering there. He has been listed in the World Economic Forum's "Global Shaper Under 30" list.

Dante Cassanego, who has a great track record as a successful engineer at Intuit. He's a recipient of the Scott Cook innovation award at Intuit and has earned a Stanford BS in computer science and an MBA from MIT.

Katie Nienow, who has a degree in physics and economics from University of Virginia and experience working in DR Congo on microfinance (translation—she's very smart, courageous, and microfinance-savvy).

Juntos is now a typical hot Silicon Valley company. Located in Mountain View across from the train station, they have a modest space with a great location. They took their design roots to heart, and the team has plenty of design

---

88   The GSMA, which tracks all telco-led mobile money projects, reports this problem through a website that gives data about the activity rates: http://www. mobilemoneyconsulting. com/2012/02/22/mobile-money/activity_rates.

talent mixed with high-tech wizards. Their relatively small team is a mix of Latin American, African, and US-born men and women. They have received lots of attention, winning contests like G20 Summit Mexico City, the Innovation Award for Financial Inclusion, first place in the Stanford Entrepreneurship challenge, Sibos Innotribe, and CFSI Best new product for the underserved. They recently got a Series A funding round from Aligned Partners VC, led by Susan Mason, who has deep experience and a successful track record in financial services investments.

THE SEEMINGLY SIMPLE SMS SOLUTION

Their challenge has been how to reach newly banked people who had never entered a bank branch and don't have internet access. They developed a service in the cloud that sends customized messages (individually customized and sensitive to the local culture) via text messages to new customers of mobile banking (bank led) or mobile money (telecom led). One hundred and sixty characters at a time is small real estate, but has proven sufficient to make the difference between use and no-use as well as change the amount of savings dramatically for frequent users of Juntos's service.

As Ben explained it in an interview with the newsletter of the Latin American Private Equity & Venture Capital Association (LAVCA):

"Juntos Finanzas supplies a suite of three SMS based personal finance tools that drive account activity and build savings for the underbanked. Juntos partners with Latin American banks and other financial institutions to help cash-based households track their spending and save towards goals. Our most popular product, a B2B platform, is scalable with dynamic intelligence that can support millions of individualized, automated conversations simultaneously in multiple languages, anywhere in the world. Our technology platform is a quickly deployable turnkey solution: it runs parallel to a bank's IT system, removing any need for lengthy integration cycles. As bank customers begin using our tools, they start to form and deepen regular savings habits as they work toward a pre-set, concrete goal. Harnessing the power of behavioral research, our SMS program motivates the creation of new savings patterns, making it easier for users to save."

Juntos' customers are financial services providers, usually banks or telcos (although they're also in discussions with a microinsurance provider). The Juntos platform is available to their clients as a tool to drive customer engagement and increase savings balances. As their customers use the Juntos "savings coach," they build new financial behaviors as they work towards personal goals.

Ben describes what they do. "Harnessing the power of behavioral research, our SMS program motivates the creation of new savings habits, making it easier for users to save. Users tell us not only that this is often the first saving success they have ever experienced, but that they feel believed in—that they no longer feel alone in their financial lives. As a result, not only do end users build new savings behaviors that they didn't have before, but the bank or telco also experiences success: an increase in activity rates, customer engagement, and deposits."

Their innovation is more than just the messaging infrastructure. From the beginnings in the d. school at Stanford, the founders decided they would connect with the specific aspirations of the people. This meant not assuming all of them had the same objectives, knowledge levels, or challenges. Instead of the bulk sending of standard outbound messages, they developed a two-way dialogue via SMS so they could begin to understand their customers' dreams, hopes, and objectives, and could be sensitive to culture as well.

To attain this level of service, their technology had to be a robust backend that could hold "big data" and mass customize the messages. Most financial service providers know your home address and ID number; Juntos wanted to know your dream was to send your son to Harvard. This required a complex back-end technology and algorithms to make customer communications automated, scalable, and low cost.

Their innovation in service was more than just about technology. They also established a radical user-centric and data-focused design process. At Juntos they believe they don't have the answers about what will make an incredible product experience for their users—they believe they should seek that information from their users.

They follow the human-centered design process taught at the Stanford d. school that cycles through empathetic qualitative user research and rigorous quantitative analysis of response rates, engagement statistics, and impact on offline behavior.

The Juntos product is iterated weekly. Some weeks they launch dozens of tests. The response rates and actual responses are analyzed immediately and product content and design is changed to optimize results on weekly iteration cycles. This agile iteration is made possible because of a radically flexible software architecture that enables iteration without code changes.

By increasing account usage and savings rates dramatically with simple 160-character messages, Juntos is a leader in breaking down the barriers between banks and the formerly unbanked. In their implementation in Colombia, the bank reported incredible results: fifty percent higher balances in the Juntos group compared to the control, and thirty-three percent higher active client rates compared to the control.

Juntos is focused on scaling to hundreds of millions of newly-banked consumers around the world who feel empowered, capable, and engaged with their financial services. They understand and use those services regularly. Juntos enables financial institutions to sustainably offer low-cost financial services to excluded populations and poor customers because Juntos enables them to connect meaningfully, personally, in a customized way, with every customer on a regular basis through a low-cost channel.

They live within the 160-character box today but are also very excited about breaking out the 160-character box. It serves them well, but one can only imagine how the relationship will even get "richer" as the end user gets a smart phone and Juntos uses mobile applications to communicate. They are agnostic about whether it is their mobile app or their service communicated via the bank or telco's mobile app. Either way, the customer can get the warm interaction they deserve.

THE TAKEAWAY

- At the BoP, being unbanked can be only part of the problem. Being newly banked presents its own set of challenges.

- The newly banked need to feel connected to their financial services provider.

- To become motivated to save, people need achievable goals.

- The connection needs to be simple and low-tech: customized SMS messages are a good solution. They can serve as "soft-sell" reminders to the customer.

CHAPTER 18:

Bitcoin's Alternative to National Currencies

For centuries, advances in technology have slowly and inexorably altered our world. Since the 1980s, changes have come at an increasingly rapid pace. Personal computers emerged from the world of centralized mainframe computing, transforming businesses and personal lives forever. A universal networking standard, TCP/IP, enabled all computers to talk to each other, creating the world of global email and network computing. With the internet browser came the world of websites and online commerce. Smartphones and their applications became ubiquitous, and now there are millions of applications and billions of downloads. Location-based services on mobile smartphones, social media sites, and real-time data access have impacted our daily lives.

Yet another technology is emerging that many believe has the potential to transform financial services. Created by an anonymous techie, bitcoin is game-changing on many fronts, including reach, utility, and very low cost for the bottom of the pyramid.

But before we talk about the potential, let's first talk about what bitcoin is, and lay the foundation for understanding what it could mean to financial inclusion.

Bitcoin has two dimensions—the currency and the technology. Because they are connected but also distinct, it's important to understand both. Both have potential but also far-reaching implications.

BITCOIN AS CURRENCY

As a unit of stored value, money hasn't always been a piece of paper with a president printed on it. Throughout history, the way humans have stored and traded value has been varied: livestock, jewels, gold, beaver pelts, textiles—you name it, if it could be traded, it was probably used as currency. But since the dawn of the industrial age, most currency has been paper, and has been both issued and controlled by individual national governments. (In a few places in the world, such as West Africa and the European Union, countries work together for a common currency.)

Given the multiplicity of national currencies, by necessity humans have developed ways of exchanging one currency for another, and ensuring that the values exchanged are equivalent. If you live in the US, you will hold US dollars. If you need to buy something in Italy, where merchants want to be paid in euros, you need to exchange dollars for euros. That exchange should be done by a licensed broker or a bank, and there will be a service fee. Individuals pay a retail fee, while businesses and banks that move lots of money pay a wholesale fee. Either way, it takes time and money to move value across currency borders.

For example, as of this writing, if you wanted to change US$100 into euros, you'd receive €74.5, out of which would be deducted a fee of roughly one to three percent—that is, one to three dollars.

Sovereign paper currency works fine, except when it doesn't. It can be challenging and expensive for businesses to take payments from people in other countries. Governments and economies can become unstable and the value of a nation's currency can change quickly, often to the detriment of the people with their money in that currency in a local bank. Government policies can impact inflation and deflation of value, interest rates, and money supply. Governments can even be accused of artificially propping up the value of their own currencies.

Many people throughout the world have long hoped for an improvement to this ancient and inefficient system.

Enter a new concept: the bitcoin, a universal digital currency that is not government controlled. It's global, universal, and can be traded like any other commodity on the open market.

How does it work? Here's a vastly oversimplified explanation of the concept behind the bitcoin.

As you know, every paper US dollar carries a unique serial number. I'll take a ten-dollar bill out of my wallet right now and write down the number: IL06530049A. Ordinarily, the consumer doesn't care about these serial numbers. You just hand over your cash to a merchant and get your change. The serial number on the bill is irrelevant.

Imagine this: Every time you pay with a paper dollar, the serial number is recorded in a vast ledger. This enormous global ledger is public. It's open for anyone to inspect.

Under such a system, the path of every dollar bill in existence—its owner-ship and all the transactions that it was used for—would be tracked and publicly recorded. The first record would be made the moment the new dollar bill rolled off the presses at the US Government Bureau of Engraving and Printing. It would happen each time that dollar bill changed hands in a transaction.

(Since the records are public, would it be easy for a hacker to figure out the identity of the persons involved in each transaction? Yes—but that's a story for another time.)

Now let's assume something else. Since we have recorded the serial numbers of each dollar bill in existence, and we make a record of each time each dollar is used to buy something, we don't need the physical piece of paper—the bill with George Washington's face on it. We can dispense with it. All we need is the serial number.

If you want to pay ten dollars for something, all you have to do is say to the merchant, "I transfer ownership of dollar bill #IL06530049A to you." The trans-action is recorded in the global ledger for everyone to see. The merchant now owns dollar bill #IL06530049A.

But wait, you say—what's to stop me from just making up serial numbers, or stealing serial numbers?

Problem solved: When you acquire the serial number of a legitimate dollar bill, you are also given a secret digital key that allows you to spend that dollar. Without that secret digital key, your dollar is worthless. Lose the key, and your dollar's value is zero.

Losing the private key is like putting your paper dollar in a box, burying it in the ground, and then forgetting where you buried it. The dollar still exists, but it's dormant and cannot be spent.

This is the basic idea behind bitcoin: a global digital currency that is trackable, whose transaction records are public, and whose security depends upon a private digital key held by you, the owner of the bitcoin. Your private digital key is proof of your ownership of that particular bitcoin.

So what's a bitcoin worth?

As of this writing, one bitcoin = US$588. Because few transactions are in the amount of whole bitcoins, you can spend fractions of a bitcoin. Bitcoins can be divided up to eight decimal places (0.0000 BTC) and potentially even smaller units if that is ever required in the future.

Like any commodity, the price can fluctuate widely. The highest exchange rate for one bitcoin was November 29, 2013, when it hit US$1,124.76. The most recent low was US$401 in April 2014.

Digital units of value existed before bitcoin was invented, and still exist today. Examples include prepaid top-up value, airline frequent-flyer miles, and Facebook credits. These digital assets had value within a limited number of uses. You couldn't buy groceries with your United frequent-flyer miles, or used prepaid top-up value to pay your utility bill. But as these digital assets became widely accepted, the uses for them expanded. For example, United allows you to use miles to book hotels. United customers in India get to use their miles just like people in the United States. And in some cases the providers of the virtual currency allowed transfers, like mobile-to-mobile transfer of prepaid top-up value. In 2006, the co-author of this book, Karl Mehta, built one of the first virtual currency platforms as founder & CEO of PlaySpan Inc. (acquired by Visa Inc. in 2011) for digital currencies for companies such as Disney, Time Warner, and Facebook.

These assets are centrally controlled by the corporation that created them, and are limited in acceptance. But they provide utility and in many cases low-friction usage.

Bitcoin is a new kind of digital asset. It is global, de-centralized "open" management, and designed for a global online commerce world. There are a limited number of bitcoins (as of August 2014, about 13 million), and as the bitcoin "miners"—the open system administrators—continue to process transactions, they are "paid" by creating more. It is estimated that by the year 2033, the arbitrary cap of 21 million bitcoins will have been reached. No more supply can be created then. The increased supply must come from splitting bitcoins, so those people who are fans of the currency are not worried about running out.

THE BITCOIN TECHNOLOGY

Marc Andreessen, co-author of Mosaic, the first widely-adopted web browser, is now a top venture capitalist. An early fan of bitcoin, he has already invested significant amounts in bitcoin companies. Early on he touted the benefits of bitcoin as a breakthrough. Here is how he explains it.

"First, bitcoin at its most fundamental level is a breakthrough in computer science—one that builds on twenty years of research into cryptographic currency and forty years of research in cryptography by thousands of researchers around the world.

"Bitcoin is the first practical solution to a longstanding problem in computer science called the Byzantine Generals' Problem. To quote from the original paper defining the BGP: 'A group of generals of the Byzantine army are camped with their troops around an enemy city. Communicating only by messenger, the generals must agree upon a common battle plan. However, one or more of them may be traitors who will try to confuse the others. The problem is to find an algorithm to ensure that the loyal generals will reach agreement. '

"More generally, the BGP poses the question of how to establish trust between otherwise unrelated parties over an untrusted network like the Internet.

"The practical consequence of solving this problem is that bitcoin gives us, for the first time, a way for one internet user to transfer a unique piece of digital property to another internet user, such that the transfer is guaranteed to be safe and secure, everyone knows that the transfer has taken place, and nobody can challenge the legitimacy of the transfer. The consequences of this breakthrough are hard to overstate.

"What kinds of digital property might be transferred in this way? Think about digital signatures, digital contracts, digital keys (to physical locks, or to online lockers), digital ownership of physical assets such as cars and houses, digital stocks and bonds . . . and digital money.

"All these are exchanged through a distributed network of trust that does not require or rely upon a central intermediary like a bank or broker, and all in a way where only the owner of an asset can send it, only the intended recipient can receive it, the asset can only exist in one place at a time, and everyone can validate transactions and ownership of all assets anytime they want."[89]

Bitcoin is much more than just a global online currency with decentralized control. It is also a protocol for transactions. It's a protocol in the same way the internet and web pages are protocols. Just like the internet, the inventor of the first web browser may have used it to build a web page, but the browsers then allowed anyone who wanted to follow along and build their own web pages.

There is a large global community of smart technology people around the world who are working on the bitcoin technology. While management of the protocol is decentralized, there is a group of eight people who are the final judges for what gets into the official protocol. But many people, companies, and groups contribute. Since this is an "open approach" to innovation, and many people are working in parallel, things are moving very quickly. The protocol is good, but not perfect. As issues surface, various groups look to tackle the issues and the community through adoption, and the eight judges decide what stays in the protocol.

Some things don't make it into the bitcoin protocol but do make it into commercial solutions that are built.

Which brings us to the second part of what is going on.

Companies, individuals, government groups, and non-profits are all working on bitcoin-based solutions to problems. For example, consider this question: "How do I give someone an account for bitcoin, let them buy and sell the currency, transfer bitcoins, encourage businesses to accept bitcoin, and do smarter transfers with bitcoin?" All of this is being worked on from many different angles by many different people and groups. It is about so much more than digital money—it is a protocol for transferring things over the internet, so the applications will be about much more than the currency and even more than just about financial services.

This superior architecture is better for global online solutions, and therefore better than the underlying architecture for many of the commerce and financial service systems that are in place today. These systems won't go away, but lots of innovation is likely to happen in this new superior arena. We saw that with the internet and mobile—Uber, AirBnB, Facebook, Netflix, M-Pesa, and Square

---

89   http://dealbook. nytimes. com/2014/01/21/why-bitcoin-matters/?_php=true&_ type=blogs&_php=true&_type=blogs&_php=true&_type=blogs&_r=2

all emerged in the new world of high-speed internet and mobile, and leveraged its advantages.

There is another advantage in the bitcoin world. It's brand new, and so there's no legacy solution that is being carried forward.

Banks and other financial actors struggle mightily to make changes to their existing systems. With legacy solutions, there's lots of code and processes that can be very difficult to change. Starting fresh has some huge advantages for innovators, which PayPal proved. While Visa, Mastercard, and Amex clearly had assets to apply to the question of internet payments, they struggled for a decade to re-task those assets appropriately. Meanwhile, PayPal rose from nowhere to become the leader in online payments.

By the nature of the protocol, bitcoin is more easily traced, more secure, and lower in cost than traditional transactions. Most credit card payments today cost between two and three percent of the value of the payment, and there is a growing amount of online payment fraud. Bitcoin's underlying cost is a fraction of the cost of card payments and fraud is virtually eliminated. This improves the margin for online commerce, lowers the cost of services to the bottom of the pyramid, and opens up the world of micro/nano transactions.

LOOKING TO THE FUTURE

Bitcoin is an open community, which means anyone globally can join in and contribute. Interfaces to the system are well documented and publicly available. Contributions can be made by anyone. There are multiple groups in every city in the world that meet to discuss bitcoin issues. There are teams in most financial service companies evaluating or building solutions on bitcoin. And then there are thousands of entrepreneurs building new companies delivering bitcoin products and services.

Investments are scaling quickly. The CB Insights blog recently reported, "Bitcoin startups raised over $76.8M in Q2 '14, almost equal to the $85M in 2013. With smart money VCs actively investing in the space, investor interest should continue to climb."[90]

---

90   https://www. cbinsights. com/blog/bitcoin-venture-capital-
      boom?utm_content=buffer49820&utm_medium=social&utm_
      source=facebook. com&utm_campaign=buffer.

With bitcoin, we believe the innovators will lead, while traditional banks and financial service providers will need to adjust—just like traditional retailers like Wal-Mart, Macy's and Nordstrom now sell online, but Amazon is the e-leader.

But what does this mean for the underserved? In many places in the world, cash is still the dominant way to pay merchants. Cash is stored at home, people struggle to buy online, and money transfer can be very inconvenient and expensive. Card and bank fees rates that are acceptable to the top of the pyramid consumers and businesses are totally unacceptable to the bottom. The middle struggles.

We believe bitcoin creates a lower-cost, lower-friction way to build solutions for these challenges.

In addition to the two- to three-percent fee for merchants to take cards, which in emerging markets is a showstopper to most small businesses, there are other issues. Many people worry about the stability of banks and currencies, and how they might suffer from the ramifications of unstable, local markets. Cross-border payments, such as the P2P and business payments from out-of-country customers (in common with the global outsourcing of individual work) are slow and expensive.

The latter problem is an increasing pain point as more and more of the emerging market workforce consists of small businesses doing piecework for global customers. On a recent visit to Nepal, a group of entrepreneurs explained this to me. A growing number of Nepalese are doing technical design work through oDesk or other websites for project work. Most of the projects are small, and it is not uncommon for a project fee to be eight or nine percent.

For local payments, there is another problem. Products and services cost less and are primarily in smaller packages in emerging markets. This means payments are often less than one dollar. This is where traditional payment systems pricing gets painful. There is a fixed cost to all traditional payments, so the pricing frequently has minimums—say fifteen cents. This is very painful if the payment is one dollar.

In addition, there are high fees and inconvenience of traditional cash-to-cash domestic and international money transfer. In some countries this is more painful than others—domestic money transfer in India is very inconvenient—with people having to travel and then stand in line at post offices to receive money. International remittances to Bangladesh are very expensive and take a long time to get to the eventual recipient because the in-country infrastructure is limited.

More and more of the world of business is moving online. Cash societies, where remote payments are not possible, will be at an increasing disadvantage. There are work-around methods, like cash on delivery or cash vouchers. But they have high costs and require a two- or three-step process for collection. This makes it harder to launch online businesses because consumers who primarily use cash for purchases aren't accustomed to paying electronically.

All of these are real-world challenges that bitcoin could and will tackle. Its architecture gives it some significant benefits:

- It's the same everywhere, and therefore especially well suited for global use.

- It's an online ecurrency.

- It's secure, a key benefit of cryptocurrency.

- It's traceable—a blockchain keeps all the information about a transfer forever.

- It's fast. In bitcoin there's no concept of overnight settlement because transactions happen in near real time.

The rapid increase in bitcoin startups and entrepreneurs is creating an investment in a whole new ecosystem. For example, companies are working on different aspects and momentum is great. Some are working on what the consumers need to buy, sell, and store bitcoin, others are working on exchanges for trading bitcoin, and still others are developing ways for merchants to accept bitcoin.

All of this innovation is distributed, and there is no central manager—like a Visa or Mastercard—dictating what happens when. It feels much more chaotic because of this. But the key benefit is the speed of innovation. Just like web pages and app stores speed up innovation on the web and mobile, bitcoin distribution, and open innovation is creating the same benefit for financial services.

Most of the bitcoin "gold rush" has been focused on the traditional bank market in rich countries like the United States. The first wave consisted of speculators and well-funded players from developed countries.

BITX: THE SUPERSTORE OF BITCOIN

Today, we're beginning to see emerging market actors like BitX, a subsidiary of Switchless, based in Singapore. BitX has implementations in a growing number of emerging markets including South Africa, Malaysia, Zimbabwe, and Kenya. The founders of BitX—an ex-investment banker and an ex-Google engineer—left their great jobs with a big passion to provide state-of-the-art financial services in countries that have very weak banking systems.

They are open to working with banks or other companies as "partners" to offer to their customers bitcoin services. But they are also operating an independent bitcoin service—a combination of a wallet, exchange, and also connections to merchants for acceptance. Focused on maximum utility for their users, they recently partnered with one of the largest traditional merchant services company so that their 20,000 merchants could start accepting bitcoin.

BitX operates bitcoin exchanges in several countries around the world. The BitX Exchange is a market platform where people can buy and sell bitcoins using local currency, securely and easily. People place orders to buy or sell bitcoins at particular prices into the system. Whenever a buy order matches a sell order, a trade occurs. BitX takes care of clearing the trades so that there is no risk of counterparty default.

Timothy Stranex, co-founder of BitX, threw some light on the potential of bitcoin.

"I think that the first useful applications of bitcoin in these markets will be related to how bitcoin facilitates international payments," he recently told me.

"First, local merchants can more easily accept payment from foreign customers. This allows them to access the global marketplace more easily. For example, the family of one of the people in our team owns a florist Windhoek, Namibia. They get quite a few orders from Germany, such as people sending flowers to their relatives in Windhoek. They're paying five percent for these international credit card payments. Bitcoin would be a lot cheaper.

"Second, B2B international payments. We've experienced that the banking infrastructure in some countries, such as Kenya, can be quite unreliable for international payments. Our launch in Kenya is currently delayed by two weeks because we're waiting for the bank to find a lost wire transfer that's meant to fund our initial float! I've also heard stories of businesses missing payments to overseas suppliers because of unreliable forex availability from the central banks.

"Third, capital controls. Many emerging market countries have capital controls, also known as exchange controls. Basically, any money moving into or out of the country has to be reported and approved by the central bank or treasury. This introduces a huge amount of bureaucracy, delays and costs. Every knowledgeable person I've met thinks they should be abolished, at least in South Africa. Bitcoin is potentially useful because it allows people to completely circumvent a government's capital controls. Of course, BitX cannot assist with this, because by definition it's illegal.

"Fourth, remittances. People working abroad often need to send money home. Bitcoin can be an efficient way to do this. However, it's not as easy as it sounds because a) the recipient wants to receive local currency, not bitcoin, so there needs to be enough liquidity available in the country to do the conversion, and b) if the recipient doesn't have a bank account (or M-Pesa wallet), then physical cash somehow needs to be delivered to the person. The BitX exchanges will hopefully solve the first issue. The second issue (cash distribution) is still quite difficult to solve."

It is the open nature of bitcoin that gives it power. "There are a lot of people trying to solve a lot of financial problems in emerging markets," says Marcus Swanepoel, co-founder and CEO of Switchless, the parent company of BitX, and which develops enterprise crypto-currency software for leading global banks, private wealth managers, and brokerage firms. "Having an open protocol with permissionless innovation is surely going to create many opportunities for people to help the poor in this space.

"Merchants in most emerging markets are not large sophisticated multinationals, so they pay higher fees, charge-backs will, in theory, hit them more, and they might not have the professional people and systems to deal with accepting on these networks.

"In these markets very few people can get credit or have credit records, so a credit-based system is not the best.

"Micropayments is also a strong theme here. In emerging markets, people transact in much smaller amounts, and these protocols can process these transactions more efficiently.

"Volatility still an issue, but it could stabilize over time. There could be further derivatives of bitcoin: hybrid currencies issued by governments, banks or telcos.

"Given the open nature of bitcoin, you might find people starting to use it at a grassroots level to circumvent government exchange controls. A lot of their trading is peer to peer, so actually it's potentially easier for them to trade in and out of bitcoin outside the normal banking system. This will be an interesting one to watch.

"Overall, while the jury is still out on bitcoin, whether it be in developed or developing markets, we believe the fundamental pros: lower transaction costs and innovation will probably be more useful in markets where there are very high fees, inefficient systems, and no existing electronic user behavior—that is, in the near future there are going to be a few billion people who have never even heard of the internet all of a sudden having access to it, so it will be interesting to see how they behave and which technology they choose.

"But even if bitcoin just solves the remittance or B2B transfer issue a little bit, it will make a massive impact."

THE TAKEAWAY

- Bitcoin has tremendous potential in emerging markets. Its architecture and open innovation model make it a) inherently better for solving tough financial inclusion challenges and b) characterized by speed of innovation.

- Although today most bitcoins are used by consumers at the top of the pyramid, we expect the future will add exciting offerings for the under-served. The potential is there, and now some of the investment in bitcoin is landing with companies like BitX.

- There is both a currency and a technology (protocol). There are lots of almost religious arguments about both. The early adopters have already jumped onto the bitcoin train. It remains to be seen whether the great promise of bitcoin will be manifested into greater financial inclusion at the bottom of the pyramid.

CHAPTER 19:

Credit Scoring for 2.5 Billion People

Before leaving this section of the book in which we have revealed successes around the world, we need to look at a few projects that are beginning to show tremendous progress. Technology is moving quickly, so even by the time you read this, these initiatives may be "moving the needle" in financial inclusion.

These projects tackle a challenge with which most Americans are intimately familiar: your credit score.

Anyone who's not at the very top of the financial pyramid knows the feeling. You go to buy a new car. After finding the car that you think you can afford, the salesperson hands you off to the finance manager. In his or her office, he "crunches the numbers." And then comes the fateful moment that you dread: when the finance manager smiles and says, "Okay, we'll just run a credit check and get this wrapped up." You sit while the credit bureau is contacted. After an eternity, the finance manager frowns. He looks up from his screen.

At the very worst, he says, "Do you know someone who would be willing to co-sign your loan?"

Or he might say, "Well, based on your credit score, the best we can offer is six percent interest." He then computes your monthly payment. It's more than you think you can pay.

Your problem is your credit score. On the standard scale of 300 to 850, your score may be in the "subprime" category (550 – 620), or even in the "poor" category (300 – 550). What this means is that commercial lenders—the people who issue credit cards, mortgages, personal loans, and car loans—may charge you a high interest rate or refuse to make a loan to you.

If you live in a cave in the mountains, pay cash for your vittles, and don't care about borrowing money, this means nothing to you. But in today's industrialized society—and increasingly this includes developing nations—consumer credit is a fact of life.

A consumer credit system allows consumers to borrow money or incur debt, and to defer repayment of that money over time. Having credit enables consumers to buy goods or assets without having to pay for them in cash at the time of purchase.

For most of modern human history, consumer credit was highly localized. Retailers offered credit directly to their known customers.

That began to change in 1950 when a group of New York businessmen introduced the Diners Club credit card. Diners Club was going to be a middleman. Instead of individual companies offering credit to their known customers, from whom they would then collect what was owed, Diners Club was going to offer credit to selected individuals on behalf of many companies. After billing the customers, Diners Club would pay the companies.

The idea was a hit, and the Diners Club credit card continued to grow more popular. In 1958, both American Express and the Bank Americard (later called VISA) arrived.

At the same time, the concept of a personal universal consumer credit rating emerged. Credit reporting bureaus had started as associations of retailers who shared their customers' credit information with each other. Initially, the credit bureaus shared information on customers who did not pay their bills and were identified as bad credit risks. Later, they expanded the data to include information on prospective customers.

As the economy grew after World War II, the retail sector expanded, and banks and finance companies took over from retailers as the primary source of consumer credit. Consumers became more mobile, and demand for a national credit reporting system increased.

The development of computers that could store and process large amounts of data enabled the credit bureaus to efficiently provide credit information to consumer lenders. Nationwide reporting of consumer credit information became possible.

Which brings us back to the all-important credit score, commonly referred to as your FICO score. Founded in 1956 as Fair, Isaac and Company by engineer Bill Fair and mathematician Earl Isaac, the pioneer credit score company sold its first customized credit scoring system two years after the company's creation. Sales of similar systems soon followed. In 1989, Fair Isaac and Equifax introduced the first general-purpose FICO score, which they called "Beacon." Prior to this, all models were custom designed just for the use of companies that wanted a scoring model. This generic version was the first to be used by vastly different types of companies.

By the 1980s, three credit bureaus had emerged as the dominant consumer credit reporting companies: Equifax, Experian, and TransUnion. All three adopted the now-ubiquitous credit score scale of 300 to 850.

Having a good credit record means that a person has an established history of paying back his or her debts on time. A person with good credit will be able to borrow money more easily in the future, and will be able to borrow money at better terms.

To determine whether to extend credit to an applicant, most creditors evaluate a potential borrower's credit report. The problem is that people who are newly banked or have never borrowed money do not have a credit history for lenders to evaluate. Such consumers experience tremendous difficulty setting up their first loans or credit cards.

The key concept to remember about credit scores is that they are based on *verifiable financial history*. It's all about your past success at borrowing and repaying money from an established institution. (For example, a cash loan from Aunt Fatima to buy a sewing machine is not included in your institutional credit history, even if you had paid back every penny.) As any user of credit knows from personal experience, it takes time to build a reputation with the banks and credit companies. Once established, you then can get access to credit.

With borrowing activity comes the credit score. The better the score, the more credit and the better interest rate.

If you're unbanked or even newly banked, and you want to borrow money from an established lender, you have a problem. And this is not just your problem; it's also a community problem because your increased financial activity leads to more community financial activity and the acceleration of wealth.

For the billions of people for whom establishment of their financial reputation will take decades using traditional methods, it's a "chicken or the egg" problem. Without good identity and data about good behavior, people can't get access to credit. Without credit, they cannot establish a financial reputation.

There are a number companies tackling this tough but critical issue. Let's look at three technology-savvy companies and their different approaches to the challenge: Cignifi, First Access, and InVenture Mobile. In some respects, they are similar. They are all focused on leveraging new technology and developing new business models. They realize the finance-based credit scoring system that's entrenched in developed countries is not easily scaled to the bottom of the pyramid.

Instead, they seek out data where it already exists. They each believe that if an unbanked person has a mobile phone, he or she already has an electronic history. It may be possible to use this existing information to build an understanding of that person and their worthiness to receive credit, and assess the risk so it can be priced accordingly.

All three startups are led by smart, impressive entrepreneurs. Two of the three are helmed by first-time women CEOs.

They are all launching their services in emerging markets—two in East Africa, and one in Asia, Latin America, and Africa.

CIGNIFI

With a bachelor's degree from Oxford University and a master's degree from the London School of Economics and Political Science, Cignifi's president and CEO Jonathan Hakim has an impressive academic background. After working as a journalist for the *Economist*, he moved into investment banking for sixteen years, based primarily in London. He then spent two years at the International Finance Corporation (IFC), which is the private sector investment arm of the World Bank. His career made another turn when he signed up as president and CEO of an early stage tech company.

But his role at Cignifi is by far his most ambitious task yet. He has set out to tap into the wealth of behavioral hypotheses that are derived out of mobile telecom data usage, and then use this information to establish initial credit scoring by financial service providers (banks or telcos) for a potential market of the 2.5 billion unbanked, "unscoreable" global consumers.

Based in Cambridge, Massachusetts, Cignifi serves lenders in two ways:

1. To overcome traditional acquisition and underwriting obstacles. In extending credit to new customers, the primary obstacle is qualifying risk. Without customer credit histories or credit scores as a reference, lenders need an alternative source of data and insight to underwrite and price products accurately. Cignifi enables lenders to avoid high-risk borrowers who default quickly, and prevent adverse selection from overpriced or untargeted offerings.

Cignifi scores enable financial providers to profile consumers with no credit histories. Cignifi models mobile phone behavior to understand lifestyle and associated financial needs and risks. As the Cignifi website says, "Cignifi scores are not like traditional credit scores that require twelve or more months of payment history to forecast credit behavior. The Cignifi approach requires no traditional payment data and can be calculated with as little as four weeks' calling history. This makes Cignifi scores ideal for pre-paid customers who comprise the majority of mobile customers in emerging markets, and are typically new entrants to the formal financial system."

2. Optimize marketing ROI. Even if they appear to be qualified, you don't want to waste resources trying to sign up customers who are resistant or have no desire for your product. When crafting customer acquisition programs, providers need to know the likelihood of prospects to respond, accept, and utilize debit or credit products.

Cignifi response optimizes return on marketing investments by enabling providers to increase conversion rates by culling mailing and marketing lists and reducing overhead, and improve activation rates through tiered product offerings to meet customers' unique needs.

Cignifi also serves mobile operators by providing the data and scoring infrastructure to help global mobile operators maximize the value of financial product offerings. Cignifi scores ensure that financial product campaigns are tailored to the diverse lifestyles, financial needs, and credit risks of a broad mobile phone customer base. The result is maximum uptake of financial product offers, stronger brand loyalty to the network, and minimum risk of alienating customers with misplaced offers.

Cignifi has attracted top tier investors like Omidyar Network (the investment group of eBay founder Pierre Omidyar and his wife Pamela) and Amex Ventures. They also recruited mobile money veteran Jojo Malolos, who was instrumental in establishing Smart Money as the leading mobile money operator in Philippines.

It's still early for Cignifi, but they have made good progress establishing the necessary telecom relationships to get access to the prepaid top-up and mobile phone usage data, and introduce new financial products to the unbanked. They have successfully executed pilot tests in Brazil, Mexico, and Africa to prove the hypotheses that mobile data usage serves as a valid proxy in establishing a consumer's creditworthiness and propensity to accept a marketing offer, and further developed new business models and use cases to extract information from the data to predict creditworthiness and risk assessment.

Cignifi is set to commercially launch key initiatives as they move to what they are calling credit score 2.0. The concept explores other non-traditional sources including social media data, government services data, and others, to predict risk and marketing response behavior towards use of financial services at the base of the pyramid.

FIRST ACCESS

Based in New York City and Dar Es Salaam, Tanzania, First Access dispenses with the need for a traditional credit history by combining financial and mobile data to reliably predict credit risk for borrowers in informal markets. The goal is to quickly produce consumer credit scores that both dramatically reduce costs and risk for lending institutions, and allow access to credit for unbanked persons who have no credit history.

When you meet First Access co-founder and CEO Nicole Stubbs, you cannot help but be impressed. She is upfront that she has set for herself an ambitious goal: to increase access to capital for the informal sector globally. She's a top performer at everything she does, whether it's academic, commercial, or volunteering.

Before co-founding First Access with Nicole, company director Duncan Goldie-Scot pioneered the use of mobile payments in microfinance institutions (MFIs) in East Africa by providing technical assistance and capacity building to

MFIs in Kenya and Tanzania. He co-founded and is now a director of Musoni BV, an MFI holding company in The Netherlands, and of Musoni Kenya Ltd. in Nairobi, Kenya. It is the first MFI that is one hundred percent cashless: all disbursements and repayments use mobile payment services such as M-Pesa.

Nicole and Duncan met after doing financial services fieldwork in nearly a dozen developing economies. They realized that across the developing world, international "know your customer" laws requiring phone number registration meant that over one billion people—many of them unbanked—had traceable financial records. These data could be a huge asset for people who had no formal documents and records.

While Nicole is not yet thirty years old, she already has global credibility as a PopTech Social Innovation Fellow, StartingBloc Social Innovation Fellow, and winner of William James Foundation Sustainable Business Competition and Pipeline Fund Competition. She has worked in Africa, Asia, Latin America, and Europe, and is working on learning her sixth language (Swahili). Her background has been a boon to the development of First Access. During her years working with loan officers and borrowers she was constantly reminded that while lenders need reliable information on risk, the irony is that even though poor people aren't necessarily higher credit risks, they pay much higher interest rates because they can't prove it.

Her big data strategy includes telecom data similar to Cignifi, but to develop a multi-dimensional view of people First Access also wants to use social media information. Given the broad use of feature phones in Africa (low-end mobile phones which are limited in capabilities in contrast to a modern smartphone), this may seem strange; but it makes perfect sense when you look at the predictions for smartphone growth in emerging markets. As people get more access, there will be more data to tell their stories. Providing these insights to credit providers will be a breakthrough in access to capital. Their data is targeted for use by retail commercial banks, microfinance institutions, insurance companies, agricultural suppliers, energy companies, and payment providers. All of these providers can increase profits with better insight.

That's the promise of First Access, and they are setting out to prove they can deliver on this promise.

With First Access's service, a loan officer can text an applicant's mobile number to the company, which in turn asks the applicant, also via text, whether they authorize the lender to tap their mobile transaction history and other demographic, geographic and financial information.

If the applicant gives the go-ahead, First Access marries the applicant's data and the lender's risk profile to generate a recommended loan amount, which First Access texts back to the lender.

The company charges lenders about $1.25 per transaction, a fee that covers the cost of the data, which First Access buys from carriers. "We can keep our prices low by serving a wide variety of financial institutions and generating a high volume of loan recommendations," said Jessica Carta, First Access's chief operating officer, in *American Banker*.[91]

- They customize an algorithm to each lender's portfolio, goals, and risk appetite.

- They can do scoring using the lender's data only (standard scores) or bringing in other sources of data (premium scores).

- A "score" is not an abstract risk level but rather a concrete recommended loan size incorporating the lender's preferences, so that the loan officers have conclusive information they can act on right away. For example, First Access will send an SMS message that reads, "Sarah Mandari is eligible for a personal loan of $800 over 14 months."

- They have also partnered with a credit bureau in Kenya to be able to incorporate outstanding debt from any institution into scores (which requires a credit bureau license). This increases accuracy and helps prevent over-indebtedness.

Privacy is a top concern. For big data businesses operating in emerging markets, understanding full disclosure and informed consent is more important than ever. First Access has conducted research in partnership with the World Bank's Consultative Group to Assist the Poor (CGAP) on data privacy and consumer protection in the context of low literacy, and has designed its service around these insights. First Access gets real-time permission in the local language from mobile subscribers before accessing mobile records, does not share

---

91   http://www. americanbanker. com/issues/178_246/first-access-cignifi-use-big-data-to-bring-economic-security-to-unbanked-1064537-1. html

information between financial institutions, and engages closely with communications and financial regulators.

The First Access team is moving quickly to prove out their value proposition. They are working feverishly in Tanzania and Kenya in East Africa. There they have partnered with telecom operators and banks to prove out this new big data model for the bottom of the pyramid. Once this is scaling there, her plans are to bring the same model to other emerging markets in Africa and beyond.

So far the results have been promising. Its accuracy has been carefully tested over nearly two years and in many cases rivals the accuracy of FICO (.85 Gini coefficient).

They have now analyzed over 400,000 loan applications in East Africa and have validated algorithms for business, agriculture, energy and housing improvements. By the end of 2014, their algorithms will span business, agriculture, energy assets, housing improvements, education, franchises and supply chain finance, all at the micro- and SME-level.

As of August 2014, First Access is working with twenty-three different institutions as clients or suppliers or both, ranging from lenders to the credit bureau to mobile network operators. Their partnership with Vodacom Tanzania allows them to retrieve data on any subscriber who applies for a loan at one of fourteen lending institutions in Tanzania.

INVENTURE

Based in Los Angeles, InVenture's goal is ambitious: to create a fair and transparent financial marketplace. InVenture wants to create a market where simple mobile tools and intelligent data can change perceptions and circumstances, and thereby open new channels where buyers and sellers can connect and create new models in which to transact.

Founder and CEO Shivani Siroya is another banker turned social entrepreneur. Her master's thesis at Columbia University was on HIV/AIDS and its effect on the Indian economy. She started out in investment banking, but later landed at the UN Population Fund, where she interviewed hundreds of micro-borrowers to see whether micro-credit had improved their quality of life. She was struck by the lack of private investment to help them grow and the lack of record-keeping tools to help them run their businesses.

So she changed lanes to found InVenture, a certified B corporation. With youthful energy, Shivani walks through walls to make things happen. Included in her accomplishments are 2013 TED Fellow, 2011 Echoing Green Fellow, and 2011 Unreasonable Institute Fellow. Especially impressive was her successful fundraising that attracted an investment from prestigious Google Ventures.

"In India, there are thirty-three million micro-borrowers, but most of them don't have access to that next step of expansion capital, so they're unable to grow their businesses, and most importantly they're unable to be a source for job creation in their communities," Shivani told *Global Atlanta* at the 2012 GeorgiaForward Forum, where she was a keynote speaker.

During a recent conversation, she explained that although the original thought was to vend the big social media data to financial actors, she was going to do loans directly for a while. This is for two reasons: to prove the analytic scoring model out, and to consider this as a longer term model for InVenture Mobile.

As she told *Forbes* magazine in 2013, "Through other work at UNICEF and learning about other organizations, I was able to see the power of phone calls and text messaging to solve social problems. So in July 2011, we began developing InSight, an accounting tool that tracks and analyzes the income and expenses of micro-business owners through SMS (short message services), enabling both borrowers and lenders to see how a business is doing. InVenture had its beta launch in December 2011.

"Here's how it works: On a daily basis, borrowers, who have undergone a training session, put their income and expenses into the system, via SMS or phone. After a month, that information is processed into credit scores that help investors assess how risky each borrower is. Lenders can have their existing and/or potential borrowers adopt the tool and then log into InVision to see borrower spending patterns and credit scores. That information enables lenders to confidently lend to and help grow the businesses of micro-borrowers."

Borrowers use the technology for free. Revenues come from providing individual credit scores to partner financial institutions and from licensing the technology to partners. The biggest challenge is getting users to share their data and get in the habit of daily accounting through their mobile phones. The company is overcoming these challenges by staying close to local NGOs and community leaders, and by making the product easier and more engaging.

THE TAKEAWAY

- Credit scoring is a foundational capability for getting access to credit. Consumers in industrialized countries take the system for granted, but in developing countries it is important to creating a scalable solution for enabling access to credit and needs to be part of the larger financial inclusion architecture.

- Traditional credit scoring will take decades to be available for the 2.5 billion people who today live outside of the traditional banking systems. That is just too long.

- Innovative thinking is required. These three pioneers are examples of what it will take to develop a scalable solution—new thinking and iterating in emerging markets.

PART THREE

CHAPTER 20:

Lessons from the Pioneers of Financial Inclusion

In this book, we've revealed both the extent of financial exclusion at the bottom of the pyramid and have seen the proliferation of imaginative solutions that entrepreneurs are introducing around the world. It's an exciting time we live in, full of the promise of increased economic opportunity for everyone. In nearly every corner of the globe, dedicated visionaries are combining new technologies with social responsibility to open doors that for centuries have been closed. Going forward, we hope—and expect—that the pace of change will not only continue but quicken.

The goal of this book is to not only describe and celebrate efforts to bring financial inclusion to the bottom of the pyramid—and to make the pyramid a little less steep!—but to serve as a resource for anyone who wants to contribute to the cause. In this chapter, we'll take an overview of the projects we've covered, as well as discuss some additional ones, and present the lessons learned by the pioneers of financial inclusion.

DRIVE INITIAL ADOPTION THROUGH VERY

COMPELLING INITIAL USE CASE

It is clear from all of the success stories that things get interesting when a critical mass of *users* and *usage* is reached. Before that happens, it feels like an experiment, with some anecdotal activity but nothing that effects real change.

Therefore, the challenge is how to create the critical mass.

One common mistake is to be too ambitious about what will drive adoption. Behind the scenes, the technology can be very complicated. But to the users, the interface needs to be incredibly simple, including a clear and compelling reason to adopt the service. For M-Pesa, it was a simple and inexpensive way to send money from Nairobi to rural Kenya. The implementation was complex and hard to execute, but the value proposition and usage were very simple and compelling. Same with Square in the United States—small businesses can use a smartphone as a better way to take card payments from customers anywhere. For BRAC and bKash, it was a better way to receive a disbursement from a business, government payment, or any other incoming remittance. For Smart Money in the Philippines, initial adoption was tied to a better way to top up mobile phones; it supported nano top-ups that consumers preferred.

Once the initial adoption happens, things can get more elaborate. But initial adoption is always driven by *addressing a compelling need in a simple way*. Less is more, especially when what you do addresses something that without your solution either doesn't work well or is too expensive for low-income people.

So we can't emphasize enough the importance of starting with a compelling use case that drives adoption and creates frequent usage. Critical mass matters. The value of a system is tied to number of users and frequency of use. All successes have come from those projects that have scaled to a) large number of users and b) frequent use.

REACH AND DISTRIBUTION ARE KEY

Rural customers want trusted, nearby access to cash-in and cash-out points. Banks want to think the answer is tied to their own distribution, but in developing countries building tens of thousands of bricks-and-mortar branches is not cost effective. This is why telecoms are so important; they have the greatest reach to the 2.5 billion underserved.

To expand financial services into rural areas, you don't need physical bank branches—the mobile phone network connects you to your customers—but you do need a low-cost network of agents who live in the villages and who can handle cash. We saw how Wing in Cambodia quickly built its network of local agents. When Wing was launched, the company wanted to establish Wing as a big and trustworthy company as quickly as possible, and signed up agents all over the country. It helped that the company was affiliated with ANZ Royal Bank. Because it was identified with one of the largest banks in the world, everyday Cambodians trusted that Wing agents would not run off with their money.

Agent networks can be built from scratch, but that means higher costs. And since most providers need a long reach to lightly-populated communities, building the network as an add-on to existing solutions is often faster and more cost effective. It is more than just the initial cost. If you take a retailer who is already running a successful business, the advantages are a) the retailer is already trusted, b) the retailer is already making money off other products and services, c) you can share the people and retail presence that is already there. This is why supermarket chains, non-banking finance companies, public sector entities like post offices, microfinance institutions, mobile telephone companies, and fast-moving consumer goods (FMCG) are all candidates for distribution roles for BOP financial services.

Existing organizations with good rural reach can retask their existing assets to create agent networks to cost-effectively reach those who need to be served. New companies like Eko and Globokas are using technology and innovative business processes to enable existing retailers. But while this does not come without a retooling cost, and requires technology support, it is clearly possible, as we have seen with Safaricom, BRAC Microfinance, Eko, Globokas, Wing, GCash, Smart, and Wal-Mart. They are showing the world that it can succeed in serving the BOP where traditional financial services struggle.

MERCHANT SERVICES ARE KEY TO PAYMENTS AT THE BOP

Much discussion about financial inclusion focuses on the end user—consumer, individual, or family. But equally important is the merchant and/or small business. At the BoP, this is true for a couple of key reasons. First, many BoP people are also small business owners. So the utility of the financial offering will be judged by how well it serves not only the family needs but also the business need. Those worlds blend together for many.

The second reason is that the utility for the end user is increased with more use cases. Therefore, those solutions that support more merchants and more use cases will be more valuable. For example, if a telco, bank, or online player offers you mobile money, the usefulness for you will be tied to how many ways you can either spend the money or receive the money. Many of the use cases are tied to businesses. If you can buy from any online store, corner store, or supermarket, then mobile money has more use in your life. The more you can do what you want, electronically and safely from your mobile, the more value there is in it for you. In addition, if your employer can pay you directly, your family can send you money from another country, or your marketplace (oDesk, eBay) can settle funds with you directly—then the more value to you.

So the overall utility and appeal of payment mechanisms for the underserved are going to be not only built on top of an initial compelling use case, it will also be tied to a rich and broad set of uses. The latter will require lots of merchants to buy into this payment method. But don't think that the merchant services that work at the middle and top of the pyramid will be a good fit everywhere. Pricing, hardware, credit, infrastructure, tools, and services will need to be tailored to those who are in the BoP or those that serve the BoP.

A good example is pricing. Mapping the pricing of payments from the US will be a showstopper. In the US it is not unusual for the merchant to spend thousands of dollars per store on hardware, with transaction pricing ranges from one to four percent, with a higher percentage from transactions under ten dollars. Most BoP transactions are under ten dollars, especially in markets like India. And merchants operate on smaller margins there. So the price of implementing and small transactions will need to be different.

In addition to a different pricing model, attracting merchants will require products and services that address the specific needs of these merchants. This is a very important audience, and their needs should be attended to just as much as the needs of the end users.

We see this focus when Kopo Kopo launched its core platform in Kenya in February 2012. The company partnered with Safaricom to bring the M-Pesa Buy Goods service to small- and medium-sized businesses throughout Kenya, and today it serves hundreds of businesses from salons to restaurants to office supply stores.

In May of 2014, Kopo Kopo announced its new merchant cash advance service called "Grow." Unlike a traditional bank loan, Grow is designed to help businesses grow and prosper by accommodating their cash flow cycles. Grow cash advances are disbursed in minutes, require no personal guarantee, and come with no late fees or penalties.

"In our years of doing business, we've seen even our best customers struggle to access capital for their businesses," said Kenya CEO Francis Mugane. "Given our mission to help businesses grow and prosper, solving this problem with Grow was a logical next step—and it's only one of many steps to come."

Businesses automatically become eligible for Grow after accepting electronic payments via Kopo Kopo for three months. The more electronic payments a business accepts via Kopo Kopo, the more cash they are eligible to receive at a lower fee. Once eligible, a business owner chooses how much they want to receive and what percentage of daily sales should be deducted via Kopo Kopo to repay the cash advance. The business owner then agrees to a simple fixed fee, and funds are disbursed to their Kopo Kopo account within minutes.

Grow is ideal for businesses looking to replenish stock, refurbish their premises, or launch a new business line. Since repayments are based on electronic sales, Grow perfectly aligns with a business's cash flow: Kopo Kopo deducts a larger amount when sales are high, a smaller amount when sales are low, and no amount when there are no sales.[92]

INFRASTRUCTURE MATTERS

For many of these complex systems to work for the consumer, the infrastructure is key, especially *national identity systems* and *inter-bank settlement*. Without modern infrastructure in these two areas, solutions will struggle with basic challenges like account opening, timely money transfer, and building acceptance networks. This infrastructure is key in so many ways. Even if you want to skip currency and go straight to bitcoin, these will matter because it will give you the local "on ramps" and "off ramps" for exchanges, support compliance, assist in fraud prevention.

There are two approaches to infrastructure. Most common is a large government-led effort like Aadhaar in India or Faster Payments in the UK. These are examples of massive efforts that are well funded and have political support

---

92   http://kopokopo.com/press-release-kopo-kopo-launches-
      grow-merchant-cash-advance-service/

behind them. The good news is that there are many other governments in the process of tackling these efforts.

But equally interesting is the other approach: the innovator tackling the infrastructure requirement. In the United States, the federal government has delayed tackling the inter-bank settlement issue for too long. The settlement system is overnight with program rules that can delay settlement from a user perspective for days. It's amazing how the United States, with so much technology and financial services leadership, can be so remiss about something as basic as a modern infrastructure for how banks settle funds. The one that is used—Automated Clearing House (ACH)—is vintage 1960 batch processing. Unbelievable.

There is a small company that has tackled this issue: Omney, started by two first-time entrepreneurs with gray hair who were both financial services technical people tired of making excuses to customers about settlement. They decided if the US government wasn't going to address this problem, they would. With the help of some large companies, they partnered with the ATM networks, MC, and VISA to "retask" other networks to do interbank settlement for business disbursements. It works today, and is being used by many A-list companies big and small to support electronic disbursements and better online experience.

So when the US government decides to upgrade the infrastructure, they will have a choice: build one at a cost of billions of dollars over many years, or just embrace one that was built in the private sector. My guess is that they will do the latter.

Another potential private sector game changer could be identity systems. Apple has already made steps to use biometrics for iPhone applications. They are opening up their interface to allow other application developers to use that fingerprint-reading capability. Google will do the same if they haven't already. Why couldn't a secure ID come from the technology sector instead of a government initiative? Might it not be better for the government to avoid the billion-dollar project and for a private entity sponsor an X-Prize for tackling these issues? We might find better solutions more quickly that way.

GOVERNMENT REGULATIONS: FRIEND OR FOE

Regulations are something that seem very boring, but they're essential. Government regulations can either propel an effort forward or hold it back. If regulators get the rules governing financial services right, there will be a tsunami of new services in the area, and the best ones will be adopted and scale. Here are the most important rules they need to get right:

- **Let non-banks offer financial services.** Allow responsible non-bank actors to provide financial services. Retailers, telcos, online companies, and Fin-tech startups should be able to be licensed to provide various financial activities like load/unload cash, move money, hold funds in trust for others, electronically pay, and lend. Many of these non-banks are not only innovative, but they have great assets like trust and distribution, which can be effectively leveraged to reach and serve customers.

- **Lower the barriers for customers to enter the banking system.** In many places in the world, people who want to open up a bank account have to go through a difficult process of identifying themselves and proving they are who they say they are. Long forms, ID checks, and in-person meetings—all of these are intimidating and take time. It puts up major obstacles to people entering the banking system. Regulators can lower these barriers for newly-banked customers and allow small deposits and basic services initially. Over time, the financial services provider can graduate the information they have about the customer to collect more due diligence information.

- **Prevent toxic behavior by existing players.** With the Internet, we have seen the benefit of net neutrality and an open playing field. Without it, a large incumbent could have stifled innovation through tricky methods. This can and does happen with financial services. Put the necessary regulations in place to prevent this from happening. This will mean there will be more competition, which will increase options and lower prices. These regulations will need to be added to the telecom regulations and the banking regulations.

Once regulators do these three things, then the change will happen quickly. New services will enter the market, people will try them, the best services will be adopted, behaviors will change, and the transformation will begin. The pain points are too great, and the innovative spirit of new and existing businesses will take hold.

Let's look at where we have seen these types of regulations deliver benefits. M-Pesa is the most dramatic success, but it was also where the regulators supported all three of the most important rules.

First, they let a non-bank, Safaricom, provide the mobile money service.

Second, they supported a sign-up process that lowered the barrier to entry for creating an account and transferring money using a government issued ID card alone.

Third, when banks pushed back, regulators listened but continued to support M-Pesa's operation. Then when M-Pesa resisted interoperability, they encourage them to be more open.

In the Philippines, government regulators are now catching up to Kenyan regulators and helping GCash to craft regulations that would spur the growth of mobile money. The government created a category called e-money, or electronic money issuer, which is how GXI is categorized. They are also liberalizing their stance on qualified agents to allow both GCash and Smart to build more geographically disbursed agent networks. This is key to reach and utility of mobile money solutions.

While India has been slow to evolve, the changes after 2010 have been significant. Their latest move is a good example. India's RBI has recognized that when it comes to making financial inclusion a reality for seven hundred million people in India, smaller banks, telecommunication providers, online platforms and retailers are in a great position. The smaller stature of small banks makes them more nimble, and their locations primarily within rural communities gives a level of trust that larger banks simply don't have. Non-banks like telecommunication providers and retailers (including online retailers) have extensive reach to people who live far from bank branches. Non-banks frequently have trusted relationships with people who have never had a relationship with a bank.

The RBI has publicly stated they are now seriously considering two new categories of financial service providers in India: Payment Banks and Small Banks. This is being considered a viable solution in India where roughly forty-five percent of the population don't have checking accounts. These new category of "banks" will offer limited services that include accepting deposits, extending credit and making remittances. Their services will be provided throughout rural areas via branch networks, business correspondents and in conjunction with networks of other payment banks. Altogether, these include:

- Supermarket chains

- Finance companies

- Non-banking finance companies

- Corporate business correspondents

- Cooperatives

- Public sector entities

- Micro finance institutions

- Local banks

- Mobile telephone companies

- Private businesses

- Pre-paid instrument issuers

As such, their influence in rural communities will be considerable, making it easier for rural Indians to access financial services that have previously been unavailable. You might even say the Indian government is banking on the creation of these payment and small banks to make financial inclusion rates blossom throughout the country.

There are other regulators that are moving also. But in our view, most are moving too slowly. Once regulators get moving and do these three things, we believe strongly it will unlock innovation in their geography, and things will happen quickly. With the smartly-crafted regulatory framework, many new services will enter the market, people will try them, the best services will be adopted, behaviors will change, and the transformation will begin. The pain points are too great, and the innovative spirit of new and existing businesses will take hold.

BE PREPARED TO INVEST IN LOCAL IMPLEMENTATIONS

Within the 2.5 billion underserved there's much diversity. Innovators need to be prepared to work locally on partnerships, leverage infrastructure (like ATM networks), and customize functionality, look, feel, marketing, and pricing to meet the needs of local consumers and merchants. As we interviewed the various innovators, we could hear the fine details of their success in their markets. They knew the local customs, infrastructure, players, regulations, and market conditions well. They talked about how that influenced their services and their strategy.

Some of these companies will scale beyond national boundaries. Some already have started. Although much of what they do, many of their local lessons will apply, there will also be new ones. Juntos is an example of a company that is already experiencing that and has planned ahead. They built their technology and their GTM strategy around local design and customization. Their software engine may be shared, but the rules about local culture are specific to each place they go. This allows them to operate differently in Mexico, Columbia, Tanzania. They know first hand that local customs are very different in these three places.

The best way is to plan for maximum reuse but prepare for local customization. Technology can support this with multi-tenant implementations and APIs for fast integration with different third parties.

BE MINDFUL OF THE BUSINESS MODEL

Steve Jobs and Apple can be credited with reinventing a few industries, from mobile phones to smart phones, music distribution to digital. We think about the iPod or the iPhone as the icons of this change. But just as important to those reinvented industries is the business model. And Jobs and Apple accomplished reinvention of the business model in both cases.

One of our favorite stories about the iPhone and Steve Jobs was told to me by someone who was actually in the room to see it in action. It was about how Steve Jobs advocated with JP Morgan Chase around payments on the iPhone through the iTunes store. Big companies—Wal-Mart, Apple, McDonald's—all pay less for card or e-payments. Think of it as the high-volume discount. Small companies have the highest priced payments, which can be up to eighty percent higher. So if Wal-Mart pays one dollar for a payment, my hairdresser is probably being charged $1.80 for the same payment, even for the same purchase amount from the same customer.

Steve asked JPMC to give the small merchants in the iTunes store the same priced payments as Apple received. JPMC pushed back and asked, "Why do you even care about this?" Steve responded firmly that he cared a lot. He wanted to help people building applications for Apple be successful, even if they were small. This demonstrated his thoughtfulness about how everyone in the system needed to be successful for the iPhone to realize its potential. He had learned the hard way that, if you don't think about this, you can miss entire opportunities. After all, Apple was the leader in personal computers but struggled for a long time in business use of PCs. Most felt it was directly tied to Apple's failure to attract application providers. When the iPhone emerged, Steve Jobs had a real focus on application providers, and part of that focus was on how the business model encouraged and supported those who built applications.

This is an important lesson, especially for mobile operators and even banks that are used to being the only one in the business model that mattered. To them, other actors frequently look like vendors and are beaten into the "right business model," which really means "pricing I demand from you" without thinking about whether it's good for the other parties.

Be willing to innovate the business model. Business models need to be refined to meet the needs of the different actors. If we try to take the model for merchant payments from VISA, MC, and Amex transactions and force-fit them into the rest of the world, it will be painful, and probably not successful. If MNOs make the business models for others too painful, they will eventually lose because the innovators and financial service providers will find other ways to be relevant with other players like Apple, Facebook, or Google.

There will also need to be some iteration on the business model until the fine points are worked out. One very innovative payment company of considerable size demonstrated how they handle this in a recent negotiation with another innovator. They said, "We want to price this service and our revenue split, but we're not sure exactly how because of too many uncertainties." So they put some boundaries on how much they would pay in year one—a floor to protect the smaller company from doing all this but struggling to cover the necessary costs to support it, and a ceiling that said after a certain level of success pricing per transaction would go down. They also suggested a one-year deal so they could come back and refine the pricing and business model. It worked for both parties and acknowledged that both had a lot to learn to get the business model right.

FINANCIAL INCLUSION IS A COLLABORATIVE EFFORT

The one over-arching theme that's woven through nearly every example in this book is that in today's digital economy, financial inclusion is not a solo act. Here's why:

Decades ago, the various industries upon which we depended for financial and communication products and services were separate and distinct entities.

To call someone for business or pleasure, we picked up the landline telephone. The phone served no other purpose but to transmit the sound of a voice from one device to another.

When we wanted a credit card, we completed an application form and mailed it to the card issuer, usually a bank. Two weeks later we learned, by mail, if we had been approved.

To watch TV, we turned on the television set and adjusted the rabbit-ears antenna.

If we wanted to deposit money in our bank account, we'd go to the bank branch, fill out a deposit slip, and hand our cash or check to the teller. If we were depositing an out-of-state check, the funds might become available to us in five to seven business days.

To transfer funds to a family member or colleague in another town, we had a few choices. We could mail a check. We could send money by Western Union, for a fee. If we had access to the hawala network, we could pay the hawala agent to have our money sent across borders.

All of these activities happened independently of each other. The phone company had no relationship with the bank. The credit card company had no relationship with the money transfer people.

And then came digital communications technology.

Almost overnight, familiar tools were transformed, none more so than the humble hard-wired rotary phone—the pride of Alexander Graham Bell. At first the phone was liberated from its copper wire, and you could carry a bulky cellular phone in the car or a briefcase. Phones quickly became smaller and more powerful, and soon the phone in your pocket was packed with more processing power than was used on the Apollo moon landing.

Computers became personal too, and the internet tied them together. People began selling products online, and then banks built websites where you could securely access your account information.

Then many of the functions of the internet—text messaging, website access, data transfer—migrated to mobile phones.

Globally, something wonderful was happening. Vast areas of developing nations—India, Southeast Asia, Africa—that had little landline phone service were ideal territory for mobile phones. While many Americans were slowly transitioning from hardwired landlines to mobile phones, billions of people in developing nations who had never had a phone found themselves leapfrogging to the forefront of mobile technology.

According to *Information and Communications for Development 2012: Maximizing Mobile,* published by the World Bank and infoDev, its technology entrepreneurship and innovation program, the number of mobile subscriptions in use worldwide, both pre-paid and post-paid, has grown from fewer than one billion in 2000 to over six billion, of which nearly five billion are in developing countries. Ownership of multiple subscriptions is becoming increasingly common, suggesting that their number will soon exceed that of the human population.

In developing countries, citizens are increasingly using mobile phones to create new livelihoods and enhance their lifestyles, while governments are using them to improve service delivery and citizen feedback mechanisms.

"Mobile communications offer major opportunities to advance human and economic development—from providing basic access to health information to making cash payments, spurring job creation, and stimulating citizen involvement in democratic processes," said World Bank vice president for Sustainable Development, Rachel Kyte.

"The mobile revolution is right at the start of its growth curve," said Tim Kelly, lead ICT policy specialist at the World Bank and one of the authors of the report. "Mobile devices are becoming cheaper and more powerful while networks are doubling in bandwidth roughly every eighteen months and expanding into rural areas."

The report emphasizes the role of governments in enabling mobile application development, which brings us to the most important lesson of the new wave of financial inclusion: the necessity for collaboration across sectors to create a new industry.

What we are witnessing today is a new synergy among industries that used to operate in their own silos: banks, phone companies, credit bureaus, NGOs, retailers, online players, and governments. These sectors are working together to re-write the rules of engagement in ways that generate profits for them (yes, profits are still a powerful motivating force!) while creating opportunity for billions of people who could not previously afford the price of admission to the financial game.

Here are just a few examples.

M-Pesa, Safaricom, Vodafone, Equity Bank, and the Government of Kenya. M-Pesa began as a partnership between Safaricom, Kenya's largest mobile provider, and Vodaphone, based in Tanzania. Then a new partnership with Kenya-based Equity Bank launched M-Kesho, a product using M-Pesa's platform and agent network that offers expanded banking services.

There's more. If not exactly a partner in M-Pesa, the federal government of Kenya is a vital facilitator because all Kenyans aged eighteen and above carry the national identity card. Citizens must provide it to open a bank account, register a business, for employment, acquire a driver's license, transact mobile phone banking, and many other uses that require proof of identity. Therefore, in Kenya the "know your customer" rule is easily satisfied, making mobile banking practical.

Smart, GCash, and Growing Relationships with Banks. In the Philippines, the Microenterprise Access to Banking Services (MABS) Program was designed to address the need of the Philippine microenterprise sector and other low-income people to gain access to a wide range of financial services and ensure that all sectors of society can participate in a growing economy. Altogether, the MABS program spanned fifteen years, beginning in 1997 and closing in 2012. The program oversight continued to be led by the Mindanao Development Authority (MinDA) under the Office of the President.

As a pioneer in the use of mobile technology to deliver microfinance services, MABS served as a bridge between rural banks, mobile network operators Globe Telecom, and Smart Communications, Inc., and assisted with regulatory approvals from the Bangko Sentral ng Pilipinas (BSP).

MABS assisted rural banks in providing mobile phone banking and mobile commerce transactions by developing new products and services. MABS worked with the Rural Bankers Association of the Philippines (RBAP) to help obtain approval from BSP for mobile money-enabled banking services and to develop appropriate operations and procedure manuals for rural banks.

MasterCard Partnerships. MasterCard's technology combined with increased engagement of governments is helping drive greater expansion of financial inclusion. Public-private partnerships, such as the social security program in Pakistan, offer the unbanked new opportunities to join the financial mainstream.

MasterCard's work with the South African Social Security Agency has helped showcase the impact of delivering government funds via electronic payments and encouraged other governments to explore these solutions.

MasterCard won the Award for Financial Inclusion at the 2014 African Banker Awards, in recognition of its far-reaching achievements in extending financial inclusion across Africa.

The Award recognized MasterCard as the company that best succeeded in delivering financial products and services to broad segments of society, thus contributing to financial inclusion, development and growth. MasterCard's broad-based collaboration with public and private sector entities is quickly bringing the benefits and security of electronic payments to the continent's largest economies, where financial exclusion is still prevalent.

In East Africa, MasterCard partnered with Nakumatt, one of the largest supermarket chains in East Africa, to roll out one million Nakumatt Global MasterCard Prepaid cards (multi-currency, EMV, contactless card), providing an entry-level solution for people who are coming into financial services for the first time.

In Nigeria, the government launched a national ID program that combines a biometric identification solution with a prepaid payment functionality powered by MasterCard, and is the broadest financial inclusion initiative of its kind on the African continent.

In Morocco, Banque Marocaine du Commerce Extérieur (BMCE) and prepaid solutions company Vantage Payment Systems (VPS) launched a MasterCard Payroll Prepaid Program to address the financial needs of interim workers, in addition to extending the cards to local security agencies and cleaning companies.

In Egypt, MasterCard partnered with the National Bank of Egypt and Etisalat to unveil the first Arabic mobile money program that enables subscribers to transfer money via their phone.[93]

First Access, Mobile Phones, and Credit Scoring. In a previous chapter, we saw how First Access combines demographic, geographic, financial, and social aspects of clients' mobile phone usage to produce information that is consumed by another industry—personal lending. First Access's customer base includes retail commercial banks, microfinance institutions, insurance companies, agricultural input suppliers, and business payment platforms operating in emerging economies.

It is clear that it takes a large community of actors to realize all the potential of providing financial services for the unbanked and newly banked.

We see that success today is created by a "mash-up" of actors and industries coming together. We not only expect this synergy to continue, but we expect more types of companies will get involved. We already see online and smart phone "over the top" players making moves in financial services. Apple has a massive initiative around iTunes payments and in-store innovation. Google has consistently invested in their Google Wallet offering. Alibaba's (the Amazon/eBay of China) Alipay is the leading way people buy online in China and is going global. Amazon has cloud payment services. New Silicon Valley born online payment innovator Stripe is making their mark on the US payment industry plus expanding globally.

Success in emerging financial services will come from various places. But no matter who takes the lead, what is going to be true is that there will be many participants in the larger ecosystem.

Sage advice: Don't think like the Lone Ranger.

---

93   http://newsroom. mastercard. com/press-releases/
      technology-and-partnership-approach-driving-mastercard-financial-inclusion-in-2014/

CHAPTER 21:

BaaP—A New Paradigm for Financial Inclusion

As we step back from the details and look forward, the global financial landscape is transforming before our eyes. Critical pieces are coming together to create exponential change in financial services. Even as we write these words, a new paradigm is being born. The financial pyramid, whose steep sides and distant peak for centuries were accessible only to those who could afford to participate in the traditional banking system, is becoming more level and its peak more attainable. Increasingly, the 2.5 billion people who traditionally could not afford to climb the steep sides and become financial actors are able to migrate upward from the bottom of the pyramid—from the land of cash transactions, payday loans, overdraft fees, and expensive funds transfers—to participate in affordable and accessible financial services.

We know that industries can change dramatically when paradigms shift. And some newly-emerged industries—like mobile applications, web 2.0 commerce, and social networking—have changed the ways we engage in commerce and interact with each other.

In the reshaping of the financial pyramid, an important force is the element of community.

The value of the new financial inclusion is tied to the diversity, reach, and functionality delivered via the community. Our old paradigm of a business built as a stand-alone service and leader in a category is increasingly less common. More and more we are seeing businesses harness a larger community to create value for their customers. Uber, Airbnb, Trip Advisor, Yelp, Twitter are popular examples. And increasingly these community-based paradigms are winning.

The financial services industry is ripe for a new paradigm. In the old one—which thrived in less dynamic times—banks, processors, networks, and program managers served those privileged few at the top of the pyramid. But now, emerging forces are applying extreme pressure for the industry to innovate:

- The new generation—mobile, highly social, and living in real time—have their own needs, wants, and desires. For them, twentieth-century financial services frequently fall short.

- The industry is facing increased demands from small businesses that need scaled services as well as traditional businesses that need improved services. Both need fast access to innovation.

- More people need to—and *can be*—served. The industry needs to shift from serving only the top of the pyramid to serving all of the pyramid.

- In the new digitally-connected world, everyone has access to data and to the financial marketplace. In the Internet-of-things, global commerce is growing and pushing beyond the limitations of traditional financial services.

Over the last few years, there have been a number of notable new companies creating successes. The Square credit card reader is perhaps the most visible, but there are many others. The venture community has responded and has started to increase the investment funds available to those who are building new companies. This is fueling even more innovation. Most large financial services players are responding with a combination of corporate investments, partnerships, increased internal development, and acquisitions.

The new paradigm that is emerging takes some elements from the traditional financial service models but is definitely morphing into one we call banking as a platform (BaaP). BaaP distinguishes the architecture of solutions into an architecture for innovation and vibrant communities. While it's simple to understand, it's surprisingly challenging to implement.

There are four layers of BaaP: building blocks, core systems, platforms, and community.

Building blocks are essential elements that make everything else work well. Examples of building blocks are settlement networks like Faster Payments in the UK, NPSI in India, and Omney in the United States. These systems allow larger networks of actors to safely perform real-time settlement of funds, which supports interoperability and timely money transfers. Other building blocks are credit rating companies like First Access, Cignifi, and InVenture Mobile. Once established, they provide credit ratings for all mobilized people.

The biometric ID system, Aadhaar in India, is a building block helping with enrollment and transaction security. These and many other building blocks make financial services and online commerce more efficient, safer, and faster.

Core systems are those elements of financial services that are the essential components of the services. For example, prepaid store value processing, core banking financial backends, insurance underwriting engines, credit account processing, virtual currency, FX, and AML are all essential functions that are needed. If you look at traditional financial services, ninety-five percent of the IT investment was in core systems. Unfortunately, most of these systems, although sophisticated, can carry a lot of legacy with them, making them hard to change and hard to adapt to a BaaP world. Similar to how SalesForce came out of nowhere to be a major player in enterprise CRM (customer relationship management), new core systems providers have that same potential. The next phase consists of the next generation systems that support a BaaP world.

Platforms combine building blocks and core systems to provide solutions. For example, Stripe is a *payment platform*, M-Pesa is a *prepaid mobile money* platform, Omney is a *faster payment platform*, and Coinbase (US) and BitX (emerging markets) are *bitcoin platforms*. All of these companies are exposing APIs to communities so they can incorporate existing applications or build new applications on top of them.

Applications are what users of financial services experience. Simple, Rush Card, Active Hours, Juntos, and Mint are all applications.

THE IMPORTANCE OF APIS AND SANDBOXES TO BAAP

The dramatic advances in software technology that have taken place over the past forty years have benefitted more than the IT industry. One big improvement is the emergence of easy-to-use application programming interfaces, or

APIs. (In computer programming, an API specifies how some software components should interact with each other.) They allow other software programs to use functionality without expensive and time-consuming programming. This has changed the way technical integrations are done. What could take years using old integration methods can now be accomplished in hours or days.

Companies that want to make it easy to integrate can do more than just have simple APIs; they also have "sandboxes," which are environments where you can test an application before deploying it to the production environment. Sandboxes are developer portals that provide documentation, tools, and API access. If done well, integrations are fast and easy, sometimes even self-service. The better the sandbox and APIs, the larger a partner community a company can build around their software.

It's best to design these APIs with mobile and web in mind. We no longer know what touch point will be used, but we do almost always know that there will be multiple touch points. Therefore designing for both mobile and web programs will make your APIs more useful for those building applications. And even though mobile and web are similar, there are differences. It can be useful to have mobile SDKs (software development toolkits) designed and available along with sandboxes and APIs. In this case, implementing the mobile SDK at the same time as designing the APIs will ensure that it has the necessary functionality to support mobile.

OPEN SYSTEMS WITH DEVELOPER COMMUNITIES

The software industry started with a proprietary mindset, whereby one company developed and owned the intellectual property, just like any conventional product. This gave them a competitive advantage and control over the system. But with this advantage and control came total responsibility for improving and extending the software.

An alternative model has emerged over the years—one of open systems. Linux is a well-known example, as is Bitcoin.

In open systems, the software is not owned or managed by one company. Instead, it is supported by a larger community of interested parties: small companies, individuals, large companies, universities. There is a governance process that decides what changes are added to the open base and which ones are not.

Iterations can be introduced very quickly because of the amount of work and different approaches that are taken. Innovation, speed, and expanded functionality can result.

There is a place for both proprietary and open systems. But some areas lend themselves very well to open systems. We believe core systems and platforms are both areas where open approaches could have significant advantage. And bitcoin—the protocol, not the currency—has a major world advantage here, with the number of actors feverishly working on applying and improving bitcoin.

SHIFT FROM "COMPLETE SOLUTIONS" TO "COLLABORATIVE BAAP MODELS"

The traditional financial services industry is struggling today to keep up with a rapidly changing world. Part of the struggle comes from the complete solution paradigm. For example, a large retail bank will offer its retail customer a set of solutions. With a large budget and many vendors, they deliver a complete solution to their customer's needs. That is the way they think about delivering value. But even with billion-dollar budgets (the largest companies spend this on IT), this approach has limited innovation and moves slowly.

Imagine if Apple said that all applications for the iPhone would be created only by Apple. In such a scenario, as innovative as Apple and other tech companies are, smartphones would be very different and more limited than they are today. Apple and Google both realize this. So they open up the phone functionality and embrace innovation—both for their innovation projects and for outside application developers.

Banks, processors, payment providers, credit providers, and MNOs need to do the same. This shift is a big one. The world is no longer just them and their vendors. They need to design their new value chains to include various players, with big and small collaborating. While this is technically not that challenging, it's a huge culture change that has implications for more than just technology. Legal, space, marketing, communications—all aspects of the business need to evolve to support increasingly diverse partnerships and communities.

Apple and Google both excel at building communities. It is visible in many ways, including their developer meeting building reception area at Apple. It invites you into the world of Apple, and you want to be part of it.

BAAP IS HAPPENING TODAY

If you look, you can already see movement to the new paradigm. Banks are starting to try to be more collaborative. New players like Stripe are opening up APIs and open sourcing their platform. M-Pesa has published APIs for value-added service providers. Bitcoin's advanced protocol is enabling innovators and new actors in core systems, platforms, and applications.

What will more quickly help BaaP become a force to address the needs of the underserved are:

- Regulations that let non-banks offer financial services. Allow responsible non-bank actors to provide financial services. Lower the barriers for customers to enter the banking system. Use graduated due diligence approaches especially for the newly banked. Prevent toxic behavior by existing players. This can be telecom, networks like Visa, traditional banks, and large financial services providers.

- Leaders who embrace change and dedicate themselves to inclusive services. Amex and MasterCard are leading the way, and others should follow.

- Venture capitalists and angel investors who aren't afraid of services for the bottom of the pyramid and emerging markets. Lots of money is chasing the next Square; why not divert some of that investment to deserving innovators working on financial services for the next billion?

- Revamp the culture of organizations from one of standalone proprietary solutions to one of collaborative approaches. Be attentive to all aspects of the business in doing this.

Banking as a platform is the next step in leveling the steep sides of the global financial pyramid. In the following chapter, we'll list just a few of the practical steps that you can take to participate in the growth of financial inclusion for all.

CHAPTER 22:

Ten Ways to Get Involved

Whether you're a financial professional or a concerned citizen, you can take action to level the steep sides of the global financial pyramid and make financial inclusion a reality for more people. Some of these ideas require only a few minutes of your time, while others need a sustained effort. However you choose to participate, the 2.5 billion people who are currently closed off from the pyramid of financial inclusion will appreciate your efforts.

Ready? Let's get started!

1. Join the conversation #SuccessatBOP and follow us @SuccessatBOP

2. Join or start a group—Bitcoin for emerging markets, financial inclusion.

3. Show a preference for companies like MasterCard and Amex that are committed to financial inclusion, and tell them that is why you are giving them your business. Also, tell their competitors why you are not.

4. Advise a start-up that is focused on the underserved.

5. Invest in a start-up that is focused on the underserved.

6. Write to your state and federal politicians and ask for regulatory changes. Almost everywhere in the world, regulations can be better.

7. Write a letter asking Visa, MasterCard, Amazon, Apple, and Google to support innovation for the underserved by a) not hampering innovation by others, b) doing more for the underserved.

8. Start a project within your company.

9. Start a company.

10. Receive updates and current articles by signing up for the Financial Inclusion Newsletter at openfininc.org

CAROL REALINI

An expert in financial service innovation, Carol Realini is a serial entrepreneur and globally-recognized technology pioneer. Attending the World Economic Forum, she led global discussions on alternative banking. Recognized as a top woman in Silicon Valley, she sits on boards and advises financial services and mobile companies. Carol and Karl, considered thought leaders by their peers, both share a passion for financial services that empower people's life and work, and have thus collaborated to present *Financial Inclusion at the Bottom of the Pyramid*.

For more information, please visit www.carolrealini.com

KARL MEHTA

Karl Mehta is a serial entrepreneur and venture capitalist in Silicon Valley. He was founder & CEO of PlaySpan (acquired by Visa), a global alternative payment network. Karl served as the White House Presidential Innovation Fellow working on the "Better Than Cash" initiative and serves on California Gov Brown's Workforce Investment Board. He is an active investor, board member in Edtech and Fintech and founder-CEO of EdCast Inc. He regularly posts his Insights on edcasting handle edcast.com/karlmehta.

For more information, please visit openfininc.org and edcast.com/FinIncBOP

CPSIA information can be obtained at www.ICGtesting.com
Printed in the USA
LVOW07*0007201016

509277LV00004B/7/P